Philanthropic Foundations in the Twentieth Century

Recent Titles in
Contributions to the Study of World History

Philanthropic Foundations in the Twentieth Century

Joseph C. Kiger

Foreword by Sara L. Engelhardt

Contributions to the Study of World History, Number 72

GREENWOOD PRESS
Westport, Connecticut • London

Library of Congress Cataloging–in–Publication Data

Kiger, Joseph Charles.
    Philanthropic foundations in the twentieth century / Joseph C.
Kiger ; foreword by Sara L. Engelhardt.
        p.   cm.—(Contributions to the study of world history, ISSN
0885–9159 ; no. 72)
    Includes bibliographical references (p.   ) and index.
    ISBN 0–313–31223–0 (alk. paper)
    1. Charities—History.   2. Social service—History.   I. Title.
II. Series.
HV16.K54   2000
361.7′632′0904—dc21   99–16097

British Library Cataloguing in Publication Data is available.

Library of Congress Catalog Card Number: 99–16097
ISBN: 0–313–31223–0
ISSN: 0885–9159

First published in 2000

Greenwood Press, 88 Post Road West, Westport, CT 06881
An imprint of Greenwood Publishing Group, Inc.
www.greenwood.com

Printed in the United States of America

The paper used in this book complies with the
Permanent Paper Standard issued by the National
Information Standards Organization (Z39.48–1984).

10 9 8 7 6 5 4 3 2 1

Contents

Foreword

The past fifty years have been a period of tremendous growth and ferment in the foundation field. Starting in 1952 with the Cox Committee hearings, Joseph C. Kiger has been an astute and disciplined observer of the evolving foundation culture. As director of research for the Cox Committee, Dr. Kiger gained firsthand experience in mining documents for their revelations about foundation operations. That committee established by Congress as the Select Committee to Investigate Tax-Exempt Foundations and Comparable Organizations, created a long and detailed questionnaire for some sixty of the largest foundations. The responses to the questionnaire not only provided evidence for the work of the Cox Committee, which concluded that "on balance, the record of foundations is good," but contributed the first real insights into how foundations in this country functioned. Dr. Kiger drew heavily on those responses in the preparation of his *Operating Principles of the Larger Foundations* (1954), the first of what was to become a succession of valuable books on foundations by him.

When I began work at Carnegie Corporation of New York in the summer of 1964, the congressional investigations of the 1950s were still sharply etched in its institutional memory. In fact, the corporation had taken the lead in establishing the Foundation Center in 1956 precisely to help ameliorate the overwhelming lack of information about U.S. foundations that the hearings revealed. As I have pursued my own career at Carnegie Corporation and the Foundation Center, my path has crisscrosed the trail blazed by Dr. Kiger

As a historian, Dr. Kiger has documented important aspects of the foundation field. In 1984, he coedited *Foundations* with Harold M. Keele, profiling the histories of 230 of the largest and best-known U.S. foundations. I authored the entry on Carnegie Corporation. He followed this with the editing of a similar work, the *International Encyclopedia of Foundations* (1990), on 145 foundations located in thirty-one countries outside the United States. I joined the Foundation Center staff in 1987 just as it was publishing Dr. Kiger's *Historiographic Review of Foundation Literature: Motivations and Perceptions*. Shortly after I became president of the center in 1991, we discussed a new study he was planning, which has resulted in the present volume.

Philanthropic Foundations in the Twentieth Century reflects Dr. Kiger's singular depth of knowledge about foundations here and abroad. It presents a cogent description of present-day structure and operations of U.S. foundations, exploring how and why they evolved in this way. Of particular interest is his account of the accelerating international activities of U.S. foundations. Included in the account is a discussion of an array of international foundations and connected organizations as they relate to their U.S. counterparts. This new work from Joseph C. Kiger rounds out half a century of examination of the changing foundation scene. In it, he makes another distinctive contribution to a field that is now cluttered with information—and misinformation—on this engrossing topic.

Sara L. Engelhardt
President
The Foundation Center

Introduction

Defining what constitutes a philanthropic foundation has presented and probably always will present, difficulties.[1] The structure and activities of foundations make it hard to differentiate them from other institutions such as research institutes, libraries, museums, hospitals, and so on. Sometimes these same structures and activities change with the passage of time, resulting in changes in definition. For example, the Carnegie Institution of Washington and the Carnegie Endowment for International Peace were established by Andrew Carnegie in 1902 and 1910, respectively, with initial endowments of $10 million each. From that time to about 1960 they were classified by most analysts as foundations. By that time, however, their operations had so changed that since then they have more properly been classified as research institutions. In any event, in the past fifty years, the following consensus as to defining foundations has emerged.

A philanthropic foundation is a nongovernmental, not-for-profit organization with funds of its own provided by a donor or donors, managed by its own trustees or directors, and with a program designed to maintain or aid socially useful activities and purposes. A corollary to this definition, however, is that a foundation must have been primarily set up not to get or make money but to make grants from such funds. Many worthwhile organizations that seek funds to carry out their purpose and bearing the title "foundation," such as the National Kidney Foundation or the American Foundation for the Blind, do not meet the definition. Yet, anomalies present themselves here. For example, fifty years ago the John Simon Guggenheim Memorial Foundation was one of the top sixty or seventy foundations in the United States in the size of its assets and in the amount and volume of its prestigious fellowship awards. Yet in 1989 its officers decided that it must augment the funds at its disposal in order to at least stabilize the number and monetary amount of the fellowships it awarded annually. The Guggenheim Foundation therefore embarked on a successful fund-raising campaign directed primarily at its former fellows.[2] Suffice it to say that this singular effort did not result in the foundation's ceasing to be categorized as a foundation or discontinuing its grant-making activities and awarding of fellowships.

The laws and terminology as to what constitutes a foundation tend to be complex and confusing within individual countries and vary enormously from country to country. Many organizations that can legitimately be designated as foundations bear other names: trust, endowment, fund, charity, institution, library, and even corporation, for example, the United States Duke Endowment and Carnegie Corporation of New York; Australia's Sidney Myer Fund; India's J. N. Tata Endowment; and the U.K.'s Wellcome Trust. Regardless of name, however, this definition generally and broadly describes an institution that, although having many and variegated historical antecedents, is largely a creation of twentieth-century United States. Subsuming and complicating the broad definition and variety of foundation names presented earlier is the problem of placing such organizations in various classifications or types for expository purposes. Efforts to do this in the past are to be found in a number of directories and similar works on foundations in the United States and abroad.[3] The latest and probably best such classification for U.S. foundations can be found on pages vii–viii in the 21st edition of *The Foundation Directory*, The Foundation Center, New York, 1999. Four major classifications of foundations are presented therein: (1) independent, (2) company, (3) operating, and (4) community.

The independent foundations have usually been set up by an individual or the members of a family and thus have sometimes been referred to or categorized as, "family foundations." Most of the larger and better-known foundations in the United States and worldwide have been of the independent type and, when properly set up and organized, have the ability to dispense large or small sums of money to individuals and to organizations such as educational and research institutions, hospitals, libraries, museums, and so on, to enable them to carry out a wide variety of programs and projects enjoying the favor of the donors or their successors. Independent or family foundations have also been referred to, or categorized as, "general purpose foundations." Because of the large assets held by some and their considerable combined assets, the wide scope of their programs and grants, and the fact that many have been set up in this and other countries, much of the attention of the public is centered on foundations of this type.

Foundations created by companies and business corporations have increased over the years, both in number and in the size of their endowments. Their source of funds from a company may be in the form of endowment, annual contributions, or both. Since the level of giving by businesses to their foundations often declines during periods of economic downturn, one of the major rationales for the creation of company foundations has been the stabilization in their level of contributions to recipient individuals and institutions during depressed periods. They are normally administered by those having an official relationship with the sponsoring business, and their grants are often concentrated in communities or regions where the funding business has plants, facilities, customers, and so on. Many operate programs, such as the awarding of scholarships and fellowships, often restricted to company employees and/or their family members.

Operating foundations employ and pay their own staffs to carry out their program. Foundations in this category, however, may have grant programs that divert some of their funds to other individuals or institutions; that is, they make some outside grants from time to time. The line between such foundations and other entities such as research institutes, universities, libraries, and museums can be a fine one.

Community foundations were originally established in cities and urban areas, but many are now located in suburban and even rural areas. Their endowment and supplementary funds are usually derived from multiple sources rather than a single or few sources, and foundation grants are normally made for local or regional purposes in the area where they were established and where their offices are physically located.

Since the passage of the Tax Reform Act of 1969, the U.S. Internal Revenue Service (IRS) has further confused the terminology used in classifying these four kinds of foundations. If their assets come from a single donor—individual, family, or company—the first three are classified by the IRS as private foundations. If their assets come from multiple sources—community foundations being among the best examples—the IRS classifies them as public foundations or charities and exempts them from certain taxes and restrictions that apply to the three kinds of private foundations.

Foundations may also be categorized by another set of factors: (1) perpetual—the donor specifies that the principal shall be held forever and the income alone be expended; (2) optional—the donor allows the trustees of the foundation the option of expenditure of principal as well as income; and (3) liquidating—the donor specifies that both principal and income shall be expended by a certain time. There are many variations within these types. The Duke Endowment, for example, established as a perpetual type, had a provision in its legal charter that restricted expenditures from the endowment until its assets grew to a specified size. Although there have been continuing arguments as to the efficacy of each type, most of the large foundations formed prior to the 1950s were of the optional type.

Although many large foundations encompassing all such classifications and types have been set up in other parts of the world, a disproportionate number of those with the largest assets and with wide-ranging programs were established in the United States in the twentieth century. The United States has provided these and all of our foundations with great freedom of action, which has resulted in a wide diversity in their programs and operation. The result has been that the larger and more significant ones often used their funds as venture capital in supporting innovative and even risky enterprises. This same freedom of action has permitted and indeed encouraged U.S. foundations to change in response to outside criticism and perceived new societal needs. Consequently, viewed historically and internationally, our larger twentieth-century American foundations are truly an innovation on the philanthropic scene.[4]

The major purpose of this work is to identify and discuss the most noteworthy developments and changes in the attributes, structure, operations, and governmental supervision of U.S. foundations and ancillary organizations in the twentieth century, particularly in recent decades. The work concentrates upon those foundations with the largest assets. It opens with a historical chapter followed by one dealing with the major investigations and studies that have been made of U.S. foundations. Succeeding chapters deal with major developments and changes involving U.S. foundations in the following areas: growth and expansion; information and the public; personnel diversification; and governmental supervision. The two final chapters are concerned with the most significant and ongoing U.S. foundation development: the prominent increase in their international activities, including their role in the formation and operation of associations and centers here and abroad serving as nexuses for national, regional, and international foundation operations.

In short, the foundation world that I was introduced to in the early 1950s is a far cry from the one that existed previously and from the one that exists today, nationally and internationally, and the present work concentrates on this changing scene. Nationally and worldwide, however, most commentators here and abroad agree that the public still knows relatively little about foundations and ancillary organizations and less about the developments and changes affecting them in the twentieth century. This book is an attempt to provide a chronicle and an explanation for these developments and changes.

In the research and writing of this work I am indebted for their advice and counsel to numerous officials of foundations and other nonprofit agencies together with those from government and corporations. I am particularly grateful to John Richardson, Director, European Foundation Centre, for his review and comments on the final two chapters of the book, which deal with the international scene. A special thanks is due to Sara L. Engelhardt, President, the Foundation Center, who critically reviewed the manuscript and graciously agreed to write the Foreword to it. Nonetheless, any errors in the book are the sole responsibility of the author.

I am grateful to officials of the University of Mississippi, particularly Deans H. Dale Abadie and Glenn W. Hopkins and Vice Chancellors Caroline Ellis Staton and Gerald W. Walton, for their interest in my work and for providing an office and other significant forms of aid. Also, I wish to thank the staff of the University of Mississippi Library for the very special help they have rendered me in this and other projects over the years.

Finally, I wish to express appreciation to Cynthia Harris, Acquisitions Editor, and other members of the staff of Greenwood Press. In their review and editing of this work, as in previous publications, they have raised questions the answers to which have contributed a great deal to the style and readability of the book.

My wife of over a half century, Jean, as in all other productions, was a patient and invaluable commentator on this one. My debt to her is inestimable.

1

Background and History

Philanthropy, charity, benevolence, and giving are all words that express the human trait or character of engaging in what are considered good or worthy actions or deeds. More specifically, they mean the desire and willingness on the part of individuals or groups to aid and help other people or causes. The actions resulting from such urges range from the giving of a coin to a beggar or food to a hungry person, to broad-scale private or governmental programs to ameliorate the woes and ills of a group, region or country and often involving an attempt to change the conditions causing such woeful situations. The term *charity* is now generally used in the United States and increasingly worldwide for the former actions, with *philanthropy* employed to characterize the latter. In other words, some individuals or groups carry out their acts of benevolence through direct aid for the hungry, sick, and wretched. With others, however, the intent is not so much to relieve suffering directly but rather to benefit people at large by striking at the underlying causes of distress. These two kinds of giving have been performed from the beginning of time and have often been intertwined.[1] The effort to benefit people at large, however, is the one more closely aligned with that of our modern philanthropic foundation.

Throughout history, religion has been the commonest direct and indirect incentive to engage in benevolent acts. No religious organization has long been in existence before its clerics enjoined believers to engage in such acts. In this area, however, there often seems to have been less than an altruistic motive involved in the case of one or both parties involved. In many cases it appears that the clerics urged believers to allocate moneys to them to be administered by them in order to secure divine favor before and after death. Even if such funds were used to relieve distress and suffering on this earth, the motive for their donation by the giver can be viewed subjectively as an act of penance rather than charity. In the case of the clerical administrators , the temptation to misuse such funds for their own purposes and such actual misuse are obvious.

THE ANCIENT WORLD

Rudiments of the philanthropic foundation we know today can be traced to various times, regions, cultures, and religions. Such rudiments were not evident, however, until a degree of civilization emerged that produced enough property or wealth beyond primitive communal needs that could be set aside or devoted to what were considered worthwhile works or projects. Such wealth was accumulated early on in ancient China and Egypt, other ancient civilzations of the Near East, and somewhat later in Europe and the rest of the world.

Roughly 2,000 years before Christ (2255–2005 B.C.) Li Ki wrote that provision by others were being made in China for the care of orphans and poor old men and women with no close family connections.[2] *The Book of the Dead*, a landmark in the religious literature of ancient Egypt, records examples in about 4000 B.C. of charitable giving, and one early writer on foundations asserted that in these ancient civilizations of the Near East we find "the earliest known efforts at projecting private will beyond life for general purposes; they constitute the most rudimentary form of the foundation."[3] Some 1,400 years before the birth of Christ the rulers of Egypt were donating wealth to priestly groups that contracted that they would protect the tombs of the ruling pharaohs from desecration and engage in ancillary religious observances. Similarly, "The Chaldean civilization had almost identical practices as is shown by a clay tablet, dated 1280 B.C., reciting how King Marouttach bought certain lands from his vassals, built a temple on it, dedicated the whole to the god Marduk, and endowed a college of priests to operate it."[4] There are records, too, of giving by noblemen in ancient Egypt to the poor and the sick.[5] It thus appears that, although pity was a motivation for many of these charitable acts, in other cases an equally important or even sole motive was a concern for the giver's well-being after death.

In 347 B.C., Greece witnessed the establishment by Plato of the famous Academy. Lacking the legal ability to convey an endowment directly to the Academy, Plato left a bequest in land to his nephew with the proceeds from it to be used for the benefit of the Platonian followers. The nephew, in turn, left the Academy (i.e., foundation) to a successor, and so on until the Academy's eventual demise in about A.D. 700. Epicurus, a contemporary of Plato, also provided a similar haven for his followers by a donation in perpetuity to ten of his disciples.

From the earliest times the records of the Hebrew people of the eastern Mediterranean show that they, too, set aside moneys for worthy causes. Thus:

Jacob saw a vision at Bethel and promised to give a tenth "of all that thou shalt give me" to his Lord. The Mosaic Code required that the land be left fallow every seventh year; the crops that grew of themselves were for the poor. In normal years the corners of the fields should be left unreaped, and the gleanings of the vineyard, also, were "for the poor and stranger." Hospitality, even for outlanders, was an obligation: "And if thy brother be waxen poor, and fallen in decay with thee; then thou shalt relieve him; yea, though he be a stranger, or a sojourner; that he may live with thee." To give was a religious duty, and to withhold might have serious consequences: "He that giveth unto the poor shall not lack; but he that hideth his eyes shall have many a curse."

The principle of giving the tithe, or tenth, was firmly established among the Hebrews, beginning with Abram's gift of the tithe to priestly Melchizedek."[6]

Centuries later, about A.D. 1180, the Jewish philosopher Maimonides listed precepts for best giving:

There are eight degrees in the giving of charity, one higher than the other.

The highest degree, than which there is nothing higher, is to take hold of a Jew who has been crushed and to give him a gift or a loan, or to enter into a partnership with him, or to find work for him, and thus to put him on his feet so that he will not be dependent on his fellow-men. . . .

Lower in degree to this is the one who gives charity to the poor, but does not know to whom he gives it, nor does the poor man know from whom he receives it. . . . Related to this degree is the giving to the [public] alms-chest. . . .

Lower in degree to this is when the giver knows to whom he gives, but the poor does not know from whom he receives. An example of this is the great scholars who used to go about in secret and leave their money at the door of the poor. . . .

Lower in degree to this is when the poor knows from whom he receives but the giver does not know to whom he gives.

Lower in degree to this is when one gives even before he is asked.

Lower in degree to this is when one gives after he has been asked.

Lower in degree to this is when one gives less than he should but graciously.

Lower in degree to this is when one gives grudgingly.[7]

THE ROMAN EMPIRE

With the rise of Rome as the great power in the Mediterranean/European area, by 150 B.C. Roman law had evolved that favored the establishment and perpetual legal status of associations (i.e., foundations) and a consequent growth in their number, kind, and assets. By that time, too, some of these associations were engaging in political activities and for a time they were suppressed by an edict of the Roman Senate, marking one of the earliest conflicts between foundations and government. Beginning about A.D. 200, however, they were again encouraged in their founding and operation by the Roman emperors of that period. Cities, towns, and eventually associations (i.e., foundations) were afforded the right to accept bequests, and the latter multiplied throughout the Roman empire. During this period there was a shift in the purposes for which these organizations were being created. Gifts and funds set aside for the preserving of their souls and for the care of the sick and needy continued to be made by those desiring to do good, but a pattern of giving emerged benefiting not just the ailing and destitute but larger groups of people and in a less direct and immediate manner. An outstanding example of such beneficence was that of the Greek Herodes Atticus, who

built a water supply system for Troas, endowed a giant stadium at Athens, and restored to its ancient magnificence the theatre of Pericles; he provided a temple to Neptune and a theatre at Corinth, a stadium at Delphi, endowed a bath at Thermopylea, and a system of aqueducts at Canusium in Italy. Inscriptions indicate that the people of Epirus, Thessaly, Euboea, Boeotia, and other cities of Greece and Asia Minor gratefully styled Herodes Atticus their benefactor.[8]

The latter years of the period A.D. 200–324, witnessed a reversal of such beneficence. The military emperors of those years engaged in broad-scale confiscation of the funds left to governmental and private institutions for good works and used such wealth for their own purposes. The reign of the Roman emperor Constantine (324–337), however, was marked by his conversion to Christianity. Simultaneously, he issued decrees that legally recognized the Christian Church as, in essence, a foundation and forbade the alienation of funds entrusted to it for purposes other than that envisaged by state or private donors.

THE CHRISTIAN CHURCH AND THE MEDIEVAL PERIOD

The Christian Church from the first decades of its existence had set up funds to be devoted to charitable purposes. Spurred by the official approval of Constantine and later state rulers of Christendom, its clergy increasingly urged the living to contribute to it funds before their death as an ethical and religious atonement for their sins. Thus, one specialist on foundations flatly stated, "The teaching of Jesus set up a new and personal ethic for givers, which became the most important single influence on the philanthropy of the western world."[9] Against this background the

funds entrusted to the medieval Roman Catholic Church for
charitable purposes increased at a continuing and prodigious
rate. The result was that the church became the overwhelmingly
chief philanthropic institution of Western Europe during the
medieval period. The stage was now set for the continuous
manuevering and struggle between this church and various
states, which, while usually portrayed in a religious or political
context, can be viewed as an epoch in the history of philanthropy.

In 453 the emperor Valentinian had to issue correctional edicts
against various Christian bishops and other clerics for violating
the decrees of Constantine by diverting supposedly inalienable
charities set up for the poor to their own use. On the other hand,
such churchmen could and did justifiably argue that the evolving
laws by which they managed their entrusted funds were ambiguous and sometimes contradictory.

About 550 the emperor Justinian set up three sequential
commissions and charged them with the task of bringing order to
the now confusing tangle of older decrees and interpretations of
empire law, including, of particular interest to us, those bearing
on philanthropy. The commissions' restatement of law resulted in
the promulgation of the *Corpus Juris Civilis*, or, as it is better
known, the Justinian Code. From the philanthropic standpoint
the code's most important effect was that it brought the earlier
laws governing philanthropy into closer conformity with changing political, economic, and social conditions. Several parts of the
code were to have lasting effects in defining what we now view as
foundations and in spelling out certain practices and remedies for
their more efficient operation. For example, one statute declared
that "the founder of an ecclesiastical establishment [i.e., founda-
tion] creates a legal person of an ecclesiastical nature whose
personality derives from that of the Church but which possesses
a legal capacity of its own."[10]

As long as the fabric of Western European Christendom held
together, the Church remained the primary agency of philanthropy, although medieval companies and guilds established in
the larger Western European cities also engaged in charitable
activities and eventually approximated what we now call founda-

tions. The Reformation, however, in the Protestant countries and particularly England provided the primary seedbed for the emergence of foundations with present-day characteristics.

EARLY ENGLISH PHILANTHROPY

Prior to the Norman conquest of England in 1066, the philanthropic mode prevailing in the rest of Western Europe was generally practiced there. The purposes for which beneficences were made were more of a concern for one's soul than sympathy for others. The Roman Catholic Church, a spiritual organization, emphasized the spiritual or religious aspects of giving, not the physical or temporal ones. After the Norman conquest, however, the newly established kings and nobles gradually began to reject the concept that wealth held for religious/philanthropic purposes was a sole concern of the church and not subject to royal and state authority. An equally important, although less tangible, concept had also been developing among the emerging merchant aristocracy and the English in general. Would-be philanthropists were questioning the religious or spiritual emphasis in giving advised by the church. A clear example of this trend in thought is found in William Langland's fourteenth-century poem *The Vision of Piers the Plowman*. Benefactors seeking to do good with their wealth were counseled to use it to:

> . . . build hospitals,helping the sick,
> Or roads that are rotten full rightly repair,
> Or bridges , when broken, to build up anew,
> Well marry poor maidens, or make of them nuns,
> Poor people and pris'ners with food to provide,
> Set scholars to school, or some other crafts,
> And relieve the religious, enhancing their rents:[11]

In the 1500s such shifts in thought eventually contributed to, and culminated in, Henry VIII's outright break with the Roman Catholic Church and the confiscation by the crown of what has been estimated as up to one-half of the total wealth of England and lodged, to a great extent, in the church's philanthropic network. Although much of that wealth was diverted from philanthropic purposes for royal purposes and the creation and enriching of most of the English aristocracy, a significant portion was still eventually devoted to the establishment of trusts and foundations by royal beneficence and by this same aristocracy. In addition to this breaking of virtual churchly monopoly of getting and giving for charitable purposes in England, the second change to now-religious and secular giving remarked on earlier accelerated. Although the religious motif was not eliminated, the new and growing secular philanthropic entities increasingly emphasized a concern for, and were devoted to, the alleviation of people's troubles and discomfort on this earth. This change is clearly revealed in the Statute of Charitable Uses passed in the year 1601 of the reign of Queen Elizabeth (1558–1603). Uniformly referred to as the cornerstone of English law concerning foundations, the act provided that foundations could be set up as follows:

Some for relief of aged, impotent and poor people, some for maintenance of sick and maimed soldiers and mariners, schools of learning, free schools, and scholars in universities, some for repair of bridges, ports, havens, causeways, churches, sea-banks and highways, some for education and preferment of orphans, some for or towards relief, stock or maintenance of houses of correction, some for marriages of poor maids, some for supportation, aid and help of young tradesmen, handicraftsmen and persons decayed, and others for relief or redemption of prisoners or captives, and for aid or ease of any poor inhabitants concerning payment of . . . taxes.[12]

In addition to the spelling out of those philanthropic uses considered good, the act simultaneously provided for the legal safeguarding of gifts and bequests to foundations created for such usage.

In succeeding centuries wealthy English merchants, gentry, and nobles devoted an extraordinary amount of their wealth in attempts to alleviate and solve the problems of a society slowly changing from a feudal\rural to a democratic\industrial one. Thus, a philanthropic historian states that "in the early seventeenth century the failure of a London merchant to settle some substantial and conspicuous charitable trust or gift was generally regarded as little short of shocking unless there had been a grievous wasting of the estate because of age, ill-health, or commercial misfortune."[13] A sequential study of English philanthropy in the period 1660–1960 conclusively shows that this tradition of giving, although changing in content and scope, was maintained throughout succeeding centuries.[14] Historians Jordan and Owen both write that the charitable trust or foundation was a favorite device and a major instrument whereby the English carried out their philanthropic giving.

DIVERGING GOVERNMENTAL POLICY

A key divergence in the history of foundations in the last few centuries has been the differing governmental-legal policy toward them of the countries in which they were organized and operated. In England and in Western European countries such as the Netherlands and later in other countries such as the United States and India influenced by English law, relatively few legal restrictions were enacted to create and then operate foundations. In France, following the French Revolution, the accompanying disestablishment of the Roman Catholic Church, and the almost immediate adoption of the Napoleonic legal system, the creation and operation of foundations from that time to this day rest on mandatory governmental authorization and a much greater degree of governmental control. Similarly, other countries influenced by the Napoleonic legal systems adopted stricter controls toward foundations.[15] Thus, these two different approaches provide one of the major explanations for the disparate number of foundations, particularly the larger ones, established in various countries and regions of the world during the past few centuries. They may also provide a major explanation for the efficiency and impact of these foundations once established.

CENTRAL AND EASTERN EUROPE

The history of philanthropic giving in Central and Eastern Europe paralleled that of Western Europe through the medieval period in that such giving was overwhelmingly channeled through the Roman Catholic or Greek Orthodox Churches. Although a few organizations bearing some hallmarks of the modern foundation were set up there by the nineteenth century, in the twentieth century the chaos and financial debacles associated with World War I together with the establishment of communist governments in countries there after World War II saw their almost complete elimination in the communist-controlled areas for ideological and fiscal reasons. The recent overthrow of communist governments there coincided with the establishment of a number of foundations or foundation offices. They have been primarily funded with moneys provided by individuals and nongovernmental agencies, such as foundations from abroad. An early example was the 1988 establishment in the former USSR of the International Foundation for the Survival and Development of Humanity.[16] Since then such foundations have been set up under the aegis of the Rockefeller Brothers Fund, Ford Foundation, and other large U.S. foundations.[17] Also, a multitude of foundations have been established in the region and funded by the international financier and philanthropist George Soros. Whether or not this augurs a lasting reversal of the communist ideological and legal opposition to the creation and operation of foundations in the former communist countries, however, only time will tell.[18] More important for the immediate future is the threat to the legal and fiscal freedom possibly facing those that are now in operation. In 1996, for example, there were allegations by some Russian legislators that the Soros philanthropies were espionage fronts for Western powers, particularly the United States.

EUROPEAN COLONIES

Countries colonized by Europeans have generally tended to follow the English or the French/Napoleonic governmental-legal approach in the establishment and operation of foundations. Those that copied the English established a greater number of foundations and provided them with more ease and flexibility in founding and operation. England's former colonies, such as the United States, Australia, Canada, and India, are outstanding examples. Those following the French/Napoleonic approach saw far fewer foundations established and more restrictions on their operation. The former colonies of France and, to a slightly lesser degree, those of Spain and Portugal, particularly in Latin America in such countries as Brazil, Mexico, and Argentina, are examples of this approach.

ISLAM AND THE NEAR EAST

The emergence of Islam in the Near East in the seventh century saw the beginnings of a civilization unlike that of Europe. It evolved with a different religious and political history and concomitant social and legal concepts. Nevertheless, even at the time of its founding by Mohammad, according to Islamic Sunna—meaning "belief"—he advocated the establishment by believers of *vaqf*, alternately spelled *vakfin, waqf, wakf,* plural *wakif*. The *wakif* were entities created in perpetuity (the word *waqf* means "to stand still"), upon which funds were settled with the derived income being used for purposes deemed laudable by the Islamic religion. Semi-invidious grades in purpose for being established were recognized and, to a considerable degree, still hold sway today. Foremost was the donors' benevolence to, or remembrance of, members of their own family; second were moneys provided for the maintenance and promulgation of the Islamic religion; and last were funds set aside for the poor and the sick plus good works of general use for the public. From the seventh century onward, in countries substantially populated by Mohammedans such as present-day Turkey, Saudi Arabia, Iran, and Pakistan, *wakif* have been established.[19] Over the years and today only estimates of their number and wealth can be made, but they did and do exist in substantial numbers, and some have had, and do have, considerable wealth.

ASIA PACIFIC COUNTRIES

Outside of the countries with ties to Great Britain such as Australia and India, the evolution of the philanthropic foundation in other Asia Pacific countries is a relatively later phenomenon, and there still appear to be considerable governmental restraints on their founding and activities. Japan, for example, early on copied Germany in its laws relating to foundations rather than English or U.S. law. Post–World War II Japan under U.S. influence witnessed a modification of the earlier more restrictive legal and fiscal laws pertaining to foundations.[20] It was not until the 1970s, however, that a significant number began to be established, and

according to a survey undertaken by the Foundation Library Center of Japan in 1992, there are 200 grantmaking foundations of any significant size in Japan. . . . According to the Library Center of Japan which compiled this statistical material, the combined assets of the 20 largest foundations in the United States (US$54.8 billion) was about 20 times the combined assets of Japan's largest foundations (US$2.7 billion), according to the 1990 statistics.[21]

The scope of activities of Japanese foundations, moreover, still suffers from restrictive legal statutes. In 1990, for example, the author of a brief history of the Toyota Foundation noted in her opening paragraph the "disadvantages" accruing to that foundation when it elected to provide significant support for the humanities and social sciences rather than concentrating on technology and the natural sciences in its grant making.[22] More recent reports in discussing the autonomy of the nonprofit sector in Asian Pacific countries "reflect concern about a tendency of the government to 'turn to' the nonprofit sector, reinforcing a hierarchical relationship where NGOs [nongovernmental organizations, including foundations] are reduced to mere subsidiaries of government agencies."[23] This same report further states:

Despite the impressive growth of nonprofit and nongovernmental organizations in Asia Pacific, they continue to face rather formidable constraints against their activities and against further growth. This is particularly true for rapidly developing economies in Asia, such as the ASEAN [Association of Southeast Asian Nations] countries, but it also applies to economically advanced nations such as Japan. These constraints include the overall attitude of government towards NGO's and a lack of qualified research staff and administrative staff in the case of policy research institutions and difficulties of raising funds, partly due to a limited number of funding sources and partly due to the absence of tax incentivies for individual or corporate contributions.[24]

Against this background and brief history of foundations let us turn now to the major developments and actual or proposed changes that have taken place regarding U.S. foundations and similar organizations, particularly in the last half of the twentieth century.

2

Investigations and Studies*

In most discussions of foundations the assumption is made that government because of its varying supervisory power over foundations in terms of establishment, operation, and so on, assumes more importance than business. Yet the public's and its governmental representatives' changing perception of business and the conduct of the business structure underlying foundations, certainly in the United States, ultimately appears to be one, or perhaps the major, determinant in foundation development and change and in fashioning governmental legislation affecting foundations.

In the United States foundations can be set up by will/bequest or chartered by the federal government. Most U.S. foundations, however, have been incorporated under the laws of particular states, though only a minority of states have made effective provision for their supervision. Thus, foundations in the United States, whether established by will, under the auspices of states, or by the federal government, are essentially supervised at the national level by the Congress and the Internal Revenue Service of the U.S. Treasury Department. The Congress, based on inves-

---

*An earlier version of this chapter was delivered as a keynote address by the author at the 25th INTERPHIL Conference-1996 in Tallinn, Estonia.

tigations and bills introduced by its cognizant regular committees, such as the House of Representatives Ways and Means and
Banking and Currency Committees and the Senate Finance
Committee, has enacted the federal laws under which foundations are operated.[1] Of equal, and in some ways of more, importance in their impact on foundations and in ultimately fashioning
such legislation has been the work of select or special committees
and commissions created by the Congress and the Treasury
Department, the parent organization of the Internal Revenue
Service, to specifically look into the history and operation of
foundations. In the years from 1915 to the present, in addition to
the work of the regular committees, there have been four special
investigations of foundations by the Congress and one conducted
by the U.S. Treasury Department.

Also, during the latter part of the period two privately initiated
and funded commissions were established to study the role of
philanthropy in general and foundations in particular in American life. The Treasury Department and several other government
agencies, however, played a large role in the second private
commission's work. Each of these investigations and studies took
place as the result of the varying economic, political, and social
conditions that existed at the time they were inaugurated and
conducted and with varying results. The governmental investigations, because of their subpoena and inquiry powers, and resultant research, hearings, and reports amassed a great deal of
unique and valuable information on foundations. Somewhat similar results from the privately sponsored commission studies are,
in large part, due to the makeup of the commission members. They
have uniformly been persons with broad-scale knowledge and
experience, more often than not with philanthropy in general and
foundations in particular. An examination of these investigations
and studies and the ancillary business role for each follows.

WALSH COMMISSION

The first congressional investigation of foundations was that
of the Commission on Industrial Relations, created by the U.S.
Congress in 1915. Commonly known as the Walsh Commission

for its chairman, Senator Frank P. Walsh, it was launched to determine the causes of the widespread industrial unrest then current, which had culminated in the violent strike at the Rockefeller-owned Colorado Fuel and Iron Company and in the so-called Ludlow Massacre.

The event that turned the Walsh Commission's interest from industrial relations to the foundations was the announced decision of the trustees of the Rockefeller Foundation to engage in an investigation of industrial relations. The juxtaposition of this intention by the foundation to investigate industrial relations and the strike and unrest at Rockefeller plants led many to believe that there was a suspect relationship between the foundations—and the Rockefeller Foundation in particular—and the business interests whose assets they held. Thus, by ostensibly investigating industrial relations the Rockefeller Foundation might, in reality, be whitewashing big business in its controversies with labor. Quite understandably, the commission shifted its attention from industrial unrest to foundations and their role in American life.

It was a period of trust busting, and feeling ran high against those who had accumulated great wealth, such as Andrew Carnegie and John D. Rockefeller. In the public mind, foundations bearing such names symbolized wealth acquired by monopolistic and ethically questionable practices. Under such conditions, it was only natural that the liberals of that time were vehement in their denunciation of foundations. John Haynes Holmes, a well-known clergyman, in a wide-ranging testimony, told the commission that the very nature of a foundation "must be regarded as essentially repugnant to the whole idea of a democratic society" and that foundations had in them "the seed of peril to our democratic institutions."[2]

Samuel Gompers, then president of the American Federation of Labor, concluded that the foundations' "efforts to undertake to be an all-pervading machinery for the molding of the minds of the people in their relationship between each other in the constant industrial struggle for human betterment . . . should be prohibited . . . either by law or by regulation."[3]

The majority report of the Walsh Commission charged that the great corporate interests were endeavoring to mold the educational and social life of the country by controlling colleges and universities through the giving of grants. It pointed out that the income from the Rockefeller and Carnegie Foundations alone was twice as great as the government's appropriations for education and social services and expressed the view that the policies of the foundations would inevitably reflect the policies of the great corporations and those who controlled them.

The majority report recommended a federal statute requiring a federal charter for foundations with assets of more than $1 million. The charter was to limit funds as to size and accumulation, limit activities to specific powers and functions, and prohibit any alteration of purpose unless empowered by Congress. The commission also suggested that the government counteract the influence of foundations by greatly increased federal appropriations for education and social service. The recommended legislation, which would have greatly increased the control of foundations by the Congress, was never passed, probably because of the war then raging in Europe and because subsequent U.S. entrance into it diverted attention from domestic problems. In any event the foundations escaped further governmental supervision and were not investigated by the Congress for a second time until 1952. By that time a complete turnaround had taken place in the general thinking concerning foundations. In 1915 the liberals believed the foundations to be a force for reaction and conservatism. In 1952 the conservatives charged that the foundations had been captured by the liberals and that foundation funds were being used to further subversive attitudes.

COX COMMITTEE

In describing the general conditions that led to the setting up in 1952 of the commonly called Cox Committee investigation, the committee's chairman being Representative E. Eugene Cox, I stated:

The second investigation of foundations grew partially out of the differences between "right" and "left" and partially out of various problems which were an aftermath of World War II.

In particular, the United States, confronted with the problems of traitors and subversives within its own borders to an extent never existing before, sought the reasons. What would cause the well-bred and educated, those who stood to benefit the most from our way of life, to embrace communism? Was our educational system at fault? Was it at fault in its interpretation, or conduct of the social sciences, and of economics and economic history particularly?

In a search for the answer to these and related questions, inevitably interested persons would attempt to assay the role played by the foundations. In view of their importance in the educational world, the diversity and range of their operations, their freedom of action, their venture-capital concept, it is understandable that a spot-light would be turned on them.[4]

In addition to these broad forces, several distinct groups provided the catalytic element for activating the investigation, and although their motivations were different they had a common purpose. One group felt that the foundations had lent considerable support to the United Nations and to allied organizations that they felt threatened to undercut our Constitution by treaties. Another was motivated by domestic political considerations. They were opposed to General Dwight D. Eisenhower as a U.S. presidential candidate in favor of Senator Robert A. Taft. They believed that Eisenhower would draw much of his support from influential persons, such as John Foster Dulles and Paul Hoffman, who were officers or trustees of foundations. If, as they hoped, they could show that communists had infiltrated and/or been supported by these same foundations, it would help to neutralize such support for Eisenhower for U.S. president by associating them all with communism. They also hoped to establish a link between Eisenhower , who was then president of Columbia University, and a faculty there that they maintained was a hotbed of communist/subversives and that was supported and tied in with the foundations. Finally, a smaller element centering in Chicago was personally distrustful of, and disliked, several key officials of the newly endowed Ford Foundation and hoped, in the course of an investigation of foundations, to show that these officials, too, were tarred with the communist/subversive taint. The individuals in these groups assembled material documenting their views and placed it in the hands of Congressman Cox, and their efforts eventually led to the establishment of the Cox Committee. Much of this story and its aftermath appeared in a 1953 article in *The Reporter* magazine.[5]

Widely expected to be a witch-hunt similar to other such congressional committees of the 1950s, the Cox Committee did not turn out that way. Much of this outcome was due to the competent staff hired by the committee. Significant, too, were the agreements reached at one of the first conferences of the committee in July 1952. With all members of the committee present except Congressman B. Carroll Reece, it was unanimously agreed that the investigation was to be the means of gathering impartial and objective information on foundations and that it would not lend its efforts to, or on behalf of, any partisan political party or group. In this connection, it was stipulated and agreed that no public hearings would be held until after the presidential election in November. At these eighteen hearings some forty witnesses testified, including a veritable who's who of philanthropists and foundation staff: F. Emerson Andrews, Chester Barnard, Vannevar Bush, John W. Davis, Charles Dollard, Marshall Field, Henry Ford II, Paul Hoffman, Robert M. Hutchins, Henry Allen Moe, John D. Rockefeller III, Dean Rusk, Alfred P. Sloan Jr., Donald Young, and others. In addition, there were key officials from the foundations' governmental supervisory agency, then the Bureau of Internal Revenue, now the Internal Revenue Service.

Long before the hearings, questionnaires were prepared and sent out to more than 1,500 tax-exempt organizations, including some seventy detailed questionnaires to foundations with capital assets of more than $10 million. The answers to the questionnaires were carefully analyzed in advance of the hearings and provided excellent preparation for them. Also prior to the hearings, conferences were held with approximately 200 persons who were well informed on foundation matters, and another 250 such persons were conferred with by telephone, telegram, or letter.

The final report of the Cox Committee,[6] which was unanimous, noted the importance of foundations in American life and that their most significant function had been the supplying of venture capital to advance the frontiers of knowledge. While calling attention to the great service that foundations had rendered in the areas of medicine, public health, education, the humanities, and the natural sciences, it noted their significant support in the controversial field of the social sciences and ventured the opinion that at a time when people's mastery of the natural sciences threatened them with possible extermination, the reward from the pursuit and mastery of the social sciences might prove even more important than accomplishments in the natural sciences.

With reference to the major criticism leveled at foundations and the one that had sparked its creation, the committee found that the foundations had not used their resources to discredit nor undermine the capitalistic system or to advance socialism; that while communists had made determined efforts to infiltrate the foundations, with a few exceptions they had not attained influential positions; and that on balance the record of the foundations was good in this respect. The committee recommended that the House Ways and Means Committee consider tax amendments to encourage gifts to foundations, as the need for foundations was greater than ever before.

A criticism that developed in the course of the Cox Committee investigation, more often than not voiced by those connected with foundations, was the crying need for all foundations to better inform the public as to their purpose and activities. Repeated references were made to the need for them to conduct their operations in a "goldfish bowl" or with "glass pockets."[7] The Cox Committee recommended better public accounting for all foundations and submitted a draft of a proposed act to accomplish this purpose.

Another criticism developed in the course of the investigation was the narrowness, especially geographic, in the trustee/staff makeup of the major foundations. Large foundations with offices located in the New York City area were particular targets in this regard, with allegations that trustees and others associated with their foundations were overwhelmingly residents of the city or living in close proximity to it. The universal explanation advanced by foundation representatives was the need to have suitable persons close at hand to draw on quickly for counsel and advice who would not be restricted by travel delays. While recognizing such explanations, in its *Final Report* the committee recommended:

Despite these considerations, all of which are persuasive, the committee feels that a wider geographical distribution would go far towards establishing greater public confidence in the foundations. . . . It is entirely possible that a sustained search for qualified individuals residing west of the Hudson River might assist the foundations to maintain the freshness of approach, flexibility, and breadth of vision for which they profess to strive. If, as the foundations maintain and the committee believes, foundations are public trusts then the public in its widest sense, including the geographical, should be fairly represented.[8]

REECE COMMITTEE

The Reece Committee investigation, chaired by Congressman B. Carroll Reece, in 1953 and 1954 can aptly be described as a fallout from the Cox Committee investigation. As soon as Congressman Reece, who had been a strong supporter of Senator Taft for president and the ultraconservative groups that had been instrumental in bringing about the Cox investigation, observed the direction in which that investigation was moving, these elements lost interest in it and began planning another. They urged Congressman Reece to launch a new, third investigation with the previously mentioned Chicago group associated with the genesis of the Cox Committee providing much of the driving force and research. The eagerness of the new Eisenhower administration to extend the excess profits tax afforded the group the opportunity they sought. Congressman Reece, who was a member of the powerful House Rules Committee, was opposed to the extension of the tax, but he traded his much needed vote in favor of it for a new investigation of foundations.

In a July 1953 speech by Reece, filling ten pages of the *Congressional Record,* in support of the resolution authorizing a new investigating committee, the direction and thrust of the proposed investigation were clearly outlined in the following brief quotations from that speech:

Some of these institutions [foundations] support efforts to overthrow our government and to undermine our American way of life. These activities urgently require investigation. Here lies the story of how Communism and socialism are financed in the United States, where they get their money. It is the story of who pays the bill. There is evidence to show there is a diabolical conspiracy back of all this. Its aim is the furtherance of socialism in the United States. Communism is only a brand name for socialism and the Communist state represents itself to be only the true form of socialism.[9]

And further:

Large foundations have a tremendous influence on the intellectual and educational life of our country. . . . Extensive evidence that I have examined shows that organizations which are primarily committed to a given ideology have received large grants from some big foundations over many years.[10]

The evidence to which Congressman Reece referred had been submitted to the staff of the Cox Committee. It had been examined and rejected for several reasons: the research was sketchy and often inaccurate; time was lacking to pursue some of the leads it pointed up; and it opened up a field of examination beyond the limits of the Cox Committee inquiry.

The Reece investigation seemed dedicated to proving certain theses instead of ascertaining facts. Its principal witnesses were members of its staff. Of the nine non-staff witnesses who testified at public hearings only one, the then president of the Social Science Research Council, could, by stretching it, be considered a representative of foundations. Also, the hearings degenerated into a pitched battle between Republican chairman Reece and Democratic minority members, particularly Congressman Wayne Hays. Most of the press vigorously denounced the manner in which the investigation was conducted, and the stormy hearings were finally adjourned by the chairman because of what he characterized as the obstructionist tactics of Congressman Hays.

Foundation officials were given no opportunity to be heard. Later they were afforded an opportunity to file written statements, and a few did so. Typical of the comment in the press is the following passage from an article in the *New York Times* entitled "Another Stupid Inquiry": "Under the conditions laid down by Chairman Reece the suspension of public hearings by the special House of Representatives committee to investigate foundations is inexcusable. . . . The history of this committee has been a disgrace to Congress. There was no need for it to begin with."[11]

The obvious bias displayed by Reece in his speech urging the creation of the committee, his failure to afford the foundations and the other organizations under attack an opportunity to be heard, and the spectacle of open wrangling between committee members were self-defeating. Moreover, the majority report was vitiated by an addendum setting forth the views of Congressman Angier Goodwin. Goodwin, who had been a member of the Cox Committee, strongly reaffirmed in his addendum his continuing adherence to the views expressed by the Cox Committee: "Nothing," he said, "has transpired in the proceedings of the present Committee to cause me to alter or modify the views expressed in the Cox Committee report. I take this opportunity to again re-affirm them."[12]

In the light of subsequent events, some of the obloquy and criticism directed at the work and report of the Reece Committee appears to have been unwarranted and wrong. For example, one of the major conclusions of the majority was that foundations exercise power far out of proportion to their respective funds. This theme, in varying forms, had often been urged by the foundations themselves. The report further found that this power was greatly magnified by an interlock in staff and personnel or a concert of action with other individuals and organizations, which, as the report admitted, the foundations might not be aware of. Irrespective of the methods used by the committee in arriving at this conclusion, it is not without merit. The committee assembled considerable evidence of a tendency of foundations to channel their support in recent years to those individuals and organizations that supported a liberal or left view. The conclusion that they drew may have been wrong, but the committee accumulated considerable evidence of definite selectivity. The Reece report did not urge the abolition of foundations; it urged reform, but reform from within, and it warned that if the foundations failed to see the need for reform, further congressional action was inevitable, even the withdrawal of tax exemption from them.

PATMAN INVESTIGATION

In 1961 Congressman Wright Patman, chairman of the Select Committee on Small Business of the U.S. House of Representatives, launched the last of the four special congressional investigations of foundations. It was different in a number of ways from the three preceding investigations, the most significant difference being its purpose. The Walsh, Cox, and Reece investigations were all ideologically oriented, were primarily concerned with the nature or content and conduct of foundation programs, and gave little attention to the economic aspects of foundations. The Patman investigation paid little, if any, attention to foundation programs and concentrated upon the economic effect or significance of foundations. The Patman investigation was unique in a number of other aspects. Initiated in 1961, it continued as an open-ended one until 1972. It was different also in that it did not appear to be a committee investigation but essentially a one-man crusade by Congressman Patman. This led to another anomaly, namely, that while there were two sets of hearings over the life of the investigation, the whole effort resulted primarily in a number of voluminous reports made by Congressman Patman as chairman of a committee. The announced intention of the investigation was to study the impact of foundations upon the American economy, particularly upon small businesses. The investigation was also to be pursued to see if new legislation was needed to provide better supervision of foundations vis-à-vis the economic scene. Patman praised the work of foundations but announced concern about the significant growth of new foundations and their economic impact. As he stated in a speech that launched his investigation:

Let us digress to say that we have nothing but praise for the work that has been done and is being done by foundations in many fields such as education, health, social welfare, scientific research, humanities, religion, international affairs, and government. So our thought today is not to criticize, but to urge Congress to take a fresh look. What has brought about this feverish growth [of foundations]?[13]

Patman called for an immediate moratorium on tax exemption for foundations and based his recommendation on failure of supervision by the Internal Revenue Service, willful abuses of tax exemption by numerous foundations, unreasonable accumulations of income, and the need for reassessment of tax exemption in the light of increased tax burdens for the public and increased need for revenue by the government.

Patman's resultant investigation produced eight reports (1962–1972) containing an enormous amount of statistical material. Seven had been prepared as *Chairman's Reports*[14] by staff of his committee and were presented to the other committee members by Chairman Patman; the eighth was a *Staff Report*[15] (1972) to the Subcommittee on Finance of the Committee on Banking and Currency of the House. The 1962 *Chairman's Report,* for example, contained over 135 pages of finely printed material and charged corporations with using the cloak of charity to evade taxes and to gain unfair competitive advantages in their business enterprises. The report contained seventeen recommendations, prominent among which were limiting the life of a foundation to twenty-five years, prohibiting foundations from engaging in business, limiting foundation ownership of the stock of a corporation to 3%, and treating contributions and capital gains as income instead of capital. The six later reports contained studies of the financial activities of particular foundations and, as has been said, an enormous amount of statistical material gathered from questionnaires and other documents obtained from foundations.

At the initial set of *Hearings* in 1964[16] only four government officials were heard and questioned about possible foundation violation of various statutes. No foundation officials or representatives were called or heard. The second set of *Hearings*[17] in

1967 was almost exclusively devoted to a not-for-profit organization called Americans Building Constitutionally (ABC) which, for graduated fees, undertook to instruct members in setting up foundations, with a heavy emphasis on avoiding the payment of taxes.

The Patman investigation was criticized at the time it was being carried on and, to a lesser extent thereafter, for inaccuracy and exaggeration in its reports; for failure to afford foundations an opportunity to be heard; for attempting, by the presentation of only certain selected material, to prove preconceived ideas; and, in short, for a consequent failure to present a fair and balanced picture of foundations. Granting these faults, the investigation did uncover and hold up to public view flagrant abuses by some foundations and did alert the Treasury Department, the Internal Revenue Service, and tax writing committees of the Congress to the existence of such abuses. Finally, it undoubtedly spurred the standing Committee on Ways and Means of the House of Representatives and the Committee on Finance of the Senate to request the Treasury Department to examine the activities of foundations for possible tax abuses and report its conclusions and recommendations to the committees.

TREASURY DEPARTMENT INVESTIGATION

The 1965 investigation conducted by the department and ensuing *Report*[18] published by it also called attention to abuses in the foundation field and made six recommendations of a supervisory nature. Their sympathetic content and character can probably be best judged from the following quotation from the *Report*:

> The recommendations seek not only to end diversions, distractions, and abuses, but to stimulate and foster the active pursuit of charitable ends which the tax laws seek to encourage. Any restraints which the proposals may impose on the flow of funds to private foundations will be far outweighed by the benefits which will accrue to charity from the removal of abuses and from the elimination of the shadow which the existence of abuse now casts upon the private foundation area.[19]

This same concern for the future was reflected in the writings of some of the more perceptive foundation officials. In 1968 Alan

Pifer, then president of the Carnegie Corporation of New York, warned:

The danger which foundations have faced in recent years, and perhaps never more so than today, is that public loss of confidence in them, occasioned by limited, but continuing and well publicized disclosure of abuses will become great enough to precipitate Congress into a hasty and clumsy piece of legislation. . . . It is evident, therefore, that the foundations which are carrying out genuine philanthropic purposes, which are well managed, and are making a strong effort to serve the public interest, must take energetic steps themselves to put the foundation house in better order. They have no grounds for thinking that because they have escaped restriction in the past they will necessarily continue to do so in the future. A field which has grown from less than 200 members 40 years ago to 20,000 today will, of course, come under even closer scrutiny by public authorities. And the concern of these officials, once aroused, may not stop at regulation which simply prevents wrongdoing or the grosser forms of mismanagement, however inappropriate more extensive government regulation may be.[20]

The foundation world did not seem to pay much attention to such warnings. Similarly, on the surface the Congress did not seem to pay much attention to the Patman investigation and for four years it ignored the abuses revealed and the reforms recommended by the Treasury Department *Report*. By 1969, however, came the revelation of grants by several foundations to fund projects that figured directly in the political and electoral process and of study and travel grants by other foundations to various out-of-job political figures. If anything further were needed to point up abuses by foundations and to further tarnish their public image, it was supplied by the spectacle of two foundations using their funds in a blatant attempt to influence two justices of the U.S. Supreme Court.

PETERSON COMMISSION AND TAX REFORM ACT OF 1969

The upshot was that 1969 witnessed *Hearings*[21] before the House Ways and Means Committee and *Hearings*[22] before the Senate Finance Committee regarding foundations. Significantly,

Congressman Patman was one of the first witnesses to be called and heard by the House Committee. Belatedly, in the same year, a privately funded, thirteen-member Commission on Foundations and Private Philanthropy was established, headed by Peter G. Peterson, then head of the Bell and Howell Corporation. The Peterson Commission's hurried deliberations and resultant publications presented facts; explored the accomplishments, role, and needs of foundations; and discussed their relationship to government. They emphasized that all foundations should not suffer for the misdeeds of a very few and drew a number of conclusions and made a number of recommendations to the foundations and to government.[23] Although Peterson presented much of the work of the commission to the Senate committee, and it probably helped to blunt the more drastic measures advocated there, it was clearly apparent in both the Senate and House hearings that a severely critical attitude toward foundations had developed. The denouement in this varied scrutiny of foundations was the passage of the Tax Reform Act (TRA) of 1969, which included a new tax and new supervisory laws for foundations. The major new laws were an excise tax of 4% of net investment income for defraying auditing costs of their operations; restrictions on grants to individuals; a requirement that disbursements of a foundation must at least equal investment income within a year, with invasion of capital if such income did not reach a set percentage, set annually by the IRS, of held assets; tightened restrictions on self-dealing between donor and foundation; and broadened and amplified reporting requirements. Also, the TRA of 1969 divided foundations into private and public categories for IRS purposes, with those in the public category, including community foundations and other public charities, receiving more favorable treatment under the legislation.

Viewed by many at the time as drastic and punitive, others regarded these measures as salutary and necessary and designed to correct serious inequities relating to the economic and reporting aspects of foundations. They were not directed at what might be called the ideological underpinnings of foundations. Furthermore, with the passage of a few years, some features of the 1969

legislation that were viewed by government and foundation officials as stringent or unnecessary were later modified or repealed.
Against this background of the recognition of the need for reform
and yet concern for the future of philanthropy in general and
foundations in particular was created the 1973 Commission on
Private Philanthropy and Public Needs, named the Filer Commission for its chairman, John H. Filer, chairman of the Aetna
Life and Casualty Corporation, with foundations providing most
of the money for the costs of its deliberations.

FILER COMMISSION

The ostensible major reason for being and the first concern of
the Filer Commission was the decline of voluntary giving in the
United States by its citizenry. The results of the commission's
labor were published in 1977 by the U.S. Department of the
Treasury under the title *Giving in America: Report of the Commission on Private Philanthropy and Public Needs,*[24] together
with Volumes 1–5 of *Research Papers.*[25] Although the *Report* and
Research Papers touch on all aspects of philanthropy, they concentrate on the economic aspects of giving and the relationship
of nonprofit organizations to the federal government. In the
sections of the commission's publications dealing with foundations, relatively little is said concerning their establishment or
operation. Much is said regarding the tax and supervisory laws
pertaining to them, particularly those included in the Tax Reform
Act of 1969. The major recommendations of the Filer Commission
proper regarding foundations included changing the 4% governmental excise tax to one based on the actual cost of audit, the 4%
generally conceded as being excessive; lowering the payout rate
required of foundations from 6% to 5%; personnel diversification;
easing the restriction on lobbying government by tax-exempt
groups; and creating a permanent semigovernmental advisory
commission on the not-for-profit and philanthropic sector of the
United States. These recommendations of the Filer Commission
eventually resulted in the following changes: (1) the reduction in
the governmental excise tax from 4% to 2% (in certain cases to
1%), the monetary return to the government from the lower

percentages being more in line with the actual cost of foundation audits, and (2) the lowering of the payout rate to the recommended 5%.

DONEE GROUP REPORT

The commission's receptive attitude toward criticism of foundations can best be seen in the fact it went so far as to provide financial aid and other help to the setting up of a self-styled "Donee Group," which had openly questioned the commission's purpose and work. That group eventually put out a report of its own, which was highly critical of the commission report. The Donee Group report, nevertheless, was published by the commission as part of its *Research Papers.*[26] The most important conclusions and recommendations of the Donee Group were that philanthropies, particularly foundations, should provide much more information about their programs and activities and more access to them by individuals and groups previously denied such access. To ensure this development, the group recommended numerous specific changes affecting foundations, which can be summarized under the following headings: (1) expanded and more broadly disseminated information about programs and activities of foundations; (2) broader geographical, public, and nonprofit sector and especially gender and minority representation on foundation governing boards and staff; and (3) a variety of changes in governmental regulations affecting foundations, particularly the removal of the IRS as a supervisory agency and the simultaneous creation of a new independent governmental commission for that purpose with direct congressional oversight provided for it.

While we did have the scandal in the 1990s associated with the Foundation for New Era Philanthropy and the present-day controversy over foundations and advocacy groups discussed in Chapter 6, from the time of the Filer Commission to the present, a span of over twenty-five years, there have been no *major* investigations or studies of foundations, public or private, in the United States. Yet during this period there has been a continuous increase in the growth and expansion of foundations in this country. Why the cessation of such probes in the United States? Granted, the period was, by and large, a prosperous one in the country, and the worldwide collapse of communism appeared to end the threat to the capitalistic free enterprise business system of the United States; still, an equally important consideration appears to have been the response on the part of foundation officials, particularly those connected with the larger ones, to the changes suggested and the criticisms leveled at them earlier by those within their own ranks and by these governmental and private investigations and studies. Specifically, most of our large foundations and many of the smaller ones have seen the need for, and encouraged the critical and objective examination of foundations per se. While advocating the efficacy and need for foundations, they have promoted and financed discussion, research, writing, and publication about them as a group, particularly their programs and operation. Tangentially, they have diversified the makeup of the membership of their boards of trustees and staff geographically, by gender, and by ethnicity. Some have advocated the establishment of a permanent national philanthropic commission. Some have urged the replacement of the IRS, which many contend is not governmentally positioned to play a proper role vis-à-vis our foundations and the nonprofit sector, with such a national philanthropic commission. Succeeding chapters dwell on these major changes and developments, which may go far to providing the answer to the cessation of large-scale probes of foundations.

3

Growth and Expansion

Against the background and history of foundations and the investigations and studies of foundations in the United States previously presented, the initial phenomenon that strikes one in any consideration of our present-day foundations is their burgeoning growth and expansion in the latter part of the nineteenth century and on into the twentieth century. After applying the restrictive definition and categorization of foundations advanced in the Introduction to this volume, the four factors best utilized in describing their growth are (1) the increase in the total number of foundations established; (2) the increase in assets held by all foundations; (3) the increase in the size of the assets held by the largest foundations; and (4) the increase in the monetary amount of grants awarded by them. Regarding expansion, two factors are best examined: (1) geographical expansion and (2) the setting up of institutionally related foundations.

GROWTH

Prior to discussing growth, it is well to point out that, because of inflation, it can be argued that assets held by many foundations have only held their own or have actually declined in value in real terms with the passage of time. For example, in his 1996 *Annual*

Report, pp. 6–7, for the Charles Stewart Mott Foundation, Chairman William S. White details this point. He convincingly documents that for the period 1963 to 1996 the Mott Foundation just about held its own in the real value of its assets. In any case, in numerical terms and on all four counts, nowhere is this foundation growth so pronounced as in the United States in the twentieth century.

In discussing the growth of foundations in the United States, it should also be noted at the outset that prior to the 1950s the statistics on the formation, number, assets, and grants of extant U.S. foundations fall considerably short of completeness. Such information on grant making is particularly lacking prior to that decade. The best sources for available information prior to that decade are cited in the Introduction (n. 3), and are the primary ones used for that period in this chapter and for the remainder of this work. In 1950 federal legislation opened returns of foundations to the Internal Revenue Service for public inspection, and in 1956 the Foundation Library Center (now Foundation Center) was established and began its work. Since then the statistical material on U.S. foundations as presented in its continuing *Foundation Directories*, beginning in 1960, has been as complete and accurate as possible and has been utilized in the present work.

PRE–CIVIL WAR PERIOD

Prior to the U.S. Civil War (1861–1865), few endowments or foundations had been set up in this country in the eighteenth or nineteenth centuries, and those that existed were generally limited in size and scope. One of the first was the Magdalen Society established in Philadelphia in 1800. It was created to "ameliorate the distressed condition of those unhappy females who have been seduced from the path of virtue, and are desirous of returning to a life of rectitude." Initially, this led to the opening up of a home for such wayward women. In 1918, however, it was reorganized as the White-Williams Foundation with a broader mandate, that is, the solution of problems affecting school-age children and youths.

More noticeable were those early foundations established by Benjamin Franklin and James Smithson. Under his will Franklin set up two trusts in 1791, of about the equivalent of $4,500 each, in Philadelphia and Boston to provide loans for "young married artificers of good character." Franklin's will specified that the principal and interest of the funds were to accumulate, and, although the trusts have changed over the years in size, investments, and uses, they have both worked for the benefit of the two cities from their inception to the present day. James Smithson, an Englishman, made a sizable bequest in 1829 to the United States "for the increase and diffusion of knowledge among men." Although no one has satisfactorily explained the reason for what was then a very large gift with such sweeping powers and purpose to a then-predominantly backwoods country, it eventually led to the 1846 creation of the Smithsonian Institution by the U.S. Congress. Augmented by governmental funds since then, the institution currently maintains an outstanding museum in Washington, D.C., and also uses its funds to support a broad research program.

POST–CIVIL WAR PERIOD

Not until after the American Civil War, however, was the first truly significant foundation established in the United States. In 1867 George Peabody set up the Peabody Education Fund with assets of over $2 million to aid the stricken South. In 1882 John F. Slater organized the John F. Slater Fund for the Education of Freedmen in the South with an endowment of $1 million. Following these two only about a half dozen more foundations of some significance were established in the latter part of the nineteenth century. An 1894 book on American philanthropy devoted a brief, ten-page chapter to the pitfalls occasioned in setting up and operating foundations and naively concluded: "We are not, of course, likely to have a dangerously large amount of property devoted to charitable uses very soon."[1]

An increasing number of post–Civil War wealthy industrialists, particularly the very wealthiest, refuted this view in their thought and actions. As early as 1889 Andrew Carnegie led the way with his gospel of wealth publications.[2] The basic premise of these works was that the capitalistic economic system established and prevailing in the United States furnished a greater and greater number of people there with a better and better standard of living accompanied by corresponding continuing and vast increases in the amount of surplus wealth held by a few. Carnegie preached that these then extremely wealthy individuals could do one of three things with their wealth: leave it to heirs, leave it for philanthropic and charitable purposes at death, or use it for such purposes during their own lifetime. Carnegie rejected the first two and concluded that the third alone afforded those of great wealth the wisest and most effective way to dispose of their wealth, and the major vehicle he adopted for this purpose was the philanthropic foundation. In doing so, Carnegie probably did more toward setting up the foundation pattern of giving in the United States than any other American. In 1902 he established the Carnegie Institution of Washington, his first important foundation, with an initial fund of $10 million. This was followed by the creation of numerous others, including the Carnegie Corporation of New York, established in 1911–1912. With a corpus of $125 million, the corporation was the largest single foundation created up to that time.

John D. Rockefeller shared Carnegie's views and, agreeing with the foundation course of action, began to set up foundations almost as soon as Carnegie. In 1901 the Rockefeller Institute for Medical Research (now Rockefeller University) was established; in 1902 the General Education Board; and in 1913 the Rockefeller Foundation. In total, about $500 million was donated by Rockefeller toward the creation of these and other foundations. Other notable foundations were established at this time: the Milbank Memorial Fund in 1905; Russell Sage Foundation in 1907; and the New York Foundation in 1909. Still, by 1929 there were only about 200 to 300 foundations of any real significance in existence in the United States. It is interesting to note that one of the most perceptive foundation executives of the period observed:

My own feeling is that we shall see few, if any, new foundations of very large size, say $100,000,000 or over, but that there will be a steady increase in those of somewhat smaller size, say from $3,000,000 to $15,000,000 in capitalization (within which figures would fall the existing Russell Sage, Milbank, and Guggenheim Foundations).[3]

Despite the Great Depression, which began in 1929, and the dramatic reduction in surplus wealth in the 1930s, some 300 more foundations were added to the foundations rolls in that decade. The more important independent ones included the Field, James, and Kellogg Foundations, together with four set up by the Mellon family. Also, the Ford Foundation, destined to become the largest U.S. foundation for many decades, was incorporated in 1936 with an initial endowment of $25,000.

POST–WORLD WAR II PERIOD

Accompanied by the advent and prosecution of World War II, the 1940s saw a surge in the establishment of foundations. Spurred, in part, by the higher tax levels attendant upon the war, some 1,800 were founded in that decade. By the 1950s there were about 4,000 significant foundations in existence in the United States with total assets of about $3 billion. Among those foundations holding the largest assets only four independent ones held assets in excess of $100 million: the Ford Foundation, Rockefeller Foundation, Carnegie Corporation of New York, and Duke Endowment. Only some fifty to sixty of all other types of foundations had assets amounting to $10 million dollars or more . In view of this continuing growth of foundations in the United States, particularly of large independent foundations, some prominent industrialists/philanthropists of the 1950s still held the view that few large foundations would be created in the United States in the future because of high tax rates and the general tendency toward a wider spread of wealth.[4] Swayed by this and earlier similar views, the 1953 U.S. House of Representatives Cox Committee's *Final Report* erroneously stated:

While there has been a tremendous growth in the numbers of small foundations in the past 10 years it is unlikely that existing tax levies will permit the creation by individuals or families of large foundations (in the sense that the Ford, Rockefeller, and Carnegie Foundations are large) after the next 10 or 15 years.[5]

THE 1960s

In 1960 the first edition of the *Foundation Directory* appeared, and it estimated that by that time there were about 12,000 foundations in existence in the United States but that only about 5,200 were significant enough in assets, programs, grants, and so on to warrant inclusion in the *Directory*. It was also stated therein that these 5,200 held assets totaling approximately $11.5 billion; that the 129 largest foundations, those with assets of $10 million each or more, held assets totaling about $8.8 billion; and that the 10 largest foundations, all of the independent type, held assets of more than $100 million each and collectively accounted for about half of the approximately $11.5 billion in assets held by all of the foundations in the United States. The *Directory* also pointed out that the 129 larger foundations accounted for about 56% of total foundation grant expenditures of $625 million and that more than 87% of all known foundations then in existence in the United States had been founded in the 1940s and 1950s.

1980–1999

The best estimate is that there were approximately 20,000 foundations in existence in the United States in 1980. By 1999 this number had doubled to more than 40,000. The latest *Foundation Directory* (21st ed., 1999, Introduction, pp. vii–xv), contains entries for 10,445 of the most significant foundations out of the approximate 40,000. These 10,445 foundations meet financial criteria of at least $2 million in assets or $200,000 in annual giving for inclusion in the volume. Their combined assets of about $304 billion accounted for 92.3% of all foundation assets, and their combined grants of about $14.3 billion accounted for 90% of all foundation giving. Historically, this group of foundations has exerted the greatest impact on society and is the one primarily considered in this volume.[6] The fourteen largest foundations in the group each held assets of $2 billion or more, and the next 86, in size of assets held, each had $419 million or more.

INDEPENDENT FOUNDATIONS

An overwhelming number of foundations falling into the preceding categories were of the independent type, with the recently established Bill and Melinda Gates Foundation leading in assets with just over $17 billion. Statistically, the *Foundation Directory* (1999, p. ix) shows that 8,884 independent foundations held some $261 billion or about 85% of total foundation assets, while their total annual giving of almost $11 billion constituted 76.1% of total foundation annual giving of about $14 billion.

COMPANY FOUNDATIONS

Although later in origin and proportionately smaller in number and size of assets held, U.S. foundations in major categories other than the independent—that is, company, community, and operating—have experienced similarly spectacular growth in the twentieth century. As has been noted, all of the earlier significant foundations established in the United States had been of the independent type and the result of funds accumulated by individuals. In the late nineteenth and twentieth centuries, independent foundations were usually the result of successful operation of companies and corporations that such individuals owned or controlled. In the earlier decades of that period, many of them believed that the primary or even sole purpose of their companies was to provide profits for their owners and shareholders and wages for their workers. Reflecting this thinking, it was held that a company or corporation had no right to channel its profits for other purposes such as charitable contributions to individuals or other organizations.[7]

The first major departure from such reasoning appears to have been in the various forms of financial aid provided by U.S. railroad corporations directly to units of the Young Men's Christian Association (YMCA). With beginnings in England and established in the United States in 1851, the YMCA was receiving financial help from the railroads for 82 of its associations in 1890, and by 1911 this number had climbed to 230 associations. By the latter year it appears that such aid had cumulatively amounted to several million dollars.[8] World War I and U.S. entry into that war saw a considerable augmentation in the philanthropic aid provided by our corporations toward various campaigns for funds mounted by the YMCA, Red Cross, and other similar organizations for welfare work among our armed forces. While the records for such giving have not been found, one writer observed in a 1952 volume that they were certainly in excess of $20 million and asserted that "enough evidence exists to pin-point 1917 as the year in which corporation contributions reached a substantial total in the history of American philanthropy."[9] The first edition of the *Foundation Directory* (1960, p. xxi) stated, "A wave of foundations of a new type had crested in the past decade." It added, "A few early examples of company-sponsored foundations exist, but they were set up in great numbers only recently, with an apparent peak in 1952 and 1953." While such a peak may have occurred for those years in the 1950s, company foundations have seen a continuous increase in numbers, size of assets held, and annual giving since then. Statistically, the latest *Foundation Directory* (1999, p. ix), shows that, among the 10,445 foundations included therein, 939 company foundations held about $10 billion or 3.4% of total foundation assets of about $304 billion, and their annual giving of approximately $2 billion accounted for 13.9% of total foundation annual giving of about $14.3 billion. That the earlier thinking about corporate philanthropy is not dead, however, can be seen from the following. A 1996 article expounded the deleterious effects of corporate philanthropy and urged the elimination of tax deductions by corporations for such giving.[10] A 1997 article concerning the Sunbeam Corporation and its chairman, known by the nickname "Chainsaw Al," observed:

Within 60 days of his [Chairman Al Dunlap] taking over at Sunbeam in November 1996, he fired half of Sunbeam's 12,000 employees. He then eliminated the company's $1-million-a-year giving program.

Mr. Dunlap's philosophy of giving is pretty simple: "The purest form of charity is to make the most money you can for shareholders and let them give to whatever charities they want."[11]

In 1997 another article appeared outlining a variant on this thinking, an approach that has occasioned much pro-and-con debate among corporate and foundation leaders as well as government officials. In its opening the article states:

For the past 16 years, Mr. Buffet [Omaha billionaire] has given shareholders in his Berkshire Hathaway investment company the power to pick virtually all the recipients of the corporation's donations. The iconoclastic Mr. Buffet, who is worth an estimated $21-billion, says he doesn't approve of the approach followed by most companies, which leave grant-making decisions in the hands of top managers and other employees.[12]

Two bills implementing such thinking were introduced in 1997 in the U.S. House of Representatives. "One of the bills would require all public companies to give shareholders a say in deciding which charities should benefit from a corporation's largesse, the other would require companies to disclose to shareholders all major donations."[13] As might be expected, the corporate response to them was decidedly negative.

On the other hand, a 1990 supplement to *The Atlantic Monthly* stated:

Over the past several years, while government funding of social services has decreased, corporate America has quietly donated billions of dollars to charitable organizations and programs [many of these donations through company foundations]. It is in order to highlight the social role that corporations are playing now, and to encourage greater corporate effort in the future, that *The Atlantic Monthly* is publishing this supplement.[14]

More recently, in a quarterly 1997 report, Chairman Don D. Jordan of Houston Industries, one of the nation's largest energy industries, announced the establishment of a charitable foundation to fund many of the charitable contributions already being made by the corporation. The announcement also stated that charitable contributions would range from $3 million to $5 million per year.[15] In the same year Lucent Technologies, a leading communications corporation newly spun off from the American Telephone and Telegraph Company, "announced the formation of the Lucent Technologies Foundation and a corporate contribution program, through which we plan to award about $20 million annually."[16]

COMMUNITY FOUNDATIONS

If the exact origin of company foundations is ambiguous in some respects, the emergence of the community foundation is very clear-cut. It is universally agreed that it can be traced to the thinking and action of an often overlooked pioneer in American philanthropy named Frederick H. Goff (1858–1923). A self-made lawyer and banker and erstwhile giver to worthy causes in Cleveland, Ohio, Goff noted and became increasingly disturbed by the number of bequests and setting up of trusts and foundations, particularly many smaller ones, for causes that had outlived their usefulness. The solution that he advocated and put into practice was the establishment in 1914 of the Cleveland Foundation, the nation's first significant community foundation.[17] Earlier community foundations often started with assets totaling a few thousand dollars and with grants in some cases totaling a few hundred dollars. Yet, as early as 1920 it has been estimated that their assets totaled approximately $7 million, and they were making annual grants totaling about $375,000.[18] The first edition of the *Foundation Directory* (1960, p. xxi) lists 101 community foundations holding assets amounting to about $340 million. Total annual grants made by them by that time had advanced to approximately $10 million. If this earlier growth can be categorized as steady but not spectacular, the period since then may be seen as at least remarkable. Statistically, the latest *Foundation Directory* (1999, p. ix) shows that, among the 10,445 foundations listed there, 318 community foundations in the United States now holding some $19.5 billion or 6.4% of total foundation assets, while their total annual giving of about $1.1 billion accounted for 8.2% of total foundation giving of about $14.3 billion.

Many officials of the larger community foundations have increasingly expressed concern about the growth in the number of so-called foundations, created and lodged in commercial enterprises such as the Fidelity Investments Charitable Gift Fund, Barnet Bank, and Vanguard Group, Inc. and often with assets as small as $10,000. Since 1993 the Gift Fund has created such foundations for a multitude of donors and with assets now totaling some $2 billion. Community foundations and other charitable organizations complain that such organizations give too much control over charitable giving to the donor and that they stress personal benefits to the donor rather than the public good. Also, as Jack Shackley, the president of the California Community Foundation in Los Angeles, maintains, "Fidelity is operating a captive charity to serve its commercial purposes."[19] By 1999 there were reports of possible congressional and IRS scrutiny of these so-called donor-advised funds lodged in the commercial entities as well as those in the communitiy foundations themselves.[20]

OPERATING FOUNDATIONS

As stated earlier, categorization and designation of operating foundations have always been more difficult than for those falling in the other categories. Indeed a 1948 directory stated, "To call any operating organization a foundation is incorrect in the view of some."[21] Nevertheless, this same directory appears to have been the first attempting to classify such foundations and providing separate statistical material on them. Close examination of this material, however, reveals that a considerable degree of omission or overlapping therein which precludes using it for comparative purposes. Earlier editions of the *Foundation Directory* (e.g., 1st edition, 1960; 4th edition, 1971; 6th edition, 1977) do not include operating foundations as a separate category and appear to have referred to, or lumped them in with, other categories of foundations.[22] The eighth edition (1981 pp. vii–xxii) of the *Foundation Directory*, as do all of the later editions, does separately categorize operating foundations as one of the four major types of foundations and lists 48 operating foundations holding total assets of about $1 billion and providing total giving of about

$33 million but does not provide other detailed fiscal data about them. Under these circumstances, comparisons over longer periods in this category of foundations are limited. In any case, the latest edition of the *Foundation Directory* (1999, p. ix) shows that of the 10,445 listed 304 operating foundations in the United States now hold some $13.5 billion or 4.4% of total foundation assets of about $304 billion. In view of the size of these assets, their total annual giving of only about $265 million or 1.8% of total foundation giving reflects the fact that many make few or no grants to other organizations. Perhaps the most telling example of this characteristic and the growth of such foundations is provided by the 1999 data on the J. Paul Getty Trust. Founded in 1953, the trust is the 5th largest U.S. foundation, with assets of about $7.3 billion, and it primarily funds and administers its own Getty Center, which consists of an art museum, five institutes, and an ongoing grants program. Total giving of the trust, however, amounted to only about $9.4 million. This is in contrast to the Ford Foundation's assets of about $9.5 billion but total annual giving of approximately $254 million.

EXPANSION

The geographical expansion of foundations in the United States in this century has been as significant as their growth. In discussing this expansion, one must begin by going where the major segments of wealth were concentrated at the beginning of this century. U.S censuses at that time reveal that wealth was overwhelmingly centered in the area north of the Mason-Dixon line and east of the Mississippi River. The earlier directories of foundations cited in the Introduction (n. 3) show that within that region an equally overwhelming percentage of the total number of foundations in the United States in the early decades of the twentieth century had been founded and/or had their offices located there. Also, as late as the 1920s the relatively small number of foundations established and/or located in other sections of the country was invariably ones with small assets. A major exception was the 1924 setting up of the Duke Endowment in North Carolina with initial assets of $40 million.

American Foundations and Their Fields (1955, pp. xix–xxii) provided an analysis and statistical summary on the location of 4,164 U.S. foundations studied, and it shows the continued predominance of this region. Of the 4,164 foundations, 2,756 or about 66% were located in the New England, Middle Atlantic, and east-north-central regions of the United States, with 1,238 or approximately 30% of the foundations in the entire United States located in New York State and with 91% of these in New York City. The regional location of the 10,445 foundations studied in the latest *Foundation Directory* (1999, p. x) shows a considerable change. The New England, Middle Atlantic, and east-north-central regions now have 8.1%, 25.4%, and 18%, respectively, located there out of the total number of foundations. The South Atlantic and Pacific regions, however, now show 15.2% and 12.2%, respectively, located there of the total foundations. The remaining five regions of the United States account for the remaining total of about 21%, with the percentage of four significant ones ranging from 3% to 7.1%. These statistics indicate that there have been a significant dispersal of the location of the wealth accumulated in the United States in the past fifty years and a concomitant dispersal in the geographic location of our foundations.

INSTITUTIONALLY AND GOVERNMENTALLY RELATED FOUNDATIONS

As advanced and discussed in the Introduction, the definition of a foundation and the four categories into which they fall have served to exclude from previous consideration herein institutionally and governmentally related foundations, that is, those created within, controlled by, or a part of other entities such as labor unions, churches, hospitals and medical organizations, universities and colleges, or government. Though often calling themselves foundations—examples are the George F. Baker Foundation of Harvard University's Graduate School of Business Administration, the Mayo Foundation for Medical Education and Research, and the U.S. government's National Science Foundation—the basis for excluding such foundations has rested on the grounds that they were created to aid or support a parent institution, that they do not have separate governing boards or have boards that are controlled to a large extent by the related institution, or whose ultimate control rests with a governmental authority. In this last connection, it bears noting that the National Science Foundation was defined and included as a foundation in the 1955 edition of the directory *American Foundations and Their Fields*. In the Introduction (p. xi) it was argued: "The National Science Foundation, although structurally no more than an agency of the Federal Government established by Act of Congress, is functionally a true foundation using its available funds to seek solutions to certain of mankind's problems. Therefore, it, too, has been included."

The noninclusion of the National Science Foundation and its sister, governmentally related foundations the National Endowment for the Arts and the National Endowment for the Humanities (discussed later), as well as the institutionally related foundations, in all of the later directories, encyclopedias, and so on, on foundations is, of course, justifiable. Nevertheless, it is true that in their makeup and method of operation these organizations have borrowed heavily from the recognized foundations and also share many of their other attributes. They tend, for example, to have more freedom of action and many fewer bureaucratic controls than their related organizations. This is true even in the case of the governmentally related foundations whose grants and expenditures are now as large or larger than those of many of the previously defined foundations.

It seems appropriate, therefore, that some consideration of the expansion and growth of institutionally and governmentally related foundations should be provided at this point. It should, however, be noted at the outset that statistical or other broad-scale information, except that for the government-related foundations, is generally lacking and, parenthetically, much in need of further study. Available information and information based on individual examples, therefore, have been relied on to show that their expansion and growth have often paralleled those of the previously defined foundations.

LABOR UNIONS

Since the 1940s a considerable number of labor union-related foundations have been established in various parts of the United States. They are usually dependent on the related labor unions or other donors for funds to carry out their programs. Some of the better known have been founded and named to honor prominent figures in the labor movement. They include, accompanied by the related labor union and date of founding, Sidney Hillman Foundation, Amalgamated Clothing Workers Union, 1946; Joseph Anthony Beirne Foundation, Communications Workers of America, 1975; Jerry Wurf Fund, American Federation of State, County and Municipal Employees, 1982; and Cesar E. Chavez Foundation, United Farm Workers, 1993. The largest and best known of the labor-related foundations, however, is the National Foundation for the Improvement of Education (NFIE), set up in 1969 by the National Education Association (NEA) when the NEA officially became a labor union. Although the NFIE receives $500,000 annually from the NEA, it has relied heavily on outside sources for support of its programs. Recently, however, the foundation has begun a drive for an NEA-raised endowment for the foundation that has been estimated to reach $30–35 million by the year 2003.[23]

RELIGIOUS INSTITUTIONS

Institutionally related foundations operating as a part of churches or religious institutions appear to have developed as early or earlier than those associated with labor unions. There appear to be forces at work, however, that do not bode well for their continuation as such in the future. For example, consider the case of the 199-year-old Presbyterian Church (U.S.A.) Foundation. With about $1.5 billion in assets and over 150 employees, the foundation is one of the oldest and largest church-related foundations in the United States. The foundation's leaders now believe, however, that charity regulations at the federal and state levels affecting the foundation are becoming so onerous and unpredictable that

[t]hey are moving the bulk of the foundation's financial-services operations out of the non-profit area altogether and reorganizing them under the same laws that regulate commercial businesses.

On January 2, the foundation opened what appears to be the nation's first charity-owned federally chartered trust company, a for-profit venture that will administer charitable trusts for churches and other religious bodies, invest the assets in stocks and bonds, and keep up with recordkeeping and disclosure requirements.[24]

President Larry D. Carr of the foundation estimates that the shift will save more than $500,000 in annual operating costs, but he adds: "While the hassles and costs of complying with regulations for non-profit groups are already bothersome, . . . he is more concerned about the prospect of harsher restrictions [on such foundations] being imposed in the near future."[25]

HOSPITALS AND OTHER MEDICAL INSTITUTIONS

The earliest and undoubtedly best known example of the hospital and medical organization-related institutions is the Mayo Foundation for Medical Education and Research. It was established in 1915 by the two famous physicians William J. and Charles H. Mayo in Rochester, Minnesota, to receive philanthropic gifts for the advancement of medical research and education. The Mayo Association, the predecessor of the Mayo Foundation, was established in 1919 by the two Mayos, and all assets were turned over to it. Thus, the Mayo Foundation today is the corporate entity for all of the activities of the Mayo Clinics and the Mayo programs in medical education and research. The Mayo Foundation now has approximately $2.5 billion in revenue from all sources and about 30,000 personnel, including physicians, scientists, staff, and students engaged in such activities and programs. The hospital and medical organization-related Mayo Foundation for Medical Education and Research conducts the development program, seeking support for the activities and programs of the Mayo Foundation. It bears noting that, with a recent bequest to it of $127.9 million, the former now has an endowment totaling $480 million.

The same forces at work causing the deviation from church-related foundations, however, appear to be affecting hospital and health maintenance-related foundations. A recent study states:

In 1981, 82 per cent of the nation's HMOs were nonprofit institutions; by 1995, only 29 per cent fell into this category. Nationally the number of nonprofit hospitals merging with or being acquired by for-profit chains climbed from 18 in 1993 to 63 in 1996. . . .

Conversions of nonprofit health care institutions into for-profit companies has already resulted in the largest transfer of charitable assets in history, according to a May 1997 *New York Times* article. Many nonprofits that have converted in the last few years have distributed their assets to newly created private foundations. So far, nearly $9 billion has been transferred to at least 80 new foundations.

The study concludes:

billions of nonprofit charitable dollars may be lost to the for-profit sector. Shareholders may benefit at the expense of community health care needs, and the public may become increasingly disenchanted with health care and its providers. With careful oversight and monitoring, however, these transactions can occur while the public's interests are protected.[26]

Interestingly enough, such conversions have resulted in the creation of significant numbers of true foundations. Such private foundations have been created in order to ensure that assets accumulated by organizations operating as nonprofits will be used to benefit the public. For example, the California Wellness Foundation, with present-day assets of over $1 billion, was established in 1990, when Health Net, a health maintenance nonprofit organization, converted to for-profit status. Similarly, when Colorado Blue Cross and Blue Shield converted from a nonprofit to a for-profit status in 1996, its accumulated funds were used to establish a foundation in 1998 with assets in excess of $200 million.

COLLEGE AND UNIVERSITY INSTITUTIONS

College and university-related foundations definitely have many traditional foundation attributes, particularly in the

greater amount of administrative and other flexibility afforded
them under their charters of incorporation. They appeal to donors
on the basis that their gifts and bequests will be wisely and
flexibly administered and used in accordance with their wishes
and in the best interests of the ultimate recipient—the college or
university. This, it appears, in large measure accounts for their
significant expansion and growth in the last fifty years, particularly among state-supported institutions of higher learning. The
prototype for institutions in this group is the Kansas University
Endowment Association, established in Kansas in 1891, but it
took more than fifty years for it to acquire significant assets:

Fifty-eight years (1891–1949) were required to bring the foundation's
managed assets to $1 million. Nine more years were required to bring
the managed assets to more than $5 million. Six years later, in 1964, the
assets had grown to $10 million, and by 1970 the assets exceeded $25
million. Since then, the value of the association's endowment has grown
to $385 million, thus confirming that the exponential growth of assets
continues unabated throughout the 1990's.[27]

Another prominent example of the recent rapid growth of
university-related foundations is the University of Mississippi
Foundation. With an endowment of approximately $4 million in
1973, the year it was organized, the foundation assets have
increased to more than $150 million in 1999.[28]

Today there are more than 1,000 such foundations at U.S.
public universities and colleges, which collectively hold considerable portions of assets at these institutions. Past and present
administrators of state-supported universities and colleges and
officials of their related foundations advance cogent arguments
and reasons for the establishment and operation of such foundations.[29] In recent years, however, there have been a number of
conflicting state court decisions in Indiana, Ohio, Michigan, West
Virginia, and South Carolina as to whether or not such foundations are public or private organizations. A major feature figuring
in such decisions was whether or not their records should or
should not be open to public inspection. Some of the cases occa-
sioning these decisions erupted over alleged lavish expenditures

of foundation funds by officials of the foundation or the parent institution. The 1990 case of the University of South Carolina, for example, ultimately resulted in the opening of foundation records and the eventual resignation of the university's president and chief financial officer, together with that of the foundation's executive director and nine foundation board members. Also, in 1998 investigations of university foundations in Virginia and Maryland were launched by state authorities there. To prevent such occurrences the counsel and advice offered by knowledgeable persons are strikingly similar and reminiscent of the cautions advanced by participants in the foundation investigations discussed in Chapter 2. The need to select foundation board members of diverse backgrounds with the ability to work with and within the parent university and college structure is stressed by these same observers. Of equal and perhaps more importance is the call for the wide and full disclosure of foundation goals, funding, and disbursements, together with openness in all of its operations. In commenting upon the erosion of trust in university and college foundations caused by such controversies, one university foundation official succinctly stated: "A demonstrated willingness to communicate openly may be the only pathway for renewal and restoration of the trust on which philanthropy was built."[30]

GOVERNMENT INSTITUTIONS

A number of governmentally related foundations, those created, governed, and funded by the U.S. government, have been created since World War II. The growth in the assets at their disposal and their grant-making ability outdoes that of many of the institutionally related foundations. The first of these government related foundations originated at the urging of U.S. scientific leaders as to the need for a new method of governmental funding of scientific research, particularly basic research, in the aftermath of World War II.

Led by Vannevar Bush, whose seminal 1945 work, *Science: The Endless Frontier*,[31] was the catalyst for its establishment, the National Science Foundation (NSF) was set up by an act of the

Congress in 1950 to initiate and support research in the sciences. This was accomplished only after considerable congressional and business opposition to the creation or expansion of more governmental programs and sharp debate over whether or not the social sciences with their touchy issues should be included under the rubric "sciences." Leaders in the social science community, particularly those at the Social Science Research Council, concluded that pushing for specific inclusion of "social sciences" in an enabling act would probably ensure defeat of the measure as a whole. As finally passed, the National Science Foundation Act of 1950 sidestepped the matter by authorizing support in "other scientific fields" in addition to that in the mathematical, biological, and physical sciences, but no mention of social sciences was made in the act. The foundation in its early years concentrated on the biological and physical sciences but in 1960 a Social Science Division was established within the NSF, and support in various social science disciplines has been provided by the foundation since that time.[32]

The 1950 act establishing the NSF limited its appropriation to $15 million annually. The actual appropriation for fiscal 1951, however, was $225,000 but was raised to $3.5 million in 1952. Advanced in 1954 to $8 million, together with the removal of the $15 million limit, by 1956 the NSF's appropriation had climbed to $16 million. Today the NSF's annual budget of some $2.5 billion, with about 95% of this amount for grants to some 20,000 projects involving some 200,000 persons, provides about 50% of all federal support for nonmedical basic research for science, mathematics, engineering, and technology education. This growth in grant-making ability exceeds the growth in the grant-making capabilities of most U.S. foundations.

The success in the funding and operation of the National Science Foundation was a significant factor in the creation in 1963 of a National Commission on the Humanities. Sponsored jointly by the American Council of Learned Societies, the Council of Graduate Schools in the United States, and the United Chapters of Phi Beta Kappa, the commission issued a 1964 *Report*[33] describing the current status of the humanities and the arts in the United States and concluded that massive additional financial and other support for them was urgently needed. It thereupon called for the establishment of a National Humanities Foundation with funds appropriated by the U.S. government for the foundation's dispersal in the arts and humanities. The commission noted the danger of political influence and control of the proposed governmental funding for the arts and humanities but stated:

It is the conviction of this Commission that the independence of the proposed Foundation's board will be the best safeguard against interference. If the directors and members of the board are men of acknowledged competence and courage, as are the director and members of the National Science Board, there should be no problem of improper control. Moreover, we feel that the Foundation, like the Smithsonian Institution, should not operate exclusively on governmental appropriations, but should accept grants from the widest range of sources—foundations, corporations, individuals. Plurality of support will generally strengthen the freedom and variety of scholarship in a democratic society.[34]

The *Report* was widely circulated, and snowballing public and political support for the measures it called for resulted in the passage of 1965 legislation establishing a National Foundation on the Arts and Humanities. Subsequently, under the aegis of the foundation, two separate government-related foundations were set up: the National Endowment for the Arts and the National Endowment for the Humanities. Initial governmental appropriations for the two endowments of $5.9 million for the Humanities Endowment and $4.9 million for the Arts Endowment were provided for fiscal 1996. In the 1990s, however, there was mounting public and congressional criticism of both endowments because of the people and projects being funded. Such criticism was directed particularly at the National Endowment for the Arts, where it was alleged that too many grants had been made to individuals and projects centering in New York and that many grants had resulted in obscene and lascivious works that were often too lurid to be publicly discussed. In 1990 the U.S. Congress passed a law that required the Arts Endowment to consider general standards of decency when it made its awards and to engage in wider diversification in making them.[35]

The 1994 national congressional elections resulted in the bringing to office of more congresspersons espousing these views of the endowments. In debates in the House of Representatives in 1995, this group urged the curtailment in appropriations and outright abolition of the Arts Endowment based on charges of obscenity. They also maintained that spending government funds for the arts and humanities was a frill that could no longer be afforded by a deficit-ridden federal government. In 1996 the U.S. House of Representatives voted to slash appropriations for both endowments and to phase out their operations completely in two to three years. The final legislation passed by both houses of Congress in 1997 and enacted into law, however, did not provide for termination of the endowments, although it did place certain restrictions on the Arts Endowment operations. Subsequent annual appropriations have provided $98 million for the Arts Endowment and $110.7 for the Humanities Endowment for fiscal 1999.

In recent years, in addition to these earlier government-related foundations, a number of others with grant-making capacities were established. For example, the Fannie Mae Foundation was set up in 1979 with about $400,000 in funding provided by a federally sponsored business, the Federal National Mortgage Association. By 1996 the thriving Fannie Mae Foundation held assets of about $373 million and made grants in that year totaling about $18 million. The Points of Light Foundation was created in 1990 and by 1996 had received appropriations and made grants totaling about $5 million in that year.

Having read thus far, the reader might ask, Why this prodigious growth and expansion in the United States of foundations of all types and sizes, including the institutionally related ones, in the last half century? Decade-by-decade studies have been made and opinions voiced as to a possible or probable slowing in growth and expansion of foundations. In addition to those previously remarked, a 1987 study also concluded, "The core of foundations that exist will continue to exist. There will be growth, though at a slower rate, and most new foundations will continue to be small ones."[36] Yet such growth and expansion in all categories, sizes, and location have taken place from the mid-1980s down to the present and seem poised to extend into the immediate future. Microsoft chairman and chief executive officer, William H. Gates III in 1999 gave $6 billion to the William H. Gates Foundation, probably the largest gift to a foundation by a living donor. Later in the year, Mr. Gates announced that the William H. Gates Foundation and the Learning Foundation were to be merged into one, the Bill and Melinda Gates Foundation. With its merged assets of just over $17 billion, this new foundation will be the largest independent/private foundation in the United States. Warren Buffet, the Nebraska billionaire, has frequently stated that he plans to leave his wealth to his foundation. An obvious answer to the reasons for such growth is the tremendous expansion in the amount of disposable wealth available to fund foundations in all segments and sectors of the United States. Governmental tax laws encouraging foundation growth and expansion are equally obvious. The philanthropic impulse with its spiritual and religious base, including memorialization, continued to play a most significant role. Less obvious are several other important factors. A changing public perception that there is a limit in the ability of government to solve societal problems is a factor. Such thinking appeared to be conducive to the decision of an increasing number of business and political leaders plus philanthropists that private institutions, in particular foundations, are more efficient and better in working toward their solution. Closely tied in with these factors appears to be the conscious emulation of the foundation structure by the institutionally related foundations, which accounts for their expansion. Even in the case of the entry of governmentally related foundations into the controversial arts and humanities, while criticism has caused restrictions to be placed on them, they have survived.

Finally, a major and what appears to be an overlooked reason for foundation growth and expansion in the United States since the 1950s is the same one advanced by this writer regarding the absence of *major* congressional and private investigations of foundations since the 1970s. In the last fifty years the largest and most significant foundations have not only questioned and criticized many aspects of their own operation but welcomed and even encouraged responsible criticism and arguments for changes in foundations from external sources, and they have embraced many of them and made changes accordingly. These criticisms, changes suggested, and the chief resultant changes pertaining to foundations form the focus of and are discussed at length in succeeding chapters.

4

Information and the Public

EARLY PUBLICATIONS

Information available to the public on foundations emanates from three major sources: (1) reports required from them by national and state governmental agencies; (2) annual reports and other publications voluntarily issued by foundations themselves, similar material provided by organizations specifically established to provide information about foundations, and, in recent years, a growing number of vehicles utilizing electronics communications technology[1]; (3) books and articles written about them, primarily based on the preceding two sources, by historians, economists, lawyers, journalists, and so on.

From the beginnings of foundations in the early twentieth-century United States, prominent philanthropists and philanthropoids[2] noted the lack of information about them. They advocated more and better official reporting on their founding and activities and pointed to the need to publicize their purpose, history, and operations. At the time that John D. Rockefeller was facing a hostile Walsh Commission in his unsuccessful 1915 bid to obtain a federal charter for the Rockefeller Foundation, allegations were presented that foundations were an increasingly baneful force on the American scene, particularly in education.[3] Philanthropists and others connected with them were of the opinion that there need be no concern about an alleged foundation menace to American life and education. They felt that adequate reports by the foundations were a sufficient check on their activities, though should the public be dissastisfied with what was being done, remedial action through their elected representatives could be effected.[4]

One of these witnesses at the Walsh Commission hearings stated:

You ask me whether the large resources of endowed foundations constitute a possible menace. In my judgment no concern whatever need be felt on that score, provided the Government will but require that all their transactions, in the minutest detail, be made public once or twice a year. I mean by this a statement showing in detail what their money is invested in, what their income is spent for, and how the fund generally is administered. If in the course of events, under such a system, the money is used for improper purposes, it will not take public opinion long to correct such a condition. I am an absolute believer in the efficiency of public opinion; I believe that nine times out of ten it is not only right but all powerful.[5]

John D. Rockefeller held the same opinion. He regarded:

the right to amend or rescind the respective charters of the several foundations which inhere in the legislative bodies which granted them as an entirely sufficient guarantee against serious abuse of the funds. Furthermore, I have such confidence in democracy that I believe it can better be left to the people and their representatives to remedy the evils when there is some tangible reason for believing they are impending, rather than to restrict the power for service in anticipation of purely hypothetical dangers.[6]

Despite such confidence, the then-president of the Carnegie Corporation of New York warned the foundations in 1930:

About one policy, there seems to me there can be no difference of opinion among intelligent people, that of the fullest publicity—and I draw a distinction between publicity and advertising—as to finances and activities. . . . In my judgment, public confidence in foundations in general may depend to a greater degree than is at present realized upon public knowledge of their operations.[7]

Yet the author of a 1936 study of U.S. foundations called attention to the fact that, and expressed astonishment that, "no substantial body of literature dealing with American foundations has as yet been produced."[8]

Prior to the 1950s, then, the best way to describe the creditable literature on our philanthropic foundations, of an official nature, from foundation publications or by organizations and observers from without, is that it was conspicuous by its absence. It is true that by the 1950s, there were the annual reports, primarily on the four-page Form 990-A, officially required of foundations by the Internal Revenue Service of the Treasury Department. The information provided therein, however, was often incomplete, was almost wholly numerical and financial in nature, and was unavailable for public examination in a central place. At the state level, only a few states provided for reporting by foundations, and the information provided thereby was generally less adequate than that provided at the national level.[9]

When I became one of the first employees in the summer of 1952, as director of research for the Cox Committee of the U.S. House of Representatives, one of my early official actions was a request to the Library of Congress to search for, and place on loan to the committee ,all of the pertinent books and other informational material available there on our philanthropic foundations. Although the catalog of the results is no longer available, my recollection is that a few bookshelves accommodated everything forwarded to us. Early on, the other members of the committee staff and I easily read through all of the books and other materials that were sent over to our offices. It should be added that a personal follow-up search in the stacks of the library unearthed very little more.[10]

Excluding the relatively few annual and other reports voluntarily provided the public by the larger foundations and those of a directory or biographical nature, a few of these books sent over were simply compendiums of caustic and biting criticism of all things foundation. By this time, however, there was a handful of judicious histories of individual foundations. A few others were of a sychophantic nature, finding nothing wrong, individually or collectively, with foundations and their operations. The remainder of a general nature were insightful and, while discussing foundation faults as they viewed them, found foundations on balance to be praiseworthy. In addition, there were a few journal articles of a perceptive nature, the pertinent volumes of the earlier Walsh Commission, and the recently published booklet on British trusts, that is, foundations, then and now referred to as the Nathan Report,[11] and that about accounted for the total provided us by the Library of Congress. A gleaning of these publications on U.S. foundations revealed the same recurring theme or belief: relatively little information about foundations was available, there had been little study of, and less publication about, foundations, and there was an almost complete public ignorance in the United States of their history, rationale for their programs, and method of operation.

A wealth of new informational material on foundations became available as the result of the 1950s investigation of foundations by the Cox and Reece Committees of the U.S. Congress. The fruits of the Cox Committee's efforts were particularly valuable because of the conscious effort of the committee staff to amass material on the historical and operating aspects of foundations along with delving into alleged subversive activities on their part. In addition to interviews and correspondence with about 450 individuals deemed to possess knowledge of foundations and testimony at the hearings from some twoscore more, short- and long-form questionnaires were sent to more than 1,500 foundations. The longer questionnaire was sent to the then largest ones, some seventy known to have assets of over $10 million. This form contained nine sections and included ninety searching questions. One question, for example, was: "C-7. List those institutions, operating agencies, publications, specific projects, and individuals, which have received aid from your organization and the amounts and years and nature of such aid since 1935." The answers to the questionnaires—the John Simon Guggenheim Memorial Foundation reply came to over 300 pages—were received well before the hearings, were carefully analyzed before the hearings took place, and figured prominently in the preparation of the final report of the committee.

The growth in information about foundations resulting from this and the succeeding Reece congressional investigation of them in the 1950s contributed greatly to a relative increase in publications about them. Still, in his Foreword to the 1956 publication of *Philanthropic Foundations,* Donald Young, then president of the Russell Sage Foundation, maintained that

two congressional investigations in recent years have emphasized the fact that the public has little accurate knowledge of what these nebulously defined institutions are and do, and within the foundations themselves there has been too little sharing of experience, procedures, and general knowledge.[12]

Suiting action to his words, Donald Young played a direct and prominent role in the convening of a trailblazing conference[13] in which the need for increased research and publication in various areas of the history of philanthropy in general and foundations in particular was discussed. He was in the forefront, too, in the deliberations that resulted in the establishment of the first systematically organized information center on foundations in the United States and, to a lesser degree, a number of other ancillary groups and organizations dealing with foundations.

THE FOUNDATION CENTER

In the years prior to the 1950s the major sources of nongovernmental general information about foundations, other than the annual and other reports of some of the larger foundations, were two specific foundations together with several commercial enterprises and a few other organizations. Since 1915 the Russell Sage Foundation, in addition to its other programs, had been collecting reports, books, pamphlets, and articles on foundations. Beginning in that year, too, based on such material, it began to publish bibliographies and directories providing increasing amounts of available information on foundations. The Twentieth Century Fund, beginning in 1930, made and published several surveys and other publications bearing on foundations and their activities. In the 1940s Raymond Rich Associates, a public relations and fund-raising firm, and its offspring, the American Foundations Information Service, took over the files on foundations that the fund had built up and continued such informational publications into the 1950s.[14] Albeit largely unheralded, another early source of such information was the philanthropic library of the Hanover Bank and Trust Company of New York. Established in 1930, the library collected books and similar material plus unique and extensive newspaper clippings on foundations in the largely unfulfilled hope that wealthy persons using the library would be influenced to make use of the trust department of the bank. The library or other bank personnel, however, never engaged in research or issued any publications based on its holdings. Thus, there was a dawning realization on the part of a growing number of those associated with, and interested in, foundations that there was a crying need to act to make accurate information about foundation history and activities more readily available to the public, also that there was a similar need to disseminate this information about them based on much broader and sounder information. Against this background an information center on foundations emerges.

Prominent figures in the establishment of the Foundation Library Center in New York City in 1956 (name changed to Foundation Center in 1968) were Donald Young and F. Emerson Andrews, president and director of publications, respectively, of Russell Sage Foundation, and John W. Gardner and James A. Perkins, president and vice-president, respectively, of the Carnegie Corporation of New York. With start-up funds of $100,000 supplied by the corporation, its operating budget in a few years was supplemented with larger appropriations from the Ford, Rockefeller, and W. K. Kellogg Foundations. The center's initial holdings consisted of the deposit with it of the Russell Sage Foundation's entire collection on foundations and philanthropy. This was soon augmented by the purchase of similar material from the American Foundations Information Service, together with the donation to the center of the major portions of the holdings of the aforementioned library of the Hanover Bank and Trust Company of New York.[15]

Some of the chief undertakings inaugurated and continued at the center included the continuous augmentation of its New York library holdings; the establishment early on of suboffices in 1963 in Washington, D.C., in the 1970s in Cleveland, Ohio, and San Francisco; and somewhat later in 1994 in Atlanta, Georgia; and depositories in major libraries in all fifty states plus Puerto Rico and the Virgin Islands; plus some 215 collections located in nonprofit research centers, community foundations, and so on— all of this with the view of making its holdings more easily available to the public. The center launched publications dealing with foundations, outstandingly the *Foundation Directory*, published in successive editions since the first in 1960, and it now publishes over fifty directories a year plus a line of monographs. The *Foundation News*, a bimonthly, was begun in 1960 and was transferred for publication in 1972 to the Council on Foundations. Until the early 1990s, when commercial publishers really entered the market, the center published a number of broad-scale monographs and books on philanthropy and foundations. In 1994 the center introduced the Foundation Center Search, its database in CD-ROM, and more recently a World Wide Web site on the Internet. After the Foundation Center was established, the formation of a significant number of information, research, and advocacy groups followed. These, too, with varying emphases and approaches, have continued to provide information on foundations and their operations. Identification of, and discussion concerning, the major organizations in this category follow.

INFORMATION, RESEARCH, AND ADVOCACY ORGANIZATIONS

The establishment of the Council on Foundations is tied up with the history of U.S community foundations. The National Committee on Foundations and Trusts for Community Welfare had been set up in 1949 as a membership organization of community foundations, and by 1957 it had evolved into the National Council on Community Foundations. In 1964 a reorganization resulted in the changing of its name to the broader Council on Foundations, headquartered in New York City, and the opening of its membership to all types of foundations. In 1972 the council acquired the publication *Foundation News* from the Foundation Center, changed in 1994 to *Foundation News and Commentary*, which it has published to the present. Reflecting the increasing intertwining of foundations, government, and public policy, this was accompanied by a 1980 move of its headquarters office from New York City to Washington, D.C. With a present-day membership of more than 1,500 large and small foundations, corporations, and other organizations, the council has become the premier agency in the promotion of responsible and effective foundation philanthropy and an advocacy organization for foundations, particularly as they relate to the national government.

Regional associations of grant makers, commonly referred to as RAGs, have now been organized in over 3,000 locations in the United States. Among the earlier ones (late 1940s and 1950s) were the Donors Forum of Chicago and Conference of Southwest Foundations. Although founded later (1979), the New York Association of Grantmakers (NYRAG) is a prime illustration of the method of operation of such organizations in other states. With over 200 foundation members spanning all foundation categories in the tristate New York metropolitan area, NYRAG's purpose is the improvement of all aspects of philanthropy through programs in three categories—information, facilitating, and public policy. It has ongoing monthly gatherings of its members devoted to various topics. Those bringing foundations and public policy makers together are probably the best known. In conjunction with the Foundation Center, NYRAG also convenes meetings for grant seekers. A number of publications serves to keep its members and others informed of its activities. Some twenty-five of the largest RAGs in other states and regions, regardless of title, for example, Southern California Association for Philanthropy or Donors Forum of Ohio, have all become referred to as RAGs and are conducting much the same programs in their areas.[16] In 1995 these twenty-five organized the Forum of Regional Associations of Grantmakers with offices located at the Council on Foundations. The forum serves to enhance individual RAGs' relationships with each other and the council, particularly at the national level, and encourages the overall growth of philanthropy.[17]

Several other organizations are noteworthy for their contributions in the effort to provide more information on foundation operations and to act as an advocacy group for them. Eleven fund-raising firms founded the American Association of Fund-Raising Counsel in 1935. From its inception the member firms and its leaders shared many obvious and natural interests with foundations, colleges and universities, museums, and so on. Many of the association's meetings and publications did much to acquaint the public with philanthropy in general and, tangentially, foundations. The association's publication *Giving USA*, inaugurated in 1956 and published annually since then, has proved to be the authoritative statistical analysis in presenting and publicizing the amount that Americans give each year for all philanthropic purposes. Some officials of the association have published books centering on philanthropy and fund-raising and also extolling foundations.[18] Of equal importance with these accomplishments was the role the association played in tandem with two other organizations, the National Council on Philanthropy (NCOP), set up in 1954, and the Coalition of National Voluntary Organizations (CONVO), formed in 1976, as the seedbeds for the 1980 emergence of Independent Sector (IS).

The key figure in the collapsing of NCOP and CONVO into the organization named Independent Sector was John W. Gardner. Former president of the Carnegie Foundation for the Advancement of Teaching and the Carnegie Corporation of New York and secretary of the Department of Health, Education, and Welfare under President Lyndon B. Johnson, he was a prime mover in setting up Common Cause and, as previously mentioned, the Foundation Center. He has been the author of a number of influential articles and books dealing with leadership and defined and called to the attention of the public the importance of the independent sector, that is, the third sector, along with business and government.

As a measure of such importance, the IS states that today, excluding religious organizations, there are anywhere from

750,000 to 2 million organizations in the United States in the independent sector. It also states that the 1990 census shows that there are approximately 8 million people, representing about 7% of all employed persons in the United States, employed in the sector, together with about 90 million persons volunteering their time to worthy causes.[19]

The following statement of purpose appears to be one of the best explanations for bringing IS into existence: "Helping Those Who Help. Connecting Those Who Care.

We are a membership organization that brings together foundations, nonprofit groups and corporate giving programs to support philanthropy, volunteering, and civic action."[20]

Based in Washington, D.C., the IS has grown to be an 800+ membership organization with a staff of approximately forty people and with an annual operating budget of about $6 million. It has an extensive research and publication section concentrating on the compilation and publication of material dealing with the size, scope, and impact of the independent sector in the United States. It convenes annual national and regional meetings devoted to much the same purpose. Much of this effort is devoted to and concerned with foundations. Several noteworthy specific projects include the establishment in 1985 of the John W. Gardner Leadership Award. The annual $10,000 award honors those Americans who best exemplify the leadership and ideals of John W. Gardner. The Give Five Program, devised by Brian O'Connell, the president of IS from its founding to his retirement in 1995, encouraged all to give 5% of their income to charity and community causes and to volunteer five or more hours per week to similar causes of their choice. In the decade of the 1990s and reflecting its concern for the independent sector, the IS has become the leading advocacy group opposing alleged attempts to impose governmental restrictions on the independent sector, including foundations. It observed in its stated goals for the years 1996–2000:

The winds of change have blown hard in Washington. Due to projected federal cutbacks, Congressional attempts to prohibit advocacy and lobbying by nonprofit organizations, and some negative media coverage, the sector can be said to be "under siege" and challenged to make a case for itself. . . . The need for greater understanding of and support for the sector has been building over several years. Educating the public about the sector is clearly a permanent need and requires a permanent commitment. Defeating the attempts to limit advocacy rights of the sector is of immediate urgency, but it is a need that will not soon disappear.[21]

The Aspen Institute for Humanistic Studies was organized in Aspen, Colorado, in the early 1950s.[22] With longtime and extensive ties to leaders in business, government, foundations, and academe, by the 1980s and 1990s the now Aspen Institute had metamorphosed into an organization with a wide-ranging mission to study, discuss, and publicize national and international challenges and issues across all disciplinary lines. Its headquarters is now located in Washington, D.C., with its programs and seminars located in and conducted from centers located in Aspen and the Wye River Center located on the outskirts of Washington, D.C., in Maryland. Affiliated centers in Germany, France, Italy, and Japan conduct similar programs abroad. With its record of successfully launching and supporting wide-ranging projects and programs, it is easy to understand why the Nonprofit Sector Research Fund was inaugurated under its auspices in 1991. In its announced policy the fund states:

Through grantmaking for research and dissemination, the Nonprofit Sector Research Fund seeks to expand knowledge of nonprofit activities, impacts and values, and promotes the use of new knowledge to improve nonprofit sector practices and inform public policy. The Fund also seeks to enhance nonprofit research by increasing the legitimacy and visibility of nonprofit scholarship; encouraging new investment in sector research; supporting the exploration of tough, neglected questions; and enlarging the number of creative scholars and practitioners interested in pursuing nonprofit studies.[23]

In addition to its grants program, the fund annually produces a number of working papers and publications bearing on the nonprofit sector, with many of these publications based on fund-sponsored research.

WATCHDOG ORGANIZATIONS

A number of organizations conduct research and information programs similar to those of the Council on Foundations, but they and the advocacy programs they engage in have different orientations. One of these watchdog organizations is the National Committee for Responsive Philanthropy. It was founded in 1976 by various charity officials associated with the Donee Group of the Filer Commission who wanted to make charitable groups, such as United Way and foundations, more accessible to minorities and others who, they claimed, had difficulty in gaining access to prospective donors. With offices now located in Washington, D.C., New York City, Milwaukee, and St. Paul, it conducts such projects as an internship program and publishes a newsletter, *Responsive Philanthropy*.[24]

Another example of this group is the Capital Research Center (CRC), located in Washington, D.C. As to founding date and mission, the CRC states:

The introduction of President Johnson's Great Society programs in 1964 helped spawn a new type of non-profit organization in America: the self-identified "public interest group." Today thousands operate at the state, local, and national levels. Some are high profile and well known. Others work in near obscurity to achieve their goals.

The proliferation of such groups and their strategic role in shaping verifiable public opinion and policy have put a premium on accurate and verifiable information about their purposes, personnel, and funding sources.

Capital Research Center was established in 1984 to study critical issues in philanthropy, with a special focus on non-profit "public interest" and advocacy groups, the funding sources which sustain them, their agendas (open and hidden), and their impact on public policy and society.[25]

The CRC also believes that these groups or organizations in the third or independent sector, including other advocacy groups[26] and many large foundations, overwhelmingly espouse a public policy point of view that is what the CRC calls politically correct and is detrimental to a free market economy and constitutional government. Such advocacy groups' activities, financed

by charitable tax exempt donations, including those from foundations, and grants from the federal government, have dramatically
expanded the power of the national government at the expense
of the private sector. The CRC's activities and those of similarly
oriented organizations such as the Philanthropy Roundtable are
purposely twofold: first, to provide information to the public,
corporations, all foundations, but particularly corporation foundations, and governmental officials—concentrating on the members of Congress—of the thrust and impact of the activities of the
independent sector described earlier, and second, to document
and explain to officials of the federal government, again particularly members of Congress, this same thrust and impact financed
by governmental grants or awards to these same independent
sector organizations. In carrying out these purposes, the CRC and
similar watchdog organizations conduct research and issue books
and a number of publications; the CRC sponsors the monthlies
Philanthropy, Culture and Society, and *Foundation Watch*, while
the Philanthropy Roundtable sponsors the quarterly *Philanthropy.*

OTHER RESEARCH AND INFORMATION
ACTIVITIES

While the CRC and the Philanthropy Roundtable were being
organized and operated, a trailblazing academic center was
brought into existence at Yale University in 1977. Established
under the leadership of professor of law John G. Simon, the
Program on Non-Profit Organizations (PONPO) was set up to
generate interest in and research on nonprofit organizations,
including foundations. In the 1980s and 1990s, under a variety of
titles, some twenty-five other of our universities and colleges
founded discrete centers for similar purposes and operate programs linking combinations of research, teaching, and public
policy, such as Mandel Center for Nonprofit Organizations, Case
Western Reserve University; Center for the Study of Philanthropy, City University of New York; Center for the Study of
Philanthropy and Voluntarism, Duke University; Institute for
Policy Studies, Johns Hopkins University; and Center on Philan-

thropy, Indiana University. In addition, approximately another fifty institutions of higher learning in all areas of the United States have developed and are offering courses on the nonprofit sector, philanthropy, foundations, public administration, and so on, usually as part of degree programs at the graduate and/or undergraduate level. These degrees, again, bear a variety of titles. A considerable factor in the origination and conduct of some of these courses was the 1980s Program on Studying Philanthropy conducted by the Association of American Colleges (AAC). The American Association of Fund-Raising Counsel, the Carnegie Corporation of New York, and the W. K. Kellogg Foundation assisted the AAC in setting up the program and took the lead in its funding, together with additional support from about a dozen other major foundations and organizations. Proposals to participate in the Program were accepted from AAC members for the purpose of developing and teaching undergraduate courses on philanthropy in American society once each year for three years. Some sixteen institutions funded over a three-year period were provided awards of $15,000 each to underwrite the effort, which generated several dozen new courses on various aspects of U.S. philanthropy.[27]

ARCHIVES

In addition to the foregoing centers, another major catalyst in the furtherance of research and resultant publications about philanthropy and foundations was the establishment of a number of archives containg documentary material on the subjects. Preceded by discussions going back to the 1950s, the Rockefeller Archive Center (RAC) was established in 1974. Located in Pocantico Hills, North Tarrytown, New York, as a division of Rockefeller University, the center's first holdings consisted of the papers and records of the Rockefeller family, its philanthropies and foundations. Opened to scholars in the summer of 1975, more than 2,000 researchers have since used its collections, resulting in the publication of hundreds of books and articles dealing with numerous aspects of philanthropy and foundations in the United States and abroad. In addition to its original holdings the center has continuously augmented them by the deposit there of the papers and records of a number of other foundations such as the Russell Sage Foundation, Commonwealth Fund, and the John and Mary Markle Foundation. Other deposits include those of such notables as Rene J. Dubos, Dean Rusk, and Albert B. Sabin. Since its beginnings the center has conducted a competitive research grant program providing stipends for scholars to engage in projects requiring substantive research in its archival collections, and ·numerous publications on philanthropy and foundations have resulted from the program. Center publications include a biannual RAC *Newsletter*,[28] published since 1982, and a number of "how-to" books: *Establishing Foundation Archives: A Reader and Guide to First Steps* (Council on Foundations, Washington, D.C., 1990), and *The Availability of Foundation Archives: A Researcher's Guide* (Rockefeller Archive Center, North Tarrytown, New York, 1990). It should be noted, too, that the center has made limited portions of its holdings available on microfilm. Finally, since 1975, the center has convened over twenty conferences devoted to various topics falling within its range of interest, with subsequent publication of some of their proceedings, for example, Proceedings, *The Art of Giving: Four Views on American Philanthropy* (Rockefeller Archive Center, North Tarrytown, New York, 1979).

The Indiana University-Purdue University at Indianapolis (IUPUI) in the early 1990s established a Special Collection and Archives on Philanthropy and in 1993 microfilmed the records of the fund-raising firm Ward, Dresham, and Reinhardt for deposit there. The historical collection of the Foundation Center has since been deposited there, together with a number of other collections on philanthropy.

Perhaps the best recognition of the perceived need for increasing these information and research efforts on foundations and similar organizations was the 1997 announcement by Harvard University that it was creating a new Hauser Center for Nonprofit Organizations in the John F. Kennedy School of Government. With an initial $10 million gift from Rita and Gustave Hauser, Harvard plans to raise an additional $20 million for the center because as Harvard president Neil L. Rudenstine said,

"The non-profit world is vastly understudied and not always understood."[29]

ARNOVA

From the 1950s on, interlaced and interlarded with the operations and activities of all of the foregoing organizations was a slowly growing body of scholars interested in teaching, research, and writing about the nonprofit sector, including foundations. Their mutual concerns and interests resulted in the 1971 formation of the Association of Voluntary Action Scholars (AVAS). In great part because of increasing interest in nonprofit organization and management, in 1990 the organizational name was changed to the present Association for Research on Nonprofit Organizations and Voluntary Action (ARNOVA). The association has convened annual scholarly conferences and has published a quarterly journal, *Nonprofit and Voluntary Sector Quarterly* (formerly, *Journal of Voluntary Action Research*) and a quarterly news periodical, *Arnova News*, since its beginnings. Critics used to say that the organization's ungainly name and the content of its publications reflected the dominance of sociologists and community and social workers in its membership. By 1997, however, sociologists and social workers together represented less than 25% of ARNOVA membership, and it has now grown to nearly 1,000 members located in forty-seven states and forty nations abroad. From its beginnings ARNOVA and its members have been interested in looking at the voluntary sector from an international perspective and have been collaborating with such organizations as the International Society for Third Sector Research (ISTR). Also, in 1994 a stable national office for ARNOVA under the direction of an executive director, Anita H. Plotinsky, was set up at the Indiana University Center on Philanthropy.[30]

COMMERCIAL PUBLISHERS

Until fairly recently, identification and commentary on commercial publishers dealing with philanthropy in general and foundations in particular would be like trying to proverbially nail jelly to a wall. The attrition rate for not only the commercial but all types of publishers in these areas was high. In the 1950s, for example, this writer recalls a periodical devoted to philanthropy that operated out of small quarters located on the top floor of the Plaza Hotel in New York City. It led a faltering life for about a year or so and then quietly passed off the scene. A more recent example, the quarterly magazine *American Benefactor* appeared in the spring of 1997. With a unique and innovative subscription approach and list and with a host of very upscale advertisers, the magazine published a number of informative and provocative articles across a wide spectrum of philanthropy, including foundations. Preceded by some internecine controversies and other problems, however, by 1999 the *American Benefactor* ceased publication. Nevertheless an attempt is made here to offer what appear to be the more important examples, in pertinent different genres, of commercial publishers.

In considering one of the early entries in this area, it is interesting to note that J. Richard Taft, who was employed by the Foundation Center in 1963 to head the Center's newly organized Washington, D.C. office, was also employed at that time as editor of *Foundation News*. In 1967 he left center employment to engage in a business venture of his own which eventually resulted in the formation of the Taft Group, now a division of the publication firm Gale Research, Inc. The Taft Group today, with primary offices located in the metropolitan Washington, D.C., area, is a leading commercial publisher of reference works on fund-raising and nonprofit organizations, including foundations.

While a few newspapers, such as the *New York Times, Philadelphia Inquirer, Wall Street Journal,* and *Washington Post,* have from time to time devoted considerable space to philanthropic and foundation topics, it was not until the establishment in 1989 of the *Chronicle of Philanthropy* that we have a semimonthly newspaper devoted in its entirety to these subjects. It has since become the preeminent news source for all those interested or engaged in the philanthropic process. Much of its coverage is devoted to providing information about foundations: establishment, assets, grants, personnel, governmental relations, jobs, book reviews, op-ed pieces, and so on.

Commercial publishers putting out books in the nonprofit and foundation category have generally taken the same sporadic approach as newspapers. From time to time, first this and then that publisher would bring out a book dealing with foundations or some other topic in the nonprofit sector. Only in the last few decades have a relatively few commercial publishers created divisions or subdivisions with expressed publication interest in these areas. Examples are Greenwood Press, John Wiley and Sons, Oryx Press, and Jossey-Bass Press.

PUBLICATIONS 1950s–1987, 1988–PRESENT

Due in large part to the organizational/foundation efforts, the decades from the 1950s to 1987 saw a relative surge in both the number and kind of publications about foundations. Scores of books and other works were authored by, among others, foundation administrators, educators, historians, lawyers, economists, and journalists.[31] Still, a highly acclaimed foundation history published in 1989 could announce in the opening to its Bibliographic Essay, "Until the 1980's, the historiography of foundations was essentially an insiders' tale, embroidered at the margins by a few critical studies that tended to be more polemical than searchingly scholarly." The author announced, however, "Happily, however, a number of new studies" [presumably including her own], "are beginning to draw the outlines for a more complete and critical history."[32]

The late 1980s and the 1990s, relative to the earlier decades, witnessed a continuing significant volume of publications about foundations, particularly the independent ones. A 1997 *Atlantic Monthly* article by a knowledgeable observer, however, sounds more like the ones of the 1950s and even has overtones of the previously cited one of 1989. Quoted in its entirety are the last three paragraphs of the piece, but note the subtitle in note 33, which aptly summarizes its content:

The press, which pays close attention to politics and government through deeply ingrained reflex, largely ignores foundations, or treats them, in a polite but faintly bored tone, as innocuous do-gooders rather than significant actors.

The influence of foundations goes uncharted. The main policy questions about them—How, exactly, should their economic and political activities be restricted in return for their tax-exempt status? Does the tax exemption still make sense?—go unasked.

That ought to change. Foundations are becoming so much more significant so rapidly that they deserve to be brought into the company of central institutions whose course is the subject of constant public scrutiny and debate.[33]

A 1998 survey of foundations commissioned by the Council of Foundations came to much the same conclusions.[34]

At this point this writer will make no attempt to speculate as to the why of these preceding observations and similar ones of the period that could be cited, because it is believed that possible answers lie in this and other changes in the foundation scene previously described as well as others discussed later. Rather, conjecture about the matter is postponed for the Commentary herein.

5

Personnel Diversification

The governing board of a foundation, where ultimate responsibility for its operation and management resides, is usually designated the board of trustees or, occasionally, board of trust, directors, or managers. The range of powers afforded trustees of such boards in the legal document setting up the foundation varies, but for legal purposes the trustees are the foundation.[1] The makeup and character of the members of the board of trustees at the time of founding also vary. Some have a designated institutional trustee or trustees consisting of a trust department in a bank or a few persons in such a bank. Other boards of trustees at the time of origin of the foundation, particularly true in the case of independent foundations, consist of the donor and/or members of his or her family together with close friends and business or social associates. Many of the larger foundations, such as the Carnegie Corporation of New York, the Ford Foundation, and the Rockefeller Foundation, followed this pattern. The number of trustees, generally speaking, is fixed or is fixed within certain limits at the time of the legal creation of the foundation. Such numbers can range from two or three to a dozen or even more. Tenure terms of trustees are also usually fixed at that time and can vary from one or two years to an indefinite number. The original trustees of foundations are usually endowed with the power to fill any subsequent vacanies and to change tenure terms.

The trustees of the corporation foundations have almost universally been chosen from the corporate officers of the company endowing it. The fact that the original funds of the foundation are, more often than not, supplemented from time to time by additional appropriations from the parent company makes it easily understandable why this tandem trustee arrangement for the foundation and the company is resorted to. Occasionally, however, one or two trustees from outside the company's officialdom will be elected to the governing board of the foundation in order to bring in an outside point of view to its operation. Examples of such foundations, including their easily recognizable, institutionally related company names, are the Alcoa Foundation, General Motors Foundation, and Shell Companies Foundation.

Community foundations, with their special giving relationship to a particular city or region and with a multitude of donors, generally lodge their funds with a bank that disburses the foundation's appropriations. The governing trustees—and such a representation is often specified at incorporation of the foundation—are invariably drawn from a broad cross-section representative of the community or region in which it is located. Such names as the Cleveland Foundation, first of this type to be set up; New York Community Trust, the largest; Chicago Community Trust; and Communities Foundation of Texas show the diversity in location and geographical scope of these foundations.

Operating foundations, because they usually concentrate their efforts on fulfilling one or a few missions and make no or few grants, tend to designate a preponderance of their trustees who have a background and expertise in fulfilling such specific missions. Operating foundations, as has been related earlier, are also more difficult to categorize and keep categorized than the other three categories of foundations. Perhaps because of this and indicative of the power of boards of trustees through trustee action, some have, for all intents and purposes, been changed from a foundation to a research or other kind of institution. The Carnegie Institution of Washington, Carnegie Endowment for

International Peace, and the Charles F. Kettering Foundation, although making few grants, were earlier listed as operating foundations but now appear to be more properly classified as research institutions.[2]

Institutionally related foundations, with the exception of the government-related foundations, generally have a mix of trustees: officials appointed from the related institution, church, labor union, university, hospital, and so on, together with others who usually have close ties of one kind or another with the related institution. Each of the three government-related institutions, National Science Foundation, National Endowment for the Arts, and National Endowment for the Humanities, has a specified number of trustees who are appointed by the president of the United States with the advice and consent of the Senate.

Professional staff, previously referred to as "philanthropoids," are employed by foundations to carry out the program and projects decided upon by the foundation trustees. The overwhelming majority of smaller, independent foundations have had no employees, a part-time person, or one person. Because of the nature of their purpose and operations the corporation and community and, particularly, the operating foundations have more. In the 1950s, even among the largest ones, fewer than a dozen foundations had paid staff of considerable size. The Carnegie Corporation of New York, for example, which at that time was the third largest foundation in size of assets held, had only about thirty staff members, and at least half of these were clerical rather than professional. Since then the paid staff of our foundations now numbers in the thousands, and a few of the larger ones, such as the Ford Foundation, have staffs of several hundred.[3]

CHARACTERISTICS OF TRUSTEES AND STAFF

The delineation of foundation trustees and staff just provided was applicable at the time of origination of the larger American foundations up until the 1950s, and with the exception of the staff growth remarked on earlier, there has been relatively little change in this delineation since. It is quite otherwise with the response to the question, What sort of persons make up the boards of trustees and staff of foundations? The answers and the eventual movement for, and accomplishment of, substantial diversification in the makeup of trustees and staff have resulted in one of the major changes in U.S. foundations in the past fifty years, particularly those of the large independent type.

Over the years various commentaries on, and analyses of, varying systemization and scope have been made of the characteristics of the trustees and staff of foundations of the time. For the most part, they are not specific as to the type of foundation being commented on or analyzed. The corporation, community, operating, and institutionally and governmentally related foundations, however, appear to play a small role in such commentaries and analyses. This lack of attention can probably be traced to their previously described differing trustee and staff needs and requirements. Consequently, they seem to be less of a target when the agitation for more diversification develops. It appears to be a safe conclusion, therefore, that the larger independent foundations form the major portion of foundations examined as to the makeup of their trustees and staff. Because of their asset size, the ever-increasing number of smaller foundations of all types has also worked to exempt them from such commentary and analyses.

A brief book published in 1911 on seven of the larger and more important early independent foundations shows the following number of trustees for each of them: Peabody Education Fund, sixteen; John F. Slater Fund for the Education of Freedmen, nine; Carnegie Institution of Washington, twenty; General Education Board, seventeen; Carnegie Foundation for the Advancement of Teaching, twenty-five; Russell Sage Foundation, nine; and Anna T. Jeanes Foundation, seventeen. The tenor and content of the following quotes from descriptions of the trustees on several of them—Peabody Education Fund, General Education Board, and Anna T. Jeanes Foundation—are revealing:

The late Daniel Gilman, himself a leading spirit and influential trustee in several of the foundations, is authority for the statement that the formulation of the original idea [for the foundation] was probably due to Hon. Robert C. Winthrop of Boston, who was a close ally of Mr. Peabody's and brought to his service wise counsel, unusual foresight, and remarkable gifts of expression.

The trustees of the Peabody Education Fund are sixteen in number. Its membership contains such names as those of Joseph Choate, J. Pierpont Morgan, and Theodore Roosevelt.

The trustees [of the General Education Board] are at present seventeen in number. Among them are ex-President Eliot, Andrew Carnegie, Dr. H. B. Frissell, and President E. A. Alderman. The chairman is Frederick T. Gates and the secretary, Wallace Buttrick.

The custody of the Jeanes Fund has been entrusted to the care of a most representative board. Among the members are President Taft, Dr. Booker T. Washington, Dr. H. B. Frissell, and Andrew Carnegie. A notable feature of the composition of the board is that it has three colored men, in addition to Booker T. Washington. These are Major R. R. Moton, Hon. John P. Napier, and Hon. Robert L. Smith. The president of the foundation is Dr. James H. Dillard, formerly dean of Tulane University, and at present general agent of both the Slater and Jeanes Foundations. The treasurer of the foundation is George Foster Peabody, and the secretary Major Robert R. Moton, of Hampton, Va. The other members of the board are David C. Barrow, Chancellor of the University of Georgia; Samuel C. Mitchell, President of the University of South Carolina; George McAneny, President of the Borough of Manhattan, New York City; Belton Gilreath, Robert C. Ogden, Walter H. Page; and Talcott Williams.[4]

Further analysis of the stated trustee structure of all seven boards reveals that with the exception of Mrs. Russell Sage, who was the donor of the Russell Sage Foundation, no mention is made of a woman on any of the other boards. The similar lack of mention of nonwhite representation on any of the boards other than the Jeanes Foundation is underscored by the "notable" reference in the Jeanes Foundation account to its four colored trustees. In other words there appear to be an almost complete lack of diverse representation by sex or race on the boards of trustees of these seven early large foundations and no comment as to approval of, or need for, such representation.

In 1930 the president of the Carnegie Corporation of New York, Frederick P. Keppel, observed that foundation trustees were almost all men. In a passing reference, he acknowledged that women had the capacity to serve there, but he did not push the matter and in succeeding pages, generally describing the foundation trustee, used the masculine pronoun exclusively. Also, the racial or ethnic makeup of trustees is not mentioned.[5]

In 1936 Eduard C. Lindeman published his *Wealth and Culture*, which in Chapter 5 provided a thorough and comprehensive analysis and profile of 402 trustees of seventy unnamed foundations. Lindeman states, however, that the seventy were "selected because of their representativeness."[6] He also states that his analysis was based on questions of the trustees as to age, educational and religious background, occupation, social affiliation and kinship. Although much more detailed information, including statistical tables in each category, on the makeup of the 402 is provided in Chapter 5, his summary provides a descriptive and accurate composite picture of the trustees he examined:

With such facts before us it becomes relatively simple to derive an adequate picturization of the type of individual who makes the decisions, influences the policies and purposes, and determines where the money invested in foundations is to go. Approximations of this sort do not, of course, furnish an adequate graph of any single individual trustee but they do allow us to describe the group as a whole from which foundation trustees are selected. With this limitation in mind, it seems fair to state that a typical trustee of an American foundation is a man well past middle age; he is more often than not a man of considerable affluence, or one whose economic security ranks high; his social position in the community is that of a person who belongs to the higher-income receiving class of the population; he is, presumably, "respectable" and "conventional" and belongs to the "best" clubs and churches, and he associates with men of prestige, power, and affluence. His training has been largely in the arts and humanities and he possesses only a slight background in the sciences and technologies. He resides in the Northeastern section of the United States and has attended one of the private colleges in that region. His "intelligence" is ranked high by various institutions of higher learning from which he has received signal honors. He receives his income primarily from profits and fees. In short, he is a member of that successful and conservative class which came into prominence during the latter part of the nineteenth and early twentieth century, the class whose status is based primarily upon pecuniary success.[7]

In Lindeman's analysis the race or ethnicity of trustees is never mentioned. Women are dismissed in the following paragraph, which appears as a footnote to the third sentence of his preceding summary: "I continue to speak of the trustee as a man. In the total group of 402 trustees there were eleven (11) women. All except one were trustees of so-called 'family' foundations."[8]

As to staff, Ayres, in his previously mentioned 1911 book, *Seven Great Foundations,* does name the general agent or secretary of each who administered or carried on its operation. They are all white males. The previously mentioned 1930s Lindeman study of foundations, however, makes practically no mention of professional staff. Keppel's work in that decade does comment on the background and characteristics that make up the professional staff members of foundations. For example, he states that most professional staff members come from universities. In such comment, however, Keppel makes exclusive use of "he," "man," and "men" in his commentary and never brings in diversification, such as geographical, gender, race, and so on, or the need for more of it.

The 1953 Cox Committee in its *Report* raised twelve major questions concerning foundations. Question number 5 asked: "Are trustees of foundations absentee landlords who have delegated their duties and responsibilities to paid employees of the foundations?" Question number 6 asked: "Do foundations tend to be controlled by interlocking directorates composed primarily of individuals residing in the North and Middle-Atlantic States?"[9] In its reply the committee stated that these questions could more conveniently be discussed together. It then acknowledged that since many of the larger foundations had their headquarters in New York and nearby areas, it was natural for many of their trustees to come from the same area. Nevertheless, the committee added:

Despite these considerations, all of which are persuasive, the committee feels that a wider geographical distribution would go far toward establishing greater public confidence in the foundations and would dispel much of the distrust which shelters under a traditional fear of Wall Street. It is also entirely possible that a sustained search for qualified individuals residing West of the Hudson River might assist the foundations to maintain the freshness of approach, flexibility, and breadth of vision for which they profess to strive. If, as the foundations maintain and the committee believes, foundations are public trusts then the public in its widest sense, including the geographical, should be fairly represented.[10]

Although the vaguely worded last sentence in the foregoing quotation hints at needed broader diversification in trustee makeup, the only specific factor mentioned there and dwelled on in the earlier portion of the quotation is geographical diversification. Also, in the hearings, interviews, correspondence, research, and so on, preceding publication of the *Report*, there was little, if any, questioning on grounds other than the geographical makeup of foundation trustees. In short, other factors in the makeup such as sex, race, ethnicity, or relationship to donor were simply not considered.

The overall impression provided in the material published by the 1954 Reece Committee investigation of foundations is that foundation trustees had abdicated their responsibilities. Control and operation of foundations had, in essence, been turned over by inattentive and lax trustees to a scheming and power-hungry professional staff. In other words, the foundation trustees, individually and collectively, come across as dupes manipulated by foundation staff.

The Cox and Reece congressional committees of the 1950s investigating foundations did consider the professional staff of foundations, but their primary concerns were not diversification in makeup. In the case of the Cox Committee the only issue was whether or not the staff had taken over from absentee trustees the guidance and control of their respective foundations. The Cox Committee reply was:

As to the delegation by trustees of their duties and responsibilities, the problem is basically the same one that confronts the directors of a business corporation. Both must rely in large measure upon their staffs. There is this one important difference, in the opinion of the committee. The trustees of a public trust carry a heavier burden of responsibility than the directors of a business corporation. In fairness it should be said that in the opinion of the committee this principle is fully recognized by the trustees of foundations and that they make a determined effort to meet the challenge.[11]

Entirely contrary, the Reece Committee majority report flatly stated that there had been an abdication of trustees' responsibility through the delegation of their powers to the professional staff of foundations, a staff that was then, in large measure, responsible for subverting the United States from capitalism to socialism.[12] As the committee *Report* states:

> The place of foundations in our culture cannot be understood without a recognition of the emergence of this special class in our society, the professional managers of foundations. They are highly paid; they ordinarily have job security. They acquire great prestige through their offices and the power they wield. They disburse vast sums of money with but moderate control, frequently with no supervision. Their hackles rise at any criticism of the system by which they prosper. More often than not, the power of the foundation is their power. They like things as they are.[13]

Discussion of diversification of staff—or, for that matter, trustees—in any manner in the *Report* is completely absent.

In 1956 an analysis of the characteristics of trustees was provided in Chapter 3 of F. Emerson Andrews' *Philanthropic Foundations*. Drawing upon the answers to the Cox Committee questionnaire supplied by seventy of the then largest foundations, those with assets of $10 million or more, Andrews' analysis was based on his selection of twenty foundations from that group. He then surveyed the 202 persons serving on the boards of trustees of the 20 foundations. The biographical data compiled on the 202 included sex, relationship to donor, age, education, occupation, geographical distribution, religion, and children. While providing much more detailed statistical information based on the data compiled in each of these categories, the description of a typical foundation trustee of the larger foundation that Andrews provides is quite similar to that supplied earlier by Ayres and Lindeman:

> The typical trustee emerging from this composite picture is a man who graduated from one of the eastern Ivy League liberal arts colleges and went into business or law. He now occupies an executive position of importance, is married and has two children; he is an Episcopalian or a Presbyterian, lives in or near New York City, is of enough eminence to

be included in *Who's Who*, has accepted membership on the boards of four or five other nonprofit institutions, and is in his early sixties.

In nearly all of these characteristics he is closely akin to the trustees of colleges and universities. He differs from the typical corporation director (though frequently he is on the board of one or several corporations) in having more academic background, though he is usually also a man of affairs with a substantial income.[14]

In his analysis, Andrews does point out that of the 202 trustees, 14 (7%) were women. This is, of course, a very slight increase from Lindeman's earlier survey, but Andrews makes nothing of them. Regarding race and ethnicity, there is no mention of it regarding trustee characteristics. Also, regarding the relationship of trustees to the donor, Andrews summarizes that few trustees had a close relationship to the donor, that usually there was not even family representation, and that no question of family control remained.[15]

Andrews devotes Chapter 5 to "The Professional Staff" in his 1956 book. He discusses the subject from various angles: recruitment, conditions of employment, and so on. Regarding the characteristics and makeup of the staff of larger foundations, he states that the key figure of the staff is the head, usually named the president or executive director. Reflecting this viewpoint, Andrews provides a biographical analysis and commentary on the heads of forty larger foundations, presumably forty out of the some seventy from which he selected the twenty for trustee analysis. While admitting that his data as to their background do not provide the complete variety of experience in individual cases, he states that of the forty, "Nine—less than a quarter—were professors or professional educators. Business and finance accounted for eleven, the law alone for seven, four each came from social work and publishing, three were doctors or dentists, two were engineers." He then adds:

If there is any common denominator for top professional staff, it is association with the donor. Exceptions exist, but at least among the newer foundations the top executive post is usually held by someone who became favorably known to the donor, perhaps as a business associate, or his lawyer, or a professional man such as a doctor who may have served the donor's foundation usefully.

Andrews concludes: "These men have grown into their jobs," and does not touch on female makeup of staff.[16] Comment or discussion as to diversification or the need for it in the makeup of staff personnel on this or other grounds is absent.

The staff analysis of Andrews and the previous ones do not provide the detail and depth characteristic of those done of the trustees. Nevertheless, what comes through is that the professional staff up until the last few decades, which would include Andrews himself, could be described in much the same way as the trustees, with the exception that the trustees had more of a "substantial income."

In 1965 the Treasury Department, at the request of the Committee on Finance of the U.S. Senate and the Committee on Ways and Means of the U.S. House of Representatives, conducted an investigation of private, that is, independent, foundations for possible tax abuse by them. Of the resulting six recommendations of the department the last one concerned the trustee makeup of foundations. This recommendation observed, "Present law imposes no limit upon the period of time during which a donor or his family may exercise substantial influence upon the affairs of a private foundation." It concluded, therefore, that

influence by a donor or his family presents opportunities for private advantage and public detriment which are too subtle and refined for specific prohibitions to prevent; . . . and it permits the development of narrowness of view and inflexibility in foundation management. Consequently, the Treasury Department recommends an approach which would broaden the base of foundation management after the first 25 years of the foundation's life. Under this proposal, the donor and related parties would not be permitted to constitute more than 25 percent of the foundation's governing body after the expiration of the prescribed period of time. Foundations which have now been in existence for 25 years would be permitted to continue subject to substantial donor influence for a period of from 5 to 10 years from the present time.[17]

The solicited, written statements in response to this donor trustee recommendation by the department, however, revealed an overwhelming opposition by some 125 organizations and individuals replying, and the latter included many not officially connected with any foundation.[18] No action was taken by the Congress on this recommendation. None of the six recommendations mention any need for gender or ethnic trustee diversification on foundation boards.

Feminists would argue that this same lack of concern for gender representation is reflected in that portion of a *Report,* appearing about the same time as the Treasury recommendations, urging the establishment of a National Humanities Foundation and the appointment of "men" to a projected board of trustees for such an organization:

It is the conviction of this Commission that the independence of the proposed Foundation's board will be the best safeguard against [government] interference. If the director and members of the board are men of acknowledged competence and courage, as are the director and members of the National Science Board, there should be no problem of improper control.[19]

The 1970s witnessed the publication of Ben Whitaker's general work on foundations, which devotes a considerable amount of space to a description of the makeup and role of trustees and staff in the operation of foundations. Foundation trustees, although not maneuvered by the staff into supporting socialistic schemes as the Reece Committee contended, come off in about the same light in Whitaker's work. The really important people in the operation of foundations were the "philanthropoids," that is, the staff, particularly the staff head. Beyond this, Whitaker's analysis of the makeup of trustees and staff is about the same as the preceding ones. As to the makeup of foundation trustees, he observes that "more than nine out of ten of them are male. Ford had no female trustees until 1971. There is no woman at all on the boards of the majority of the largest foundations." Also,

a characteristic of trustees is that, with very few exceptions such as Dr. Henderson at Ford and the late Ralph Bunche and Whitney Young at Rockefeller, they are all conspicuously white. The Rosenwald Fund and the American Fund for Public Service many years ago were pioneers in having trustees from minority groups, but very few have followed them since.[20]

As to staff, he states that this powerful group is extremely small
and that:

> The great majority of foundations, however, still operate without any
> professional staff at all. Only 212 American foundations (about one per
> cent) employ any full-time officer, and of the total of 1,062 full-time
> foundation administrators, twenty-five per cent are employed by Ford
> and fifteen per cent by Rockefeller. The huge Pew Memorial, Longwood,
> Irvine, and Max Fleischman Foundations have no professional staff; the
> Richardson and Brown Foundations, each controlling over $100m., have
> a staff of only one. . . . Of foundation administrators, merely [nearly]
> eighty-five per cent are male."[21]

Although dwelling on the makeup of foundation trustees and
staff, Whitaker's description does not include any strictures or
urging for diversification of any kind in their makeup.

The 1970s also witnessed the first concrete expressions calling
for the need for a diversification in the makeup of foundation
trustees and staff. The Peterson Commission spoke out strongly
in this regard. Surveying twenty-five of the twenty-six largest
foundations, the commission report observed:

> We found that only four of these foundations have boards whose
> members might be considered broadly representative of the nation's
> various geographic regions. The remainder tend to represent only single
> regions with the New England-Middle Atlantic regions in the clear lead.
> Moreover, half of the trustees of the twenty-five largest foundations
> attended Ivy League colleges, and roughly two-thirds have business,
> banking, or legal backgrounds. Of the foundation trustees for whom
> information was available, none had a background in organized labor.
> There were few Catholics, Jews, or Negroes, or, for that matter, women
> or young trustees. An overwhelming majority of the trustees of the large
> foundations are white, Anglo-Saxon, and Protestant.[22]

The commission concluded: "It is fair to say that these boards
lack diversity."[23] It strongly urged and recommended greater
diversity of foundation boards of trustees as being in their and
the public's best interest. Also, although it did not recommend a
legislative enactment, it urged the need for more independent

trustees in addition to those closely tied to the foundation's donor.[24]

The recommendations of the Donee Group of the 1973–1977 Filer Commission on Private Philanthropy and Public Needs called for:

a phase out of donor control over charitable organizations. Specifically, *the governing boards of all foundations should be required by law to have no less than one third public members immediately and no less than two thirds public members after five years. Public members would be defined negatively to eliminate donors, their relatives and business associates.*[25]

The Donee Group also recommended compulsory legislation to expand foundation trustees to include significant representation from not only the public and nonprofit sectors but also—and particularly—women and minority ethnic groups.[26]

The commission proper, however, did not endorse or recommend the need to make legal changes regarding alleged donor control of boards of trustees; indeed, it pointedly observed:

The Commission has considered and rejected the principle that all voluntary organization boards be "representative" of the public at large or of any particular community. A principal virtue of the nonprofit sector is that it reflects different priorities, differently arrived at, than does representative government. To impose representativeness on the control of voluntary organizations would, the Commission believes, undermine an important distinction between the voluntary sector and government.[27]

The Commission, however, did exhort tax-exempt organizations to

deliberately examine and if need be broaden their boards and staffs so that a wide range of viewpoints is reflected in each organization's very governance and management. Exempt organizations, like other institutions in our society, should be especially aware of the importance of having participation—more than token participation—of minority groups and women in their governance and management.[28]

To repeat, these expressions in the 1970s by the Donee Group and the commission of the need for the diversification of boards and staff through the addition of more women and minorities, legally by the former and voluntarily by the latter, along with the earlier Peterson Commission Report, were the first clear-cut calls for more such diversification of foundation personnel. From that time on there were ever-increasing calls, in all publications dealing with foundations, that increased action was needed in this regard.

As a result, by the 1990s, a significant diversification in the gender and racial and ethnic makeup of foundation trustees and staff, across a broad spectrum of foundations, had taken place. Thus, a Foundation Management Survey was conducted by the Council on Foundations in 1990. The survey was based on 723 foundations representing holdings of about $63 billion in assets and making annual grants of about $3 billion. The survey showed that women by that time constituted about 29% of these foundation governing boards of trustees. The boards' ethnic and racial composition stood at about 93% white, with about 5% black, and other minorities forming the remaining 2%. The racial and ethnic composition of the professional staff of foundations underwent an even more dramatic change. Women staff were in a clear majority (57%) by that time. Blacks now held 8%, with Hispanics, Asians, and other minorities accounting for 5%, for a total of 13% nonwhites in foundation staff positions. Perhaps of more importance was the change reported in the makeup of the chief executive officers of the foundations: "Of the 378 full-time chief executive officers on whom information was compiled, the survey said, 43% are women—up from 26% in 1982. In addition, 13 chief executive officers (3 per cent) are black, 2 are Hispanic, and 1 is Asian."[29]

These increases in feminine, minority, and ethnic representation have been augmented since that year. A 1994 study, while concentrating on foundations and their impact on public policy, contended: "The foundation elite today is not quite the repository of the WASP establishment that scholars picture it to be. While there are very few blacks or Hispanics in our sample, one-fifth are women, roughly one-tenth are Jewish, and only one-third are white, Anglo-Saxon Protestants."[30]

A 1997 Foundation Management and Governance chart issued by the Council on Foundations shows that women by that year constituted almost 31% of governing boards of foundations. Nonwhites, including about 6% blacks, now constituted approximately 10% of their makeup.[31] Another survey of 571 foundations and corporate giving programs made by the Council on Foundations in that same year revealed that women totaled almost 65% of all professional staff and held over 50% of all chief executive officer positions and that minorities held chief executive officer positions in 6.4% of the responding organizations.[32]

INDIVIDUAL EXAMPLES OF CHANGE

A concluding and probably more striking revelation of the diversification of foundation staff that has taken place in the twentieth century is the change in the makeup of the presidents of some of the largest and most influential foundations and of the chief information and advocacy groups associated with them. The history of the Ford Foundation in this regard is a prime example.

Established in 1936, it was about 1950 that the foundation received the major portion of its assets from members of the Ford family, which catapulted it into its number one position in the United States in size of assets. Before listing and categorizing its CEO makeup, however, an examination of the document *Report of the Study for the Ford Foundation on Policy and Program, 1949*, launching the giant foundation, is most revealing. The Study Committee that produced the *Report* consisted of eight members and a staff of five members and comprised entirely white males. In a concluding section of the *Report* (pp. 100–137), which outlines how the foundation's projected program was to be administered, one searches in vain for a reference to females or the need for gender, racial, and ethnic, or other representation in the description of desirable prospective trustees and staff together with their projected reponsibilities and duties. The masculine language used in the specifications for the principal officers is quite illustrative. As to the president:

He should have full responsibility for presenting recommendations on program to the Board, and full authority to appoint and remove all other officers and employees of the Foundation. . . . On his staff, the President will need a number of officers to help him consider program questions. . . . The principal program officers are the men on whom the success of the Foundation program will largely depend.[33]

Turning back to the makeup of the presidents of the Ford Foundation, in the late 1940s there was Henry Ford II, followed by Paul G. Hoffman, who resigned in 1952 and was succeeded in 1953 by H. Rowan Gaither, Jr. Henry T. Heald was elected president in 1956 and served to his resignation at the end of 1965, when he was succeeded by McGeorge Bundy. Each one of these men can best be described as white male members of our Establishment. Bundy's successor in 1979 was a black, Franklin A. Thomas, and he was followed as president in 1996 by Susan V. Berresford, a white female who has continued to serve to the present.

Other prominent examples of the diversification in the makeup of foundation CEOs include the John D. and Catherine T. MacArthur Foundation. With present-day assets of about $4 billion putting it in the top ten in size, a white female, Adele Simmons, served as president of the foundation for ten years prior to her resignation effective September 1999. A white female, Rebecca W. Rimel, has served as president of the Pew Charitable Trusts, with assets now of over $4 billion, from 1994 to the present. In both cases their predecessors were white males. Also, the Carnegie Corporation of New York in 1997 selected a male Armenian emigrant, Vartan Gregorian, from Tabriz, Iran, as its leader, while in 1998 the Rockefeller Foundation named a British male, Gordon Conway, as its new president.

The story is the same with the major information and advocacy groups associated with foundations. For example, the CEO of the Foundation Center from its origination in 1956 down to his retirement in 1967 was F. Emerson Andrews. He was followed by Manning J. Patillo and Thomas R. Buckman. Each of these officers was a white male. In 1991 Sara L. Engelhardt, a white female, became president of the center and remains so today.

A similar pattern emerges with the Council on Foundations and Independent Sector (IS). The National Committee on Foundations and Trusts for Community Welfare, set up in 1949, evolved into the National Council on Community Foundations in 1957. A 1964 reorganization saw the emergence of the present-day Council on Foundations. Down to 1982 the CEOs of these organizations were all white males. In 1982 a black male, James A. Joseph, was appointed and continued to serve as president until 1996. In that year a white female, Dorothy Ridings, was appointed president and continues to serve as such to the present. Brian O'Connell, a white male, was the president of IS from its founding in 1980 until his retirement in 1995. He was succeeded by Sara E. Melendez, a Hispanic female, who has served as president since then.

A comparison of the earlier commentaries and surveys with those of the last few decades clearly shows that there has been an almost complete change as to the perceived need for increased diversification on the boards of trustees and staffs of U.S. foundations. A similar comparison shows that this perception has resulted in a dramatic change in that regard in the makeup of such boards and staffs.

6

Governmental Supervision

As a British colony the United States derived its ideological and legal bases for charitable giving through philanthropic foundations from the English system. Following independence, however, our state and national governments had to make adaptations in their provisions for the origination and supervision of foundations in the light of their differing circumstances. In doing so there eventually developed three major departures from English precedence that have prevailed down to the present. Major proposals in the past few decades for changes in supervision have largely derived from examination and study of the British experience in the light of these departures. A brief examination of the history of the English supervision of foundations is needed, therefore, in order to put the pros and cons of such proposals in better perspective.

SUPERVISION IN THE ENGLISH SYSTEM[1]

As described in Chapter 1, during the medieval period the Roman Catholic Church was the preeminent charitable agency in England. As that period came to a close, it was accompanied in England by the Reformation and the dissolution of church holdings, many of which were devoted to religious/charitable purposes. At the same time, English charitable giving became more secular in purpose and was an important factor culminating in the 1601 passage of the Statute of Charitable Uses. This statute envisaged two purposes, which were embodied and spelled out there. First, the statute specified giving that was to be deemed charitable, and second, it aimed to reform the abuses in the administration of charitable gifts, including those of foundations.

In the following centuries the first purpose of the statute was carried out more or less satisfactorily through successive parliamentary modificatory acts and judicial decisions. The most famous of such decisions was the 1891 restatement in unfettered modern terms of the Statute of Charitable Uses as provided by Lord Macnaughten:

"Charity" in its legal sense comprises four principal divisions: trusts for the relief of poverty; trusts for the advancement of education; trusts for the advancement of religion; and trusts for other purposes beneficial to the community, not falling under any one of the preceding heads.
He [Macnaughten] added:
The trusts last referred to are not the less charitable in the eye of the law, because incidentally they benefit the rich as well as the poor, as indeed, every charity that deserves the name must do either directly or indirectly.[2]

The administration of the second purpose of the Statute of Charitable Uses and its modificatory acts was more troublesome. In carrying out its purpose, provision was initially made for the appointment of ad hoc commissioners to look for maladministration of charitable funds or their diversion for noncharitable designs. One of the major thrusts of their efforts was the ensuring of speedier identification and faster remedial judicial action when such cases were found. By the beginnings of the nineteenth century, however, despite several legislative rectification attempts that were failures, it was generally agreed that this part of the supervisory system was not working well. It was also agreed that there was a pressing need for a thorough review of the existing unsatisfactory situation with the view of arriving at serious modification of it. The upshot was the creation in 1815 of a parliamentary commission headed by Lord Brougham to do just that.

The Brougham Commission, which continued its inquiry for nineteen years, resulted in the publication by 1834 of imposing and copious volumes of reports. The inquiry also unearthed many trust situations crying for reform. More long-range in importance was its recommendation that a more systematic governmental supervision of charities and foundations was needed. There was opposition, however, from some larger charitable organizations and foundations to an increase in any form of governmental supervision; plus there was legislative division over the need for a permanent separate and effective supervisory body other than Parliament and the courts. Such opposition resulted in no legislative action until 1853, when the Charities Trust Act was finally passed. With subsequent amendments, the act established a permanent independent regulatory Charity Commission, which, however, carried on consultation across the board with Inland Revenue (England's equivalent of our Internal Revenue Service), particularly as to what was and is charitable. The act conferred broad quasi-judicial powers on the commission and also provided for it to conduct and maintain a national registry of charities. The commissioners called for came to consist initially of two paid professionals plus a parliamentary member inevitably a backbencher. This lack of parliamentary clout, plus the absence of penalties to enforce the registry, was accompanied by a completely inadequate administrative/legal staff to carry out its work. For example, the number of senior staff available to the commissioners in the late 1940s was less than what it had been in 1860, although the number of charitable trusts had more than doubled.[3] Not surprisingly, what resulted was that about two-thirds of the foundations did not bother to register, and most action by the commission to correct wrongdoing came about in large part when extreme situations of this character were bruited about and brought to public and eventually governmental notice.

Increasing dissatisfaction with this situation was exacerbated by the tremendous expansion following World War II of governmental social welfare programs that displaced many in that area that had previously been the province of private voluntary efforts. Lord Beveridge brought the whole matter to a head with his post–World War II study and resultant publication of *Voluntary Action*[4] which included as a major recommendation the need for a thorough investigation of the charitable and voluntary sector by a Royal Commission. In 1950, therefore, a committee was set up "to consider and report on the changes in the law and practice (except as regards taxation) relating to charitable trusts [foundations] in England and Wales which would be necessary to enable the maximum benefit to the community to be derived from them."[5] The resulting investigation culminated in the 1952 publication of *Report of the Committee on the Law and Practice relating to Charitable Trusts*, commonly called the Nathan Report for its chairman, Lord Nathan. After reviewing the existing supervision of charitable trusts, the *Report* recommended several major changes: the reorganization and strengthening of the powers of the Charity Commission, making it the effective arbiter of what constitutes charity; and provision for, and the setting up of, an effective system for the reporting and maintenance of a registry of charitable trusts. Embodying these and other recommended changes, a Charities Act of 1960 was passed by Parliament. With subsequent modifications,[6] the latest being the Charities Act of 1993, it has continued to the present to be the legislation under which English foundations and charitable trusts are supervised. In the ensuing decades an important by-product of such supervision has seen the Charity Commission develop into a governmentally paid advisory and facilitating body for these same organizations. In other words, unless they are the relatively few foundations or other charities involved in chicanery and fraud, the commission to a marked degree is now viewed by foundation and government officials and the public as a counselor and adviser for foundations and other charitable organizations rather than an adversary.

AMERICAN BACKGROUND

During the colonial period individual colonial assemblies generally adopted English procedures in the legal origination and supervision of the relatively few foundations established at that time, including the tax exemption afforded them. Following independence individual states and localities continued such practices over the years, although not without some dissent. In recent years such state and local tax exemption for foundations and other charitable organizations has come under fire, particularly in Pennsylvania, which has resulted in the levying of property and sales taxes on them as recently as 1995.[7] To the 1900s individual states became the major architects in the legal setting up and supervision of foundations, primarily as charitable, tax-exempt corporations. With the tremendous economic expansion in the United States following the Civil War the growth of for-profit business corporations accelerated, but the federal government did not play a major founding or supervisory role regarding them until 1932 during the economic collapse and depression.

The belief that irresponsible acts of officials of business corporations had played a large part in bringing on the economic collapse led to the passage of the Securities Act of 1933, designed to prevent such acts in the future. This act was closely modeled on the long-standing British Companies Act and Directors' Liability Act and eventuated in the 1934 creation of the U.S. Securities and Exchange Commission to supervise for-profit corporations and businesses. Foundations and other nonprofit organizations, however, remained beyond the commission's purview.

Although the first 1894 income tax on corporations was declared unconstitutional, its statutes first enunciated and carried over into federal law the tax exemption provided by the states for foundations. The language of the Corporation Excise Tax of 1909 substantially followed that of 1894 in stating that the tax would not apply "to any corporation or association organized and operated exclusively for religious, charitable, or educational purposes, no part of the net income of which inures to the benefit of any private stockholder or individual."[8] Following the 1913 adoption of the Sixteenth Amendment to the Constitution legalizing income taxes, the first U.S. income tax law passed in that year contained similar exempting language with the addition of the word "scientific." Beginning in 1916–1917 corollary laws were

passed that permitted taxpayers, including for-profit corporations, to deduct from income taxes within certain allowable percentages those funds made to or for the setting up of such exempt
organizations, including foundations. Donees who received grants
for charitable purposes from such donors were also afforded tax
exemption. Also, in 1934 a qualification regarding political activity was added and was amplified in 1954 by an IRS ruling that,
in effect, barred tax-exempt groups from entering the political
arena at the risk of losing such exemption. This limitation has
caused continuing dissension since. Up to the 1960s the list of
exempt purposes has been increased to include "prevention of
cruelty to children or animals," 1918; "literary," 1921; and "testing
for public safety," 1954. Through the years these exemption and
deduction privileges together with the aforesaid political limitation have been included in every income tax law passed since that
time. It is significant and should be noted that all of such legislation was passed in the course of and became a part of various U.S.
revenue acts and codes. Consequently, Section 501(c) (3) of the
IRS Code, providing tax exemption for the setting up of foundations and for their donees, reads in its entirety that such exemption shall be granted to

Corporations and any community chest, fund, or foundation, organized
and operated exclusively for religious, charitable, scientific, testing for
public safety, library or educational purposes, or for the prevention of
cruelty to children or animals, no part of the net earnings of which inures
to the benefit of any private shareholder or individual, no substantial
part of the activities of which is carrying on propaganda, or otherwise
attempting, to influence legislation, and which does not participate in,
or intervene in (including the publishing or distributing of statements),
any political campaign on behalf of any candidate for public office.[9]

As at the state and local level there has always been some
questioning of the value or need of such federal tax exemptions
and deductions. There has also been some questioning among
organizations eligible for and receiving such benefits. In the
1950s officials of the Rockefeller Foundation objected to allegations that a large part of the money that it distributed would, if
it were not for its tax exemption, belong to the government. They

pointed out that the average income of the Rockefeller Foundation in the 1950s was about $15 million annually and added:

We are advised that if the Federal income tax exemption were withdrawn, the tax payable by the Foundation on the basis of the above figures, under the present corporate income tax structure, would be about $865,600, or at a rate of between 5 per cent and 6 per cent rather than 90 per cent.[10]

Recent examples include a 1992 article by a professional fundraiser that opened with the statement, "Sooner or later, Congress will end the tax deductibility of contributions to charitable organizations. I won't mourn the loss."[11] A book[12] published in 1993 by two reporters for the *Philadelphia Inquirer* maintained that the public loses much more than it gains by the tax exemption policy. In the same year there was a failed U.S. Senate Budget Committee proposal to place a cap on the amount of income taxpayers could write off as a charitable deduction.

CONTRASTING AMERICAN AND BRITISH EXPERIENCE

Thus it was that the U.S. government, while largely continuing the British precedent of tax exemption for charitable purposes, made three major departures from English practice in the philanthropic area: (1) in the type of national agency supervising foundations and other charitable organizations; (2) in the tax deduction incentive extended by the U.S. government to those giving funds for charitable purposes; and (3) in imposing a specific limitation on political activities by charitable/tax-exempt organizations.

SUPERVISORY AGENCY AND TAX DEDUCTION

Regarding item 2, in England tax deduction as an incentive to give for charitable purposes was and remains practically nil. In the United States the allowance of tax deduction for charitable gifts at the national level has been present since 1916–1917. Thus U.S. individuals, corporations, and estates can deduct from taxable income, in varying percentages, the value of gifts made for designated charitable purposes, including the setting up of foundations. Similarly, the recipient of philanthropic funds is given greater relief from the burden of taxation in the United States than in Great Britain. The impact of such tax policy on the character and amount of charitable giving in the United States, however, has been argued ever since.

Turning back to item 1, government supervision of foundations, the Brougham Commission by 1853 had completed its nineteen-year study and had published its voluminous reports, and the resulting permanent Charity Commission had been supervising English foundations, with a few legislative modifications, on into the twentieth century. In 1915 the U.S. Walsh Commission did conduct exhaustive hearings and did make various legislative recommendations anent foundations, although they were not acted on by the Congress. Yet one searches in vain in the transactions of the Walsh Commission for any expression of interest in pursuing the English course of setting up a supervisory body similar to their Charity Commission. It is true that this and the succeeding legislative investigations conducted under the chairmanships of Congressmen Cox, Reece, and Patman were set up with varying specified missions and announced goals affecting foundations, business, and the capitalistic system and without specific mandates to make broad studies of foundations. With hindsight, however, it seems remarkable that none of them touch on the possibility of looking into or adopting some form of an English Charity Commission to right alleged wrongdoings of foundations. Also, there is little or no questioning of the continuance of the tax deduction for charitable giving.[13] Thus, it can be said that the fundamental question of where national supervision of foundations and other charitable organizations should be located simply wound up by continued default being lodged in the Treasury Department's Bureau of Internal Revenue, later the Internal Revenue Service. As one writer on government supervision of foundations noted in the 1960s, "The Internal Revenue Service has only indirectly and quite reluctantly become the major source for government supervision of foundations in the

United States." She added, "Its proper role is still not clear, nor have any real attempts been made either to separate or to consolidate the enforcement powers and programs of the states and the federal government."[14] In the 1970s another study on the same subject similarly concluded: "The tax laws having provided the original nexus between the federal government and philanthropy, the Internal Revenue Code has become—more by accretion than design—the principal vehicle for federal oversight of philanthropy."[15]

Such accretion may have been a major contributing factor in the apparent lack of effective oversight of foundations by the service. Other than the brief informational Form 990s submitted annually by foundations—and often not done or incomplete—any significant oversight was simply not there. To paraphrase, such oversight can best be characterized as continued neglect. It is the belief of this writer that, certainly in the 1960s and 1970s, much of the congressional and public distrust of foundations can be traced to their belief that many of these organizations were operating in secret, illicit, and clandestine ways. A case can also be made that much of such distrust stemmed from the lack of information about them, as discussed in Chapter 4, plus a perception that a weak and inattentive IRS had permitted such a deficiency from neglect or collusion. Of course, the IRS could make an effective case that the Congress in the last analysis was responsible for this situation. Also present was the not-as-much-discussed view that the avoidance of taxes through the deduction provision was as much or more of a consideration in foundation formation than a charitable or philanthropic purpose. In any case, such attitudes seem to have provided much of the impetus for the passage of the Tax Reform Act of 1969, which for the first time in American history provided a form of national tax on an American philanthropic institution—the foundation. Finally awakened to, and alarmed by, antifoundation pronouncements and by the tenor and tone expressed at the congressional hearings accompanying the passage of the act, two nongovernmental commissions to consider philanthropy in general and foundations in particular were organized. These two studies with resultant publications were conducted during the periods 1969–1970 and 1973–1977, respectively.

The first of these studies (Peterson Commission) presents in the Preface of its 1970 report the answer to why the commission was set up:

By remaining a kind of closed society in an era when openness is a byword, the foundations excited public suspicion that they were engaged, not in a great range of activities that promoted the general welfare, but in secret things done in a dark corner. By their reluctance to discuss publicly their failures as well as their successes, the foundations foreclosed the right to their own frail humanity. They became instead symbols of secret wealth which mysteriously used the levers of power to promote obscure, devious, or even sinister purposes.[16]

The leaders setting up the commission and the time in which this took place are identified in an opening chapter:

In late 1968, in response to these conditions, John D. Rockefeller III brought together other concerned people for a series of meetings focused on two main questions. Was it possible to secure an independent appraisal of American philanthropy? What should be the long-range role of philanthropy and foundations in American life? At one point in the discussions, a suggestion made by Alan Pifer, president of the Carnegie Corporation, was endorsed by other participants: that an independent commission be formed to study all relevant matters bearing on foundations an private philanthropy and to issue a report containing long-range policy recommendations with respect to them.[17]

One of its recommendations was also presented in the Preface. This marks the first time that a responsible and knowledgeable American assemblage clearly enunciates that there was a need for the establishment of a new entity for the oversight of American foundations. Although this recommendation called for only a private advisory, rather than public supervisory, group, it was a significant harbinger of things to come:

One across-the-board recommendation made by the Commission merits a special mention. It is the proposal for the creation of an Advisory Board on Philanthropic Policy. A private body of this sort, though set up under public auspices, could have a continuing influence on every aspect of American philanthropy. It would be an ongoing mechanism and would stay abreast of changing circumstances, of unresolved and emergent questions, of new concepts of philanthropy's function in society. It would extend into the future the kinds of studies and recommendations made by this commission, but would do so under conditions which promised a more thorough analysis and a continuing reevaluation.[18]

Although approving the existing tax incentive provisions as beneficial for the creation and operation of foundations, other charitable organizations, and philanthropy in general, the Peterson Commission rather lamely observed, "Much work must be done before the flawed tax incentive system as it now exists can be replaced by something better."[19]

Before considering the second study (Filer Commission), it is informative to examine one of a number of conferences and meetings that took place at about the same time, specifically, the Ditchley, England, Conference of 1972. This conference was preceded in the 1960s by several other European conferences on foundations and philanthropy, involving delegates from various European countries, England, Canada, and the United States. Those conferences of the 1960s were devoted, in large part, to a consideration of the domestic and international roles of foundations, their legal and fiscal position in those countries, and particularly their supervision by governments.[20]

The Ditchley Conference of 1972 concentrated on Anglo-American philanthropy and foundations in the preceding regards and was attended by philanthropic and foundation leaders from only England and the United States. Moreover, it was convened against the backdrop of the earlier European conferences, the Peterson Commission report, and the 1969 congressional hearings and resultant Tax Reform Act of that year in the United States. The conferees at the 1972 Ditchley Conference devoted their discussions generally to "[f]inance, legal regulations, and all the other organizational problems of charities and foundations, including their relations with government."[21] Specifically, there was much discussion of the three major differences in the relationship of British and U.S. foundations with their respective governments: (1) supervision of foundations, (2) tax deduction,

and (3) political activity. The prevailing attitude of all participants on item 1, against the backdrop of the events of the 1960s
and 1970s in the United States, was summarized as follows:

The discussion did not make clear why American foundations had not
"set their own house in order" before having new requirements imposed
upon them or why, since tax and audit requirements existed before 1969,
these had not been enforced. American members in turn regretted there
was no body in the United States equivalent to the British Charities
Commissioners which could advise and assist tax-exempt organizations
as well as regulate them. The conference members were told that the
Peterson Commission recommended the formation of an Advisory Board
on Philanthropic Policy to oversee the whole field of philanthropy, but
members were not hopeful that decisions about the charitable status for
tax exemption could be wrested from the Internal Revenue Service. Even
so, they agreed that some kind of special advisory agency, perhaps along
the lines of the British Charity Commission, would be desirable.[22]

Regarding item 2, the tax deduction incentive difference, a
succinct statement of the facts is made:

The manner and extent to which private giving is induced or encouraged by statutory provisions differ markedly between Great Britain and
the United States. . . . In England and Wales the individual is not
granted any relief in his personal taxes as an inducement to give. . . . In
the United States (individual, corporation, or estate) deducts the value
of gifts from taxed income.[23]

Much less clear as perceived by the discussants was the effect
of these differences:

Discussions of these two contrasting legal systems yielded no consensus as to whether the more liberal American provision for deductibility
of contributions induces more generous giving than the less liberal
provision in the British law. It was suggested that the more skeptical
attitudes of American tax authorities toward givers offset the more
liberal provisions of law; in Britain, conversely, perhaps the friendly
attitude of the authorities makes up for less liberal provisions of law.
The data required for a reliable assessment of the effect of either system
upon the volume of giving simply do not exist.[24]

In short, the discussants favored adoption in the United States of some form of the British system to supplant or amplify the governmental supervision of the U.S. Internal Revenue Service, but there was no consensus as to changing the U.S. liberal tax deduction provisions to bring them into line with British practice. Such tax deductions however, have and are continuing to present problems for the IRS. A recently developed method of giving under which charities use tax-deductible gifts from donors to pay for life insurance policies on the donors and then share in the proceeds is a good example. Such insurance setups are already being used by some 1,000 donors with sums involving more than $1 billion. These and other so-called split-dollar plans will cause untold damage to donors and charities if they are found to be illegal by the IRS.[25]

The establishment of the 1973 Filer Commission followed hard on the heels of the Peterson Commission deliberations and report and the 1972 Ditchley Conference. A goodly number of those named to the Filer Commission or utilized as advisers had been involved in the organizing of, or had participated as conferees in, some of the earlier philanthropic studies groups. The conferees, particularly those associated with the second Ditchley Conference, had become cognizant of, and many had developed general approval of, the English supervisory method and tax approach. These views were carried over by them to the Filer Commission. Thus the Filer Commission concluded in Chapter 8 of its *Report*:

After considering various existing and proposed alternatives, the Commission feels that a regulatory agency with full governmental status and wide authority, modelled on the British Charity Commission, is not transferable into the American context and that the present pattern of enforcement and oversight of nonprofit organizations should, with the changes proposed in the previous chapter, be maintained.

Yet the Commission does feel that there is indeed a need for an organization with analysis and advancement of the non-profit sector as a central purpose . . . we do see considerable merit in quasi-governmental status for any national organization on the non-profit sector . . . the Commission accordingly, in terminating its own work, puts forward as one of its major recommendations: That a permanent national commission on the nonprofit sector be established by Congress.[26]

Some of the changes referred to in the previous quotation recommended increased foundation accountability and accessibility, but in regard to a governmental body responsible for supervision of them the commission *Report* flatly opined "[t]hat the Internal Revenue Service continue to be the principal government agency responsible for the oversight of tax-exempt organizations."[27] This did not satisfy two dissenting members of the commission. One, Graciela Olivarez, argued that "the regulatory functions of the IRS should be transferred to another agency, specifically the proposed commission on the nonprofit sector. Recent questionable activities of the IRS alone make that agency suspect. . . . Philanthropy . . . should fall within the regulatory purview of a special entity created for and sensitive to that purpose."[28] The other, Frances T. Farenthold, in arguing for a similar transfer, alleged that the politicization of the IRS under five previous presidents had taken place with deleterious impacts on various segments of the nonprofit sector.[29] She added:

The Commission's own study in this area says that the officials who are responsible for regulating exempt organizations are "handicapped by a) cumbersome procedures which were designed generally to meet the needs of the tax-collecting branches of the Service; b) inadequate authority in relation to other officials near the top of the Service's hierarchy; c) the understandable emphasis of the Service on its role as tax collector rather than as overseer of a non-revenue producing activity; and d) the generally weaker qualifications and training of the Service's field staff as compared to the National Office staff.

All of this leads to conclude that all ruling and audit functions regarding exempt organizations should be removed from IRS and placed in a new independent regulatory commission.

This new commission would also have greater credibility and more potential for performing the research and advocacy function envisioned by the Commission report for the proposed national commission on philanthropy.[30]

The commission's ad hoc Donee Group, in addition to other criticisms of the commission's findings and recommendations, strongly opposed the commission's endorsement of a continued governmental supervisory role for the IRS. It rejected as futile previous and recent attempts by administrative changes to upgrade the personnel and work of the IRS in the nonprofit sector and stated:

It is our view that the I.R.S. is institutionally incapable of regulating and rendering adequate service to charitable organizations since exempt organizations are by definition excluded from the agency's main area of concern, which is raising revenue. The I.R.S. has given little attention, minimal funds and utilized the least skillful employees in their exempt organizations activities. . . .

As one of the participants in the post-Ditchley group stated in a letter to the Donee Group, "The fact simply is that the principal objective of the Service has to be revenue raising. It is, as Sheldon Cohen [former commissioner of the IRS] has often observed, the name of the agency. Little revenue is to be found among investigations of charities. Hence this activity will always take second, third, or last place among the priorities of the people at the Service." . . .

We therefore recommend *the removal of all ruling and audit functions regarding exempt organizations from the I.R.S. and creation of a new regulatory commission with a presidentially appointed board reflecting all elements of private philanthropy, including donees.* . . . In the absence of a staff or congressional advocate for philanthropy with some "turf" to protect, . . . We therefore recommend *a permanent, staffed, standing committee or subcommittee in the House and Senate having oversight responsibility over any permanent regulatory or oversight agency and power to review any legislation affecting the nonprofit sector.*[31]

The Filer Commission conducted extensive research and discussions concerning the effect of the tax exemption and deduction privileges afforded donors and donees and particularly as incentives for philanthropic giving and activity. It concluded, "On balance, the Commission believes that the virtues of the charitable deduction significantly outweigh its defects as both virtues and defects have evidenced themselves over six decades of the deduction's existence."[32]

What resulted from the findings and recommendations of the Peterson and Filer Commissions? Success as regards the continuation of the governmental tax exemption and deduction incentives for philanthropic purposes and continued failure as far as their advocacy of a philanthropic quasi-governmental advisory group separate from or above the IRS. For example, on January 7, 1977, the Treasury Department announced the appointment of a twenty-four-member "blue ribbon," "high-powered" Advisory Committee on Private Philanthropy and Public Needs to "to advise the Treasury on tax aspects and standards for private philanthropy." Significantly, the committee adopted the same title as that of the immediately preceding Filer Commission. The committee held one meeting in early January. At its second meeting on April 7, 1977, however, the secretary of the Treasury abruptly announced to the members that the committee was being done away with because newly elected President Carter felt that there were already too many advisory committees in existence. The secretary suggested that the committee might reorganize itself as an "informal" organization, but this proposal was rejected by committee members as robbing it of its legitimacy.[33] The latest form of such proposals was advanced at a recent meeting of the American Assembly and rejected by the assembly.[34] It has been rumored that a 1994 IRS ruling was designed to ensure continued rejection, particularly congressional, of such proposals in the future. Thus: "In a ruling that surprised many tax experts, the IRS has declared that campaign committees of Congressional candidates can give excess funds to private foundations—without subjecting the candidates to tax. . . . Some say the IRS bent the law to win favor with Congress."[35]

Also, disclosure legislation in 1996 and rules affecting foundations and other tax exempt groups in 1997–1998 revealed an IRS sensitive and conciliatory toward their problems in meeting such rules.[36] There was the IRS response in 1996–1999 to earlier allegations of excessively high salaries and benefits paid to officials of large charitable organizations and foundations, the most notorious cases being that of the earlier head of United Way and the former trustees of Hawaii's Bishop estate. The IRS published guidelines as to such compensation and proposed intermediate sanctions, including fines and taxes, for those organizations found guilty of violations. At the same time it called for public response to its proposals prior to issuing final regulations. In general, the response from the philanthropic community appears to be favorable to these regulations.[37] In 1998 an IRS modernization included consolidating its operations into four units, one of which would be a newly operationally enhanced and beefed-up tax-exempt sector.[38] By that year, too, the service provided that all informational Form 990s, including those of foundations, be sent to a single office located in Ogden, Utah. This change has made it possible for a number of organizations to make many of such returns available to the public on the Internet, a service that the IRS hopes to eventually do on its own Web site.[39]

POLITICAL ACTIVITY—DONEE GROUPS

In addition to the preceding differences between the United States and Britain on government supervision of foundations and tax deductions there remains the third, the U.S. ban on substantial activity by foundations and other charitable organizations involving the carrying on of propaganda or otherwise attempting to influence legislation, that is, engaging in political activity. This third difference has occasioned as much or more past and present-day congressional and public attention in the United States than the other two.

The British approach has been one of not defining or using restrictive legislation in this area. Rather, the approach has been defining what constitutes "charity" and "charitable" and then measuring whether a particular organization or organizational activity falls within that definition. The United States legislatively forbids "substantial political activity" but does not define exactly what it forbids. It might be said that the British approach is positive, and the U.S. negative. The British in a general way define "charity" (positive) and measures against it. The United States limits "substantial political activity" (negative) and says, Don't do it. It may be that the acrimonious and partisan debate in the United States on the whole issue has resulted in part from this difference.[40]

Any consideration of this issue in the United States must open with some attempt to define the various terms and words, in addition to political activity, that have been and are being bandied about in discussing such alleged activity by tax-exempt organizations. What is lobbying? What is advocacy? What is public policy? A definition joining the last two terms would be that advocacy is the act of advocating, pleading for, or supporting an aspect of a public course or policy to be followed by government. The older word, lobbying, although it has had some usage, has tended to become a pejorative, old-speak word that essentially means the same thing as advocating public policy. These words and terms and their meanings are important because any democratic government must have some lawful means by which individuals and groups can lay their views and perceived needs before government. At first glance, it would seem that governmental regulation of what is "lawful" and what is "unlawful" lobbying or advocacy would be easy. A century or so ago in the United States such regulations were standard and direct and involved the states much more than the federal government. They also were clear-cut and outlawed bribery or intimidation and other such actions aimed directly at legislators or other officials. The passage of years and the increasing role of the federal government in the political/electoral process, however, and the emergence of what might be called group lobbying or advocacy made the earlier regulatory approach simplistic. A particular regulatory problem affecting foundations developed as to the distinguishing by the IRS of what constituted illegal advocacy on the part of foundations. In the case of donees, whether funded by foundations or by grants from governmental agencies, similar judgmental problems developed and were compounded by whether or not their advocacy was substantial. It should be noted in passing that the IRS devotes some thirty-nine pages to explain its rules on this subject. These problems are futher complicated by defining what a foundation is and what a donee group is, many of the latter having assumed and bearing the title foundation.

In any consideration of problems of advocacy and public policy involving foundations one must start with the universally acknowledged role of foundations as instruments for effecting social change.[41] This role, of course, is legislatively restricted by that portion of the IRS Code that states that a foundation or charitable donee group will lose its tax-exempt status if a "substantial part" of its activities consists of "carrying on propaganda, or otherwise attempting, to influence legislation." The complete statute, however, provides no definition of these terms. In interpreting them, the IRS not only has been reticent about defining them but has, on numerous occasions, reversed its decisions in denying tax-exempt status, often when confronted by a foundation or advocacy group with supplemental arguments and information.[42] Continuing attempts to differentiate distinctly and exactly between propaganda/influencing legislation and education have also proved fruitless. Foundations, by the very nature of the broad mandates of many to work for the betterment of mankind, if their grants—particularly those for educational purposes—are successful must often have an influence on governmental legislation.

With the exception of the Reece Committee investigation, the congressional investigations of foundations did not delve deeply into this controversial topic. The Reece Committee's coverage of the subject is banal and unexplanatory and serves only to illustrate the difficulties of defining these terms and tangentially the difficulties presented to the IRS in interpreting and enforcing them.[43] Both the private Peterson and Filer studies of philanthropy and foundations, while conceding the difficulties presented in defining these terms, recommended continued prohibition of such activities by foundations but argued for their allowance by donee advocacy groups. The Filer Commission report forthrightly stated:

That nonprofit organizations, other than foundations, be allowed the same freedoms to attempt to influence legislation as are business corporations and trade associations, that toward this end Congress remove the current limitation on such activity by charitable groups eligible to receive tax-deductible gifts.
The only major restrictions in this area that the Commission believes can be fully justified are:
Those that would prevent a person or group from being able to set up an organization to campaign for a particular piece of legislation and then deduct from income taxes the expenses of running such an operation. Therefore, the Commission recommends that organizations receiving tax-deductible gifts must be required to have broader charitable aims and functions apart from any immediate legislative activities.
Prohibitions against a nonprofit organization's supporting or opposing a candidate for public office.
Maintaining the current total prohibition against lobbying by private

foundations.

Otherwise, the Commission believes that there should be no restrictions, linked to tax deductibility, on what the Commission feels has become an increasingly important role of the nonprofit sector and a major part of the philanthropic process.[44]

In addition to these investigations and studies centering on foundations, another earlier one bears examination: the 1950 U.S. House of Representatives Select Committee on Lobbying Activities, chaired by Representative Frank Buchanan. Although touching only tangentially on foundations, the *Reports* of the Buchanan Committee are of particular interest today because they are devoted to and elucidate this present-day philanthropic hot topic.[45] In 1950 individuals and groups associated with conservatives, such as members of the Dupont family, J. Howard Pew, and the Alfred P. Sloan Foundation, were singled out for examination as to their alleged lobbying and advocacy activities.[46] By the 1990s, however, some scholars argued: "Most foundation spending for public policy projects tilts towards the left, despite all the talk among foundation professionals on the virtue of philanthropic pluralism. . . . In terms of actual public policy funding, however, liberal grants outnumber conservative grants by roughly four to one."[47] This may be part of the explanation as to why liberal public policy advocacy groups occasion more congressional targeting today than conservative ones. On the other hand, a 1991 study cited major foundation support in the 1970s for neoconservative think tanks. A prominent illustration was a 1972 grant from the Ford Foundation for the support of the American Enterprise Institute (AEI).[48] In any case, solutions advanced at the earlier time appear to have pertinence whether the advocacy groups being targeted are conservative or liberal. In regard to lobbying or advocacy with federal funds, the *Report* counseled:

Congress retains absolute power over agency budgets. This power over the purse strings can be asserted first through careful investigation in advance of the appropriation of money; and second, through the withholding or detailed earmarking of funds. Congress has frequently exercised this power, as in the numerous appropriation acts specifically

forbidding the expenditure of appropriated moneys for designated lobbying activities.[49]

The *General Interim Report* of the committee in its conclusions
also observed that the investigative authority of Congress,
through standing and select committees, such as its own, constituted another safeguard against advocacy abuses. An alert press
was also cited as a check on an expenditure of public funds in
questionable advocacy activities. Finally, it emphasized as the
sixth, last, and longest of the conclusions:

We need more information on lobbying and lobbyists. This, at the
moment, is the most feasible approach. Every group has the right to
present its case, but at the same time Congress and the public have a
right to know who they are, what they are doing, how much they are
spending, and where the money is coming from—in a word, full disclosure of the relevant facts. . . . Congress and the public have the right to
full information on those who actively attempt to influence the decisions
of government.[50]

The minority Part 2 of *A Report of the Select Committee on
Lobbying Activities,* while differing in some minor respects with
the majority portion of the *Report,* generally wholeheartedly
concurred with the majority and stated: "We do feel that those
individuals whose principal purpose is to attempt to persuade
individual members of Congress to follow a certain course of
action might well be required to identify themselves and their
source of support."[51]

In the 1996 U.S. presidential campaign, the Republican Party
platform stated:

We will end welfare for lobbyists. Every year the federal government
gives away billions of dollars in grants. Much of that money goes to
interest groups which engage in political activity and issue advocacy at
the taxpayers' expense. This is an intolerable abuse of the public's money.
A Republican Congress will enact legislation, currently blocked by Bill
Clinton's Congressional allies, to make groups choose between grants
and lobbying.

We will establish Truth in Testimony, requiring organizations which
receive government funds and testify before Congress to disclose those

funds. Our "Let America Know" legislation will force public disclosure of all taxpayer subsidies and lobbying by groups seeking grants.[52]

In the 1990s, too, much of the congressional investigative and legislative activity in the area of advocacy and public policy has centered on foundations and on the donee individual or groups receiving grants from them or funds from the government. Specific targets for examination have been the donee groups with the major portions of their operating funds coming from governmental, that is, public, grants or contracts. A 1993 book argued that such large-scale government funding has turned many social service groups into virtual state agencies spending in excess of $15 billion a year.[53] Various 1990s legislative proposals, such as those advanced by Representatives John Bryant, Robert Ehrlich, Ernest Istook, John Mica, and David McIntosh, together with a similar one in the Senate introduced by Senator Carl Levin entitled "The Lobbying Disclosure Act of 1993," would have forced such groups to reveal the source, duration, and amount of such funding when engaging in a variety of "political activities" such as advocating the passage of particular legislative programs by the Congress. Proponents for revealing such information contended that the officials and others connected with many advocacy groups have a built-in incentive, because of previous funds awarded them, to advocate for an extension and/or an augmentation of such programs and resultant funds to them. The proponents contend, too, that large and inordinate portions of such funds have been or would be used for future advocacy purposes or for high salaries and other perks for advocacy officials rather than the worthy purposes advocated and intended. Opponents countered that they are already required to report such information to the IRS. Too, the duplication of such called-for information to the Justice Department in some proposals would be an onerous and time- and money-consuming task resulting in a significant diminution in the funds available for the advocated worthy purposes. They also argued that the measures called for were an infringement of freedom of speech and association by advocacy groups.[54] Following a great deal of acrimonious debate, a complicated Lobby Disclosure Act of 1995 was passed and went into effect in 1996, but more stringent provisions were still being urged by some congresspersons after its passage. Amid this welter, one former congressman eventually became so incensed over what he viewed as illegal political and other activities by tax-exempt groups that he stated: "To oversee compliance with all those activities, Congress needs to create a national office—a 'czar,' if you will—for tax exempt groups. That position must be given strong powers to enforce the tax law."[55]

POLITICAL ACTIVITY—POLITICAL LEADERS

The semifarcical denouement in this tale of controversy over what constitutes illegal political activity has been that those who write and pass our tax laws have gotten caught up in it. Tax-exempt organizations have a number of features appealing to politicians in their campaigns to seek and hold public office. Such groups can skirt stricter campaign finance laws. They do not require the degree of disclosure as to the names of supporters, nor are their contributions limited. Thus, politicians of differing political persuasions have used their interpretations of what constitutes substantial political activity to gain the financial means to further their own political ends. On the contrary, many of these same political figures, conservative or liberal, Republican or Democrat, have argued that their respective opponents have used tax exempt organizations, called foundations, institutes, advocacy groups, or what have you, in illegal ways.

In the 1990s there was a surge in the development of these relationships between politicians and tax-exempt organizations. At the beginning of that decade, amid calls by politicians of all stripes for tighter IRS regulation of them, a "sampling" of such organizations alleged that fourteen Democratic and eight Republican incumbent senators and congresspersons had close ties with such organizations. A former IRS commissioner somewhat cynically observed at the time: "What has happened is, that like all other political areas, people have become more sophisticated. . . . Everybody tries to squeeze what they're doing under the heading of education, or some other charitable denomination. . . . Everybody knows the rules and everybody tries to bend them, I can't say that either side is pure in that respect."[56] He might have added, as has been alluded to earlier, that retiring congresspersons were quietly putting their excess and heldover campaign funds into tax-exempt foundations, funds often totaling more than $0.5 million.

Although other political figures, such as Senator Alan Cranston, had been accused of, and criticized for, improper usage of tax-exempt organizations for political purposes, the best-known recent one has been Congressman Newt Gingrich, former Speaker of the House of Representatives. In this well-publicized 1996–1997 case, for a time it appeared that his tenure as Speaker was held in the balance. The major issue in the case was the solicitation for donations to several tax-exempt organizations, particularly the Progress and Freedom Foundation, that were engaged in supporting a number of his activities, including his teaching of a college course. It was alleged, too, that these tax-exempt organizations had close ties with a political action group that the Speaker had set up and that he ran. His critics argued that such actions were violations of law, in particular that such activities, including the college course, were political rather than educational in character. Supporters of Gingrich argued that the course and other activities were indeed educational, that their propriety had been cleared with an appropriate congressional committee, and that identical activities had been carried on in the past by other congresspersons. The upshot was an investigation by an ethics committee of the House. The Speaker's political opponents called for his censure, which would have made it virtually impossible for him to continue in the office. After much political jockeying in the ethics committee and in the House as a whole, the Speaker was eventually reprimanded and fined $300,000 by the House, in large part for providing inaccurate information on one aspect of the matter. He was reelected as Speaker, and the IRS eventually ruled in 1999 that the Progress and Freedom Foundation had done nothing wrong in sponsoring Gingrich's college course. Such confusion as to the rules governing political advocacy involving individuals and organizations underscores the need for the government and the nonprofit sector to clarify such rules.[57]

In addition to such issues, there is considerable present-day advocacy of the abolition or severe modification of the Internal Revenue Service by presidential candidate Steve Forbes and several congressional leaders in the Senate and the House of Representatives. Measures under such a plan call for the substitution of a flat tax or sales tax for the present income tax. This would be accompanied by the abolition or modification of the tax exemption and tax deduction laws under the present IRS statutes. Much attention has been given to the impact on charitable giving if such measures were adopted. Opponents of such changes, such as the Council on Foundations and Independent Sector, argue that such abolition or modification would result in a drastic curtailment of charitable giving.[58] Proponents argue that the tax incentive factor was not as important in giving as pictured by opponents and that increases in available wealth for charitable giving would more than offset such projected declines. Amid this welter of discussion, there appears to have been little said as to the effect on, or what might or should be done about, the U.S. nonprofit sector or philanthropic foundations in the event of such a change.

In contrast has been the Canadian response when faced with proposed changes in Revenue Canada, their counterpart to the U.S. Internal Revenue Service. Since the fall of 1997 a panel composed of interested persons has been engaged in intensive study of what changes should be recommended for the nonprofit sector, including foundations, when this comes about. A preliminary report[59] of the panel, in addition to other possible alterations, included a major one proposing four alternative models for a new voluntary sector governance agency: (1) strengthening and revamping the present supervisory system lodged primarily in Revenue Canada; (2) and (3) a federal Voluntary Sector Commission modeled on the U.K. Charity Commission; or (4) a new nongovernmental commission placed in the private sector.

The final report of the Panel, named the Broadbent Report[60] for the panel's chairman, Edward Broadbent, which Canada's

Voluntary Sector Roundtable reported has been well received by the federal government, includes dozens of proposed changes for the nonprofit sector. The report urged that four of these should be quickly implemented: (1) development and distribution of a code of ethics and handbook of good practices for nonprofits; (2) creation of new cabinet-level positions for the nonprofit sector at the national and provincial levels; (3) establishment of a parliamentary committee to determine which groups should qualify for charitable status, a determination that should be reviewed every 10 years; and (4) creation of a Voluntary Sector Commission modeled after the Charity Commission of England and Wales. In discussing the function of such a commission, the report stated:

The principal goals of the proposed Commission would be to support and enable the sector in improving its governance and accountability practices, to promote transparency, and to help ensure compliance with federal rules governing their conduct. It would supplement rather than replace the monitoring role of Revenue Canada.[61]

Summarizing the Broadbent Report, Vice President Gordon Floyd of the Canadian Centre for Philanthropy observed:

The panel has opted for a series of recommendations that have more to do with supporting and strengthening the sector than with policing it. . . . It's clear that they're more impressed with the way policy affecting the sector is moving in Britain than in the United States.
While Americans' first impulse in insuring greater accountability is to add more regulations, . . . the attitude in Britain, when charities are not living up to the letter of the law, is that it's more because they lack the knowledge or the skill to do so rather than that they're trying to pull a fast one. . . .
The Broadbent panel has reached the same kind of conclusion about Canada's voluntary sector: that accountability deficits are most effectively addressed through preventative measures rather than by stepping up the policing.[62]

7

International Activities

EARLY INTERNATIONAL ACTIVITIES

Prior to the opening of the twentieth century, for all practical purposes there were no international philanthropic activities carried on by Americans through foundations.[1] A notable exception was one of the beneficences of George Peabody. An American resident in London, by the 1860s Peabody had amassed a fortune largely as the result of the Civil War banking between Britain and the United States. At that time Peabody established the Peabody Donation Fund, which was a foundation set up, organized, and operated under English law. This fund provided some $2.5 million toward the planning and construction of cheaper and better housing for the working classes in London.[2]

1900s–1950s

One of the earliest foundations active in international activities was the American-Scandinavian Foundation, which was established in 1911 to provide fellowships for study and research by Americans and Scandinavians. Two American philanthropists, Andrew Carnegie and John D. Rockefeller, however, ushered in overseas philanthropy by our twentieth-century U.S. foundations on a significant scale. Guided by the freedom of action embodied in their mission statements, in the case of the Carnegie Corporation of New York "the advancement and diffusion of knowledge" and in the case of the Rockefeller Foundation "to promote the well being of mankind throughout the world," these two foundations dominated the pre–World War II international programs conducted by U.S. foundations. Inspired in part by his love and affection for his boyhood home in Scotland and guided by the overall goal of attaining international peace, Carnegie launched a multitude of international programs. He spent millions in Scotland, Great Britain, and the British Commonwealth nations in educational, social welfare, and health programs, primarily through foundations. These included the Carnegie Dunfermline Trust, Carnegie Trust for the Universities of Scotland, and Carnegie United Kingdom Trust. Nine separate Carnegie Hero Funds were set up in nine countries. Churches and libraries all over the world also benefited from his largesse. In 1910 Carnegie established the Carnegie Endowment for International Peace. The Carnegie Endowment together with the World Peace Foundation contributed a great deal of information in an area characterized by a lack of knowledge and gave much needed stature to a movement that had been regarded by some in this and other countries as somehow subversive to national well-being. In 1911 the Carnegie Corporation of New York was established, and its Commonwealth Program, particularly in South Africa, became a major supporter of activities in the international area.

The year 1913 witnessed the birth of the Rockefeller Foundation. With the ending of World War I this foundation was to spend $20 million initially for such foreign activities as famine relief in Belgium, demonstration hospital units there, and aid for the medical faculty of the University of Brussels. In the period between the two world wars the Rockefeller Foundation and its sister agencies the Rockefeller Institute for Medical Research, now Rockefeller University, and China Medical Board of New York became famous for their international programs in health and medical research. While the Rockefeller Institute was attracting a research staff from all over the world that was to make it one of the world's greatest research-teaching centers in the medical-biological field, the China Medical Board was aiding the development of medical education in China, culminating in the establishment of the Peking Union Medical School in 1921. In its efforts in this area, however, the Rockefeller philanthropies' greatest contribution was their work in preventive medicine. Campaigns were launched against hookworm, yellow fever, and malaria that, in addition to following known practices in treating these diseases, encouraged new methods of combating them. Following procedures developed in U.S. programs, the directors of the Rockefeller Foundation's international medical programs insisted that a portion of the initial costs be assumed by the local host government and that it ultimately assume complete responsibility for subsequent support.

In conducting its international health and medical programs, the Rockefeller Foundation soon discovered that these were inextricably combined with problems in the nutritional and agricultural areas. The foundation, therefore, inaugurated a number of foreign programs designed to produce more and better food. The Mexican program of this type, for example, which was launched in 1941 in association with Mexican leaders, scientists, and agricultural producers, removed that country from a deficit position with respect to its basic food requirements and enabled Mexico to enter new areas of agricultural enterprise. The Rockefeller Foundation, like the various Carnegie philanthropies, was also active in the promotion of international education through gifts to various foreign universities. Some $2 million was granted for the expansion of Oxford University's Bodleian Library, and sums were also appropriated for such universities as Oslo, Copenhagen, Dalhousie, London, and Tokyo.

In addition to the Rockefeller and Carnegie philanthropies, other U.S. foundations began operating international programs prior to the 1950s, particularly in the areas of medicine and public health. The Near East Foundation, incorporated in 1930, continued its public health program, which had been inaugurated during the post–World War I turmoil in Turkey. The Commonwealth Fund, established in 1918 by the widow of Stephen Harkness, carried on a three-year program following World War I of supporting European relief work. In 1925 the fund inaugurated a fellowship program to enable citizens of the United Kingdom, Australia, and New Zealand to pursue graduate-level studies in the United States. The W. K. Kellogg Foundation, for many years after its founding in 1930, funded projects in agriculture, education, and health in Canada, Latin America, Australia, New Zealand, and selected European countries.

A number of other foundations established international programs during the period. The Kosciuszko Foundation, founded in 1925, fostered relations between the United States and Poland through personnel exchange and other programs. The Tolstoy Foundation, established in 1939, aided immigrants to the United States from Russia. The Watumull Foundation, another smaller foundation set up in Hawaii specifically for work in one geographical area, India, began work in 1942. It pioneered an exchange program of scientists and students between the United States and India and also led the way in studies and projects dealing with population problems of the subcontinent.

The John Simon Guggenheim Memorial Foundation at its beginnings in 1925 restricted its fellowships to the United States and some of its possessions. In the 1930s it extended them to include several South American countries. By the 1950s and since, fellowships were made available to all of the countries in the Western Hemisphere. The Henry Luce Foundation was established in 1925 by the famous publisher Henry R. Luce as a memorial to his father, Henry W. Luce, a nineteenth-century missionary to China. Its primary interest in its early years was in Protestant churches, schools, seminaries, and other programs in the Far East. Since then the foundation has gradually broadened the scope and increased the magnitude of its activities to include the United States. However, the foundation's Luce Fund for Asian Studies, which since the 1970s has included China, still absorbs about half of the foundation's annual appropriations.

1950s–1980s

Until the late 1960s, despite the pre–World War II international activities by our foundations described earlier and a few others, the available statistics show that they formed a small portion of total foundation giving and were overwhelmingly concentrated in grant making by the Rockefeller, Carnegie, and Ford philanthropies. Lindeman in the 1920s and 1930s calculated that 100 foundations included in his study devoted only 1.3% of their total expenditures in 1921 to what he called international relations, and 1.6% in 1931. Harrison and Andrews in 1944 in their analysis of 335 foundations stated that only 26 showed programs in international relations and recorded an increase to 7.8% there of their total expenditures. Again, shifted proportions were recorded by Rich in a 1954 study of 620 foundations, where she found an increase to 42 foundations active in the area but a decrease to 6.8% there of their total expenditures.[3]

In 1952, of the fifty-four largest foundations of the time responding to the Cox Committee *Questionnaire*, approximately only one-fourth stated that at that time or previously they had engaged in some foreign activities. Prominent among their number were the three largest: Ford Foundation, Rockefeller Foundation, and Carnegie Corporation of New York. Only six of the fifty-four foundations maintained offices and staffs in foreign countries. The foreign staff employed by them at that time was small and averaged five or six persons per foundation. The number ranged from several informal representatives of the John Simon Guggenheim Memorial Foundation, who received small amounts of money for expenses, to the forty-six full-time staff members employed by the Rockefeller Foundation in its various foreign offices. During the period 1947 to 1952, the proportion of the total amount expended abroad by the fifty-four foundations to that expended in the United States averaged 10%. Highest, again, was the Rockefeller Foundation, which averaged approximately 25% for the period.[4]

In the late 1950s and 1960s, however, there was a significant increase in international programs and expenditures on the part of a number of the major foundations and a growth in the number of smaller ones active in the area. The Rockefeller Foundation stepped up its operations, particularly in support of the green revolution, an agricultural development in the so-called Third

World countries. In the late 1950s, this foundation was dipping into capital for additional millions to be spent on its various programs in Asia, the Middle East, and Africa, and by the late 1960s the foundation was operating in fifteen nations with a combined professional staff of over 140 persons.

Continuing its earlier international programs the W. K. Kellogg Foundation in the 1960s enlarged its health and agricultural programs in the countries of South America. Established in 1940, the Rockefeller Brothers Fund in the 1950s inaugurated its flexible special program, including grants in the area of international relations and understanding. Throughout the period of the 1950s through the 1980s these "included grants for South American and Asian agricultural development, education in the Near and Middle East, improved Asian-American relations, and the economic development of West African nations."[5] In 1959 the Tinker Foundation was set up and began a broad program of grants for fellowships, visiting scholars, conferences, and endowed chairs at major universities in the United States designed to promote better understanding among the peoples of the United States, Ibero-America, Spain, and Portugal.

Still, in 1968 a Foundation Center study, reported in the Peterson Commission *Report*, showed that only 9% of all U.S. foundation grants were for programs in international activities. Also, during the period 1967–1968 our total foundation support for international activities came to about $221 million. Of this sum, about 82% was accounted for by expenditures from seventeen of the then twenty-five largest foundations. The study also showed that the largest share of foundation money was spent on programs dealing with Asian, African, and Latin American countries.[6]

In 1972 the German Marshall Fund of the United States was set up and began the conduct of a broad-scale program concentrating on the problems of industrial societies and their relations with developing ones. Also in this period the Josiah Macy, Jr. Foundation launched its programs for medicine and pediatrics in developing countries and in 1965 decided to spend up to 20% of its annual income in this area.

Carnegie Corporation of New York, which had a continuing interest in Africa since its first African grant was made in 1925, reached a policy decision in 1960 to concentrate its Commonwealth Program of international activities there, a policy that was continued to the 1980s. The corporation concluded that the economic development of the new African nations would turn on the strength of their educational bases. Funds were therefore granted in the next decades for a wide variety of educational projects there, with particular emphasis upon planning and manpower studies and involving joint cooperation by institutions of higher learning in Africa, Great Britain, and the United States.

Similar to the 1970s–1980s Commonwealth Program of the Carnegie Corporation of New York but broader in scope was the Rockefeller Foundation program in those decades called University Development and then Education for Development. Reflecting the foundation's long interest and expertise in agriculture and the medical, natural, and social sciences, the program consisted of assigning foundation staff and U.S. academics to key universities in Africa, Asia, and Latin America, where they worked in collaboration with faculty there to upgrade the host university. By the early 1980s this effort was viewed by all as successfully completed, and the program was terminated at that time. Parenthetically, in terms of staff employed and money spent, this was one of the largest programs undertaken by the foundation up to that time.[7]

Noting that religious/spiritual achievement was not recognized in awarding the Nobel Prizes, in 1972 the American financier Sir John Templeton created the Templeton Prize for Progress in Religion to be permanently funded through the Templeton Foundation. The prize has been awarded each year since then to a living person who has shown extraordinary originality in advancing humankind's understanding of God and/or spirituality. Selections have been made on a worldwide basis, and the first recipient was Mother Teresa. The amount of the Templeton Prize is calculated each year so as to exceed that of the Nobel Prizes and now stands at approximately $1.24 million; it was and remains the world's largest annual monetary prize.

Overshadowing all of these foundations in the size, range, and scope of its overseas activities in the post–World War II period was the Ford Foundation. Reorganized in 1950, as the result of the extensive and thorough work of a special study committee that stated flatly that "the most important problem confronting the world today is to avoid world war,"[8] the Ford Foundation thereupon launched an Overseas Development Program, together with an International Training and Research Program. Initially concentrating on Asia and the Middle East, by the 1960s the foundation had expanded its activities to help the new African nations and those in South America. In addition to establishing increased food production and health and medical programs, the foundation broke new ground in supporting joint economic-social research and planning programs with governments all over the world. In a special 1961–1962 review of its operations, designed to guide the foundation's activities in the 1960s, it was pointed out that from 1950 to 1961 grants totaling $61.7 million had been made "to advance international understanding and cooperation, particularly among nations of the Atlantic area." Perhaps of even more significance, the report stated that for the same period:

The Foundation expended $152.6 million to help forty less-developed countries and territories in South and Southeast Asia, the Near East, Africa, and Latin America and the Caribbean area. This assistance was largely in support of educational, training and research institutions and activities essential to the recipient countries' own programs of social, economic, and educational enhancement.[9]

Also, in line with its 1960s style of giving large block grants to institutions in the United States, the foundation in 1965 provided a grant of $72 million to develop international studies programs at various U.S. universities.

The Ford Foundation continued to concentrate a larger percentage of its activities on international relations than any other American foundation in the 1970s and 1980s:

Gradually, the foundation's international interests expanded to virtually every region of the globe. At one point, the foundation maintained more than twenty field offices in the developing countries, each with resident staffs and an array of project specialists. Indeed, in many places the foundation was the major, if not exclusive, aid-giving agency. Among the foundation's special interests abroad were, agriculture, education, strengthening government institutions, rural development, and language problems.[10]

Beginning in the 1980s, however, the Ford Foundation, while stilll continuing to spend 30–40% of its then annual expenditures of about $250 million on international activities, reduced its overseas locations, maintaining, among others, Dacca, Bangladesh; New Delhi, India; Jakarta, Indonesia; Lima, Peru; Rio de Janeiro, Carne, Brazil; Planco, Mexico; Nairobi, Kenya; Cairo, Egypt; and Lagos, Nigeria. At the same time, the foundation fine-tuned its efforts by concentrating on fewer programs in these and other areas of the world.

1980s–1990s

A large portion of the earlier international programs engaged in by our foundations centered on what might be called physical aid to other countries, such as programs in health and agriculture. Explicitly or implicitly, however, the desire to prevent future global conflicts and concomitantly to promote peace and understanding among nations underlay many, perhaps most, of these and other programs. Also, a good percentage of these programs in the period 1950 to 1980 were conducted in neutral noncommunist and non-European countries and areas of the world and were operated during that period in the context of the Cold War with Russia and the other communist dominated countries. By the 1980s a slow and almost imperceptible shift in foundation emphasis took place. While continuing, often on a reduced scale, many of the earlier programs, new ones were launched, in ways and with some foundation endeavors not yet clearly delineated, aimed at reducing or even eliminating the possibility of outright conflict, that is, ending the Cold War and preventing or at least ameliorating possible or actual conflicts at the local or regional levels.

A good description of this shift is provided by David A. Hamburg, who was appointed president of the Carnegie Corporation of New York in 1983. In his last annual report essay when he retired in 1997, he stated, "In 1983 the Corporation returned to one of the most fundamental of all Andrew Carnegie's interests, his passion for international peace."[11] The essay then describes the successive major Carnegie Corporation programs created under the following titles: Avoiding Nuclear War, Prevention of Proliferation, and Preventing Deadly Conflict, titles that reflect their effort to ensure peace. The course of events finally resulted in the ending of the post–World War II Cold War and the almost simultaneous overthrow of the communist governments in the Soviet Union and other communist-dominated countries. A paragraph interspersed in the Hamburg essay is revealing in regard to corporation activities at the time:

Unforgettably, we had the privilege of linking Mikhail Gorbachev with Western experts during his crucially formative early years in office. In 1985 a remarkable new generation of leadership took control in the Soviet Union. Building on my contacts with leaders of the Soviet scientific community that led to an enduring relationship with Gorbachev, the Corporation launched a vigorous attempt to expand cooperative projects between its U.S. grantees and their Soviet counterparts. The Soviet scholars and analysts who were involved in these contacts included several who were key advisors to Gorbachev in the early years of his reform efforts.[12]

Equally revealing when viewed from a foundation context is the emergence in 1988 of the Soviet Union's Foundation for the Survival and Development of Humanity, with the direct encouragement and support of then secretary-general of the Communist Party Mikhail Gorbachev. As this writer wondered at the time, "Whether or not this augurs a lasting reversal of the Communists' ideological opposition to the creation and operation of foundations in the USSR and other Communist countries, however, only time can tell."[13]

In any case, a growing perception that the Cold War was ending is revealed by the strong support provided by 1988 by numerous other U.S. foundations to help the process. In that year a study showed that 171 foundations made about 2500 grants in the fields of peace, security, and international relations—much of them centered in the Soviet Union and Central Europe. Such grants totaled $124 million and formed about 7% of the total amount awarded by these foundations in that year. Seventeen of the 171 awarded grants amounted to $1 million or more each and accounted for about 80% of the total awarded in the fields. Leaders included the third-ranked Carnegie Corporation, which made grants totaling about $10 million, while the John D. and Catherine T. MacArthur and the Ford Foundation were first and second, with each making awards approximately double that amount.[14]

These and other foundation efforts then and earlier were undoubtedly indirect contributing factors to the revolutions of 1989 and the eventual collapse of communist control in the Soviet Union and other countries of Eastern and Central Europe. This collapse coincided with a subsequent dramatic reorientation among U.S. foundations in the late 1980s and 1990s not only to include these countries in older programs conducted by them but to inaugurate new ones for the region and, in numerous cases, conducted by foundations new to international grant making. The dominant goal of almost all of these programs was the elimination of potential and actual conflict within and without these erstwhile totalitarian countries through the rebuilding of democratic societies within them. A wide variety of programs was launched by a relatively large number of U.S. foundations to achieve this goal. The larger foundations preeminently supported the establishment of new political units, particularly ones concerned with conflict resolution, and the setting up of a wide number of nonprofit, nongovernmental, third sector organizations. In many cases this involved a building almost from the ground up for such organizations and in many areas taken for granted in the United States, like education, the arts, religion, journalism, and, yes, foundations.

A 1997 commentary on the plans, sweep, and activities of the Ford Foundation by its newly elected president, Susan V. Berresford, serves to highlight its commitment to international activities. In that year Berresford announced that, while continuing to operate sixteen other field offices all over the globe, Ford had established its latest one in Moscow, Russia, in 1995. She also announced that the foundation then employed about 600 employees worldwide; that approximately 25% of the total were non-U.S. citizens; that overseas grants accounted for about 40% of its annual giving of approximately $430 million; and that giving was planned for international activities in approximately that percentage in the future. She added though that $15 million was to be made available to major American universities to strengthen their international studies and exchange of scholars programs.[15]

A 1997 study conducted by the Foundation Center in cooperation with the Council on Foundations more broadly illustrates this commitment and, at the same time, shows that a striking change in the amount of giving and the geographical emphasis in international activities by many large and small foundations has taken place. Based on a comparative analysis of some 800 foundations engaged in international activities in 1990 and about 1,000 in 1994, the study concluded that international giving by these foundations rose by 18% during that period. Fifteen of the largest givers and the approximate amount each gave in 1994 as shown by the study were Ford Foundation, $122 million; W. K. Kellogg Foundation, $56 million; John D. and Catherine T. MacArthur Foundation, $51 million; Rockefeller Foundation, $49 million; Pew Charitable Trusts, $36 million; Andrew W. Mellon Foundation, $31 million; Open Society Fund, $26 million; Carnegie Corporation of New York, $23 million; Central European University Foundation, $22 million; Lincy Foundation, $16 million; William and Flora Hewlett Foundation, $13 million; Charles Stewart Mott Foundation, $12 million; W. Alton Jones Foundation, $9 million; Rockefeller Brothers Fund, $8 million; Starr Foundation, $8 million. A dramatic finding in the study is the significant shift during the period 1990–1994 in the amount of money flowing to countries in Central and Eastern Europe, including the former Soviet Union, as compared to other overseas areas. These countries received about $53 million in foundation giving in 1994, but this figure reflected a percentage growth from 1990 of 548%. Only two areas of the world exceeded Central and Easten Europe in giving from our foundations in 1994: Latin America, about $70 million, and sub-Saharan Africa, about $60 million. However, their four-year percentage growth in the amount of foundation grants, 121% and 52%, respectively, was much less.[16]

A review of the preceding amounts reveals the noteworthy fact that, if one totals the amounts for the Open Society Fund with that of the Central European University Foundation, the $48 million in grant money is the foundation largesse of one living man, George Soros. Perhaps more striking is that Soros, after eventually moving to the United States in 1956 from his native Hungary, amassed his fortune here in foreign exchange dealing. Reflecting his interpretation of history and by this time his beliefs and preferences, in the 1980s he began setting up the score of philanthropic organizations for the furtherance of what he called the Open Society. This term, which calls for the creation and sustaining of democratic structures in countries lacking them, now permeates his and indeed other foundations' international programs.[17]

In view of their repressive history from the end of World War II to the late 1980s, it is obvious why much of the giving for such purposes as that by Soros and our other foundations would center in the years since on Central and Eastern Europe. In Soros's case there is the additional factor of his native-son interest in Hungary, where the Central European University, which he largely created, is located. A recent book by a former director of public policy at the Pew Charitable Trusts comments on Soros activities. The book is an insider's view that is rich in detail and provides a balanced interpretation of the successes and failures of foundation programs in the area in the past ten years. For example, in a chapter significantly titled "George Soros: Leader of the Band," the author states, "Soros and his foundations have perhaps done more than any other individual or institution to promote democracy in Central Europe." Yet he admits:

The large sums provided by Soros, such as the $65 million investment in CEU [Central European University], may also have had a distorting effect. . . . Soros's support has distracted attention and siphoned off resources from existing institutions, many of which are in desperate circumstances. The large sums involved may make it difficult for some of the Soros-sponsored institutions to integrate themselves into their local communities. A critical, and as yet unanswered question, is to what extent are the best practices of these institutions replicated in other institutions? If not widely replicated, CEU and other Soros sponsored institutions may simply become opulent islands in otherwise empty seas.[18]

The prelude to the latest entry of a large-scale foundation into international activities was the 1997 announcement by the communications mogul Ted Turner of Atlanta of his pledge of $1 billion in Time Warner stock over a ten-year period to causes supported by the United Nations. Funded by this pledge to the United Nations Foundation created in January 1998, the first grant made by the foundation in 1998 of over $22 million was primarily directed toward twenty-two international projects in three broad categories: children's health ($6.5 million); women and population ($9.3 million); and environment/climate change ($1.4 million). The following programs also received support: land-mines, ($2.6 million) and food security ($1.2 million), together with smaller amounts for drug control and poverty alleviation. Since one of the foremost announced reasons for the United Nations is planning for and action toward the maintenance of peace and concomitant prevention of war, Turner's grant to the United Nations Foundation appears to be in line with the other foundation programs for a similar purpose.[19] Similar giving by U.S. and foreign foundations to another international organization, CIVICUS, was made at about the same time. These and other grants to other international organizations are discussed in more detail in Chapter 8 herein.

In some ways perhaps the most striking revelation of the continued interest of our older and larger foundations in international activities was the 1998 announcement of the Rockefeller Foundation that it had set up and was operating a course designed to educate the wealthy in the most effective methods in giving their money away abroad. Titled Course in Practical Philanthropy, it considered a variety of philosophical and practical topics such as what donors are trying to accomplish, mission statements, and evaluation of grant proposals. Participants pay a $10,000 tuition fee, and an additional $10,000 is charged for the cost of travel to, and lodging in, the country or region abroad of interest to the potential grant makers.[20]

OVERVIEW

In looking over the foregoing description of the role and functioning of U.S. foundations active in international affairs from the beginning to the present, it seems that one particular policy and goal adhered to by them throughout the period stands out: concern on the part of their founders and administrators for the well-being of humankind outside the United States and, explicitly or implicitly, the desire to further world peace and reduce international tensions. Their earlier programs, from the early 1900s to the 1980s–1990s, were designed to aid in accomplishing this goal by concentrating on the twin development of material and human resources abroad. While certainly enlisting the support of local governmental, scientific, and educational leaders, however, they tended to utilize a disproportionate number of noncitizens there in carrying through on their agendas. Geographically these programs at that time were centered in the main in non-European regions of the world. Also, significant funds were spent at home for educational purposes dealing with non-European countries and regions, particularly in the so-called area programs in U.S. colleges and universities.

The work of U.S. foundations in international activities has come in for a small amount of criticism both abroad and at home. For example, the earlier foundation programs in food production and health were alleged by some abroad to be semirevolutionary. The foundation reply to such criticism was that they had developed and adhered to operating principles that dramatically differentiated them from earlier philanthropic organizations and that, rather than merely relieving distress, the foundations believed that they should attack the root causes of distress by improving agricultural production rather than simply feeding the hungry, and by preventing illness rather than caring for the ill. Another earlier example was some questioning of foundation insistence upon local support and cooperation in the conduct of foreign programs. The foundation reply was that this approach had been tried and tested successfully in U.S. programs and that unless such local support was freely given abroad, the long-range prospects for the success of any programs were negligible. On the other hand, certainly in Central and Eastern Europe, the criticism today appears to be that more such local support in the form of the involvement and the turning over of more of the conduct of programs to local citizenry is needed.

Finally, during the years of the Cold War and since, there have been charges that foundations that operate programs in international affairs are merely disguised agencies of the U.S. government. Charges of a similar nature can and have, of course, been leveled at religious bodies, business organizations, and even social and athletic clubs and organizations It is true that, at the height of the Cold War in the 1960s, a few smaller foundations— the J. M. Kaplan Fund and the Hoblitzelle Foundation are two examples—were used as "cover" for operations of an intelligence nature. Such operations, however, seem to have been minuscule relative to the overall international activities of all of our foundations and at the time were roundly condemned by many, including those associated with other foundations.[21]

These earlier accusations of foundation involvement in spying were disclosed internally and based on U.S. Internal Revenue Service information. Today, similar allegations emanate from abroad and are particularly directed at the Soros foundations set up in Central and Eastern Europe. Although such rumblings have, for the most part, been dismissed, they have resulted in the effective closing of Soros' foundation operations in Belarus and Serbia by their governments' actions. Such closings took place despite the continued objections of Soros that these and all foundations funded by him involved grant-making programs with a nonpolitical and nonpartisan purpose. Also, such objections were seconded by the U.S. Department of State.

International activities of U.S. foundations have also been objected to domestically on the grounds that such money would be better spent in the United States than abroad. A succinct rebuttal to such objections was that provided by George Eastman in the 1930s to such criticism of his establishment abroad of dental clinics for needy children: "What I have contributed for dental dispensaries abroad is but a very small percentage of what I have given in our own country; whereas my money has been made in the Kodak business which is carried on all over the world."[22] In the 1950s the industrialist Paul Hoffman was a major architect in the launching of the Ford Foundation's program of international activities. He expressed the opinion then that all foreign expenditures should be related to the goal of international peace; that being the foundation objective, it made no difference whether the money was spent at home or abroad. In the final analysis, Hoffman concluded, every dollar spent abroad would repay the American people many times over if permanent peace were obtained. Similarly, in 1963 President Henry T. Heald of the Ford Foundation gave these reasons for that foundation's decision to maintain and expand its activities abroad:

First, that the resolution of our domestic problems would be a hollow victory if two-thirds of the world continued to be racked by deprivation and unrest.

Second, that the Foundation has sufficient resources to make a significant contribution. (The overwhelming majority of American foundations confine their activities to the United States and in most cases lack the funds for meaningful assistance abroad.)

Third, as a private institution the Foundation has certain advantages of independence, flexibility, selectivity, and perseverance in its assistance abroad.[23]

In the congressional investigations of foundations there was little criticism of foreign funding by U.S. foundations. The Cox Committee flatly stated: "The committee believes that these international activities and foreign expenditures of the foundations are motivated chiefly by consideration of the welfare of the American people and as such are entirely praiseworthy."[24]

The majority report of the Reece Committee stated that it was not able to come to a final evaluation of foreign use of foundation funds but tentatively suggested that such grants be limited to 10% of annual income. But even here, they opined that exceptions might be made. Congressman Wright Patman in his 1960s–1970s investigation of foundations, however, assailed the foundations on the grounds that they were giving millions for projects outside the United States—in India, Mexico, and other foreign countries—but practically nothing in Utah or Wyoming. Patman also contended that these foreign grants were an important contributing factor to the deficit in the country's balance of international payments.[25]

Since that time such criticism by congressional or other knowledgeable persons has effectively stopped, undoubtedly due to the dawning realization by congresspersons and the public of our present-day and growing environmental, economic, political, and social international intertwining with foreign nonprofit organizations, including foundations.[26]

In retrospect, in the 1980s and 1990s six major changes from the previous decades appear to have taken place in grant making by U.S. foundations for international activities: (1) an increase in the overall number of foundations engaged in such grant making and in the percentage in total foundation giving; (2) more emphasis upon, and interest in, the creation of just and stable societies in all countries; (3) targeting of Central and Eastern Europe as major areas for giving, particularly to implement the second change; (4) greater utilization of local organizations and individuals in the operation of foundation programs abroad; (5) larger foundations encouraging and helping smaller ones contemplating or desiring to engage in international giving; (6) increased willingness by U.S. foundations to encourage and support the foreign nonprofit sector, particularly foundation centers and international organizations. Although this last change has been touched on in this chapter, its potential for future impact on development of the foundation field appears to be so great that the entire next chapter is devoted to it.

8

Foreign Foundation Centers and International Organizations

The increasing involvement of U.S. foundations in international programs and activities has been described in the preceding chapter. Highlighted have been the six major changes in such activities since World War II. The last major change listed, has been the process wherein our foundations developed closer ties with foundations established and operating abroad. These ties have gone hand in hand with, and have been interwoven to a large degree with, foreign foundation centers, bearing different titles, that provide information and support for foundations located there. Similar ties have been forged with a number of international organizations. Many of these foreign and international organizations have received financial and other forms of support from U.S. foundations at the time of their creation and later and U.S. foundation officials have served over the years in official and consultative capacities in and to them. There follow identification and description of the major organizations of this type in Europe, Near East Africa, Asia Pacific, and the Americas and the foundation directories that many of them and individual foundations have issued.

Identification of these organizations was based on extensive personal and written consultation with knowledgeable persons in this country and abroad. Of course, there are many countries where none have yet been founded. Locating information on the extant organizations has always been a problem. There is, however, a growing body of information available about the longer and better established of them, such as the Charities Aid Foundation and the Hague Club. Still, multiple problems (linguistic, legal, etc.) and the difficulty of interpreting their role and function in changing and diverse settings make completion of satisfactory accounts of them difficult. With this caveat, it is believed that this chapter includes enough individual and collective information about these organizations to effectively enlarge the body of knowledge of individual ones and of the group as a whole. In the account that follows, in addition to as much other information as possible, the place and date of founding, the naming of past and present key officials, location of offices, description of programs and activities, and discussion of the relationships of these organizations with similar ones, including foundations, at home and abroad, are presented. An attempt has also been made to provide insight into how the working of these organizations has been associated with U.S. foundations' international programs and activities abroad; often including funding by U.S. foundations for their founding and subsequent activities.

EUROPE

One of the most active of the European organizations, which in the 1990s became international in its scope, is England's Charities Aid Foundation (CAF). Undergoing a number of name changes in its early history, the CAF grew out of organizations extending back to 1924. It was reorganized under its present name in 1974 and is an apt illustration of the nomenclature difficulties in describing foundations and similar organizations. In its purpose and operation this foundation is literally an organization to aid charities and, inferentially, other foundations. In its own words, "It offers services to donors and support for the voluntary sector to encourage a greater flow of funds."[1] In addition to its other activities, it has published numerous works dealing with philanthropy including, from 1968 to the present, the authoritative U.K. *Directory of Grant-Making Trusts*, and, since 1995, the international quarterly magazine, *Alliance*.

CAF officers, particularly its director, Michael Brophy, represent the interests of British foundations in many of the deliberations and actions of the governmental Charity Commission and the Inland Revenue. Also, he and they act in a similar way in other national, regional, and international philanthropic organizations. Brophy has, for example, figured prominently in setting up the European Foundation Centre (EFC), International Standing Conference on Philanthropy (INTERPHIL), and World Alliance for Citizen Participation (CIVICUS) and has served over the years in official capacities in them. The CAF acts also as a foundation. It had assets in 1994 amounting to about £8.7 million, from which it made grants in that year amounting to about £500,000 for its stated purposes. The CAF is centrally administered from offices located at Kings Hill, West Malling, ME 19 4TA, England. In 1993 it established a U.S. affiliate, CAF America, and at the same time opened offices in the United States. By 1997 it was stating, in full-page ads:

CAF (Charities Aid Foundation), a leading non-profit in the UK with offices and related organizations worldwide, is committed to increasing the substance of charity. The CAF family facilitates tax-effective giving, advises on international grant-making and operates across international boundaries to match need and resources by providing information, advice and assistance to both non-profit organizations and donors.

CAF produces a range of publications which are designed to assist and support donors involved in international grant-making activities and provide information and funding advice for non-profits working worldwide.[2]

Another such organization located in the U.K. is the Association of Charitable Foundations. Founded in 1989, with purposes similar to the CAF but zeroing in on foundations and trusts, the association is a membership organization of approximately 300 foundations and trusts. Headquartered at 4 Bloomsbury Square, London WC1A 2RL with Nigel Siederer as its director, the association officials stay abreast of legislation affecting foundations and charities and convene conferences and seminars on matters affecting its members. The association publishes the bimonthly *Trust and Foundation News* and numerous other publications.

England's Ditchley Foundation and some of the impact of its sponsorship of the Ditchley Conferences of the 1970s have been described in Chapter 6. Located at Ditchley Park, Endstone, Oxford, England, the foundation was set up to provide a place for persons from the Atlantic community to hold meetings where problems of common concern such as philanthropy and foundations could be discussed. The physical facility for the use of such persons is a commodious manor house in the countryside near Oxford and is maintained and staffed by the foundation. The longtime provost of the foundation was H. V. Hodson. In addition to heading up its conference operations for years, he was a pioneer in the gathering and providing information about foundations on a worldwide scale. He edited the first edition of *The International Foundation Directory* in 1974, to be followed by successive ones by him, including the latest, eighth edition in 1998. Each edition provides vital information on the major foundations operating internationally plus bibliographical references. The multipage introductions to the successive editions provide succinct accounts about the past and contemporary status of foundations worldwide. Too, they thread their way through and discuss foundations' intricate, changing, and often perplexing relationships to each other and to other international organizations.

Two other organizations of this type merit attention: the Salzburg Seminar and the Bellagio Study and Conference Center. Founded in Salzburg, Austria, in 1947 to promote dialogue and understanding among American and European youth following World War II, the Salzburg Seminar since then has vastly expanded its focus and geographic scope. Financial support from the 1950s on has come from numerous foundations, such as the Ford Foundation and the Hauser and Nippon Foundations. Such support was capped in 1997 by a $10 million endowment grant from the W. K. Kellogg Foundation. Since 1947 some 17,000 participants in its conferences and other activities have considered a wide variety of pressing issues, including some devoted to philanthropy and foundations. Such deliberations and the administration thereof are carried on from the Seminar's headquarters at Schloss Leopoldskron in Salzburg.

The Bellagio Study and Conference Center is located on the shores of Lake Como in the Italian Alps. The genesis of the center was the 1959 bequest by an American expatriate, Ella Holbrook Walker, of the Villa Serbelloni, in Bellagio, Italy, to the Rockefeller Foundation. The donor wanted her gift and the villa to be used to promote international understanding. In its administration of the center, the Rockefeller Foundation launched a series of programs to implement that wish. The result has been that the center has served as a meeting place for more than 21,000 residents and conferees since inception. Many of these participants have been officials of, or associated with, the Rockefeller Foundation and other foundations all over the world. Similarly, although there has been the widest range of topics considered there, many have dealt directly with, or touched upon, philanthropic and foundation developments worldwide.

Ireland has no foundation center or association. A 1994 publication, however, in Part One, provides an overview of the charitable sector, while Part Two consists of a directory of grant-making foundations and other bodies in the Republic of Ireland and Northern Ireland.[3]

Two major associations in Germany provide a focus for German foundations. The Donors' Association for the Promotion of Sciences and Humanities is commonly referred to in English as Donors' Association or in German as the Stifterverband. An earlier version of the Donors' Association was launched in Germany in 1920 but a new start was made after World War II announcing its purpose:

Since its beginnings at the end of the forties, the aims of the Stifterverband have been to promote science and technology in research and teaching and to support talented young researchers and technicians. . . . [T]he Stifterverband concentrates on six areas of concern: international scientific cooperation; support of young academics; medical research; economic research; research in the sciences, technology, and mathematics; and research in the arts and humanities.[4]

In addition to financial support for such activities, the Donors' Association "performs some functions as a service for its members or in the interests of the scientific community at large." Prominent among the latter endeavors is:

Operating a Foundation Center: Documenting the world of foundations in the Federal Republic, publishing foundation directories and related literature, consulting would-be donors and fund-raisers from the science community, and influencing the lawmakers in favor of liberal laws regulating foundations, including fiscal laws, as well as arguing vis-a-vis the public at large to make use of the foundation or trust instrument.[5]

In this connection, the Stifterverband published a survey of European foundations in 1972 in English and a ninety-nine-page directory in German in 1992 containing profiles of its members.[6]

The other foundation association in Germany is the Federal Association of German Foundations, in German, the Bundesverband Deutscher Stiftungen (BDS). The BDS was founded in May 1948. With half of the approximately 8,000 active foundations in Germany set up in the past twenty years, the latest association effort has been to work for the continuation and even augmentation of this growth. Its current chairman, Alex von Campenhausen, recently maintained that German tax law must be revised to provide tax write-offs of up to 20% of gross income in order to maintain such growth. At the same time, the BDS has called for the rewriting of the statutes governing foundations' use of income so as to permit them to build reserves against potential falloffs in such income.[7]

As described earlier, foundations in France have not achieved a prominent position there. Consequently, there is no foundation center as such in France, although the Fondation de France, set up in 1969, with its network of ancillary foundations performs such a function.[8] Also, directories of French foundations have been published by the French government.[9] Despite such relative inattention to foundations, an early post–World War II conference on foundations of trailblazing importance and a harbinger of even more important ones to follow was held at Royaumont, France, in 1961 under the joint auspices of the Royaumont Foundation, the

Ford Foundation, and the European Cultural Foundation. Convening in a renovated thirteenth-century Cistercian abbey, which is now the headquarters for the Royaumount Foundation, seventeen participants from the United States and participants from seven European countries plus representatives from four international agencies attended the conference.[10]

In Belgium the King Baudouin Foundation, founded in 1976, has developed a foundation center function similar to that of the Fondation de France.[11]

A situation similar to that in France prevails in Italy. A 1971 guide to European foundations, however, was issued under the auspices of the Giovanni Agnelli Foundation, together with one by it in 1973 on Italy, both edited by Franco Agnelli.[12]

Spanish foundations are focused around the Foundation Center, in Spanish the Centro de Fundaciones (CF), and a recently established Confederation of Spanish Foundations. Founded in Madrid in 1978, one of the Foundation Center's major efforts has been the publication of the *Directorio de las Fundaciones Espanolas* (Directory of Spanish Foundations). The 1986 first edition of 247 pages contains information, addresses, officers, and programs, together with pertinent indexes on over 1,300 major Spanish foundations. A subsequent 1994 edition of the directory was expanded to 539 pages and contains information on over 2,700 Spanish foundations: addresses, names of officials, information on activities and annual grant making, and pertinent indexes. Both editions are in Spanish.[13]

The confederation presently includes about 500 foundation members of various types, including institutionally related educational, health, and cultural ones. One of the confederation's major purposes has been encouraging and advising the formation and operation of foundations in Spain. Its officers and staff represent Spanish foundation interests in Spain, Europe, and internationally through a variety of activities, for example, meetings, publications, and so on.[14]

Spain's immediate neighbor Portugal, has a Portuguese Foundation Centre, established in the 1990s. A Portuguese foundation directory, in a Portuguese and English side-by-side translation, was published by an individual Portuguese foundation in 1993.[15]

As described earlier, foundations in Central and Eastern Europe were virtually wiped out by World War II and the advent of the communist takeover in the area. The gradual ending of the Cold War and the eventual overthrow of the communist regimes, plus the surge in U.S. foundations' international activities, saw an accompanying renewal of philanthropic interest and activity there. A 1977 directory of foundations in Finland was compiled under the auspices of an individual Finnish foundation.[16] By the 1990s a number of foundation centers were opened in Central and Eastern Europe. Many of these centers grew out of the European Foundation Centre's Orpheus Program and were financed, in large measure, by U.S. foundations. For example, the Rockefeller Brothers Fund in 1995 made support funds available for the newly established Information Center for Foundations and Other Not-for-Profit Organizations in Prague, Czechoslovakia, and made similar funds available to the newly established Non-Profit Information and Training Center, located in Budapest, Hungary. By this time the Hungarian Foundation Centre had published two directories of Hungarian foundations.[17] With continued support for their activities from these same U.S. sources, these Central and Eastern European organizations appear to be achieving some success in their goal of becoming self-sustaining entities.

There are several associations and centers located in Europe whose officials and activities span the continent and include strong international ties. Among this group are the Hague Club, the European Foundation Centre (EFC), and International Standing Conference on Philanthropy (INTERPHIL).

The Hague Club grew out of a series of meetings beginning with a conference in Berlin in 1964 initiated by the Ford Foundation and attended by representatives from eight European foundations. There followed somewhat similar meetings in 1965 in London and at Ditchley, Endstone, England, in 1966. The impact of the Ditchley Conference on the thinking of U.S. representatives in attendance about governmental supervision has been discussed in Chapter 6. This same conference was an important milestone among European conferees in the steps leading to the formation of the Hague Club. Succeeding and similar conferences of major European foundation executives then followed: 1966 (Rome, Italy); 1968 (Bad Godesberg, Germany); and 1969 Villa Serbelloni (Bellagio, Italy). The Bellagio Center meeting was arranged under the joint auspices of the Ford Foundation and the Rockefeller Foundation and was attended by representatives from ten American and ten European major foundations.[18] At this Bellagio meeting the plans for the Hague Club jelled. There then followed two preparatory meetings, one at The Hague, Netherlands, in 1970 and another at Hannover, Germany, in 1971, which were climaxed at a 1971 meeting in Turin, Italy, where the "Founding Members"[19] announced the birth of the Hague Club, named after the Dutch city where most of the legal and associated preparatory work had been carried out under the guidance of Willem Welling. Then and since, he has been popularly referred to as "Papa" Welling by fellow members because of his continuing efforts in the Hague Club's behalf. Until his retirement in the 1990s, he served the club in numerous capacities, including two terms as chairman.

The Hague Club was organized as an association of chief executives or officials of European foundations, rather than the foundations they headed or were associated with. Its main objective was to provide a continuing small forum where members could discuss, in a mutual-trust atmosphere, foundation matters on a European and international scale. It was correctly felt that member discussions based on mutual trust would be of inestimable benefit in the operation of all foundations concerned. The Hague Club has never maintained a permanent secretariat; instead, it relies on a rotating Steering Committee, consisting of a chairman and three other members, to handle its finances, meetings, and so on. The original members of the club came from European foundations and meetings centered on European issues. Gradually a few more foundations and associated organizations worldwide were involved. By 1995, Hague Club members consisted of executives from twenty-six foundations from twelve

European countries and seven corresponding members, foundation executives from Australia, Brazil, Italy, Israel, Japan, Mexico, and the United States. Since 1971 the club has published six editions of *Foundation Profiles*, which provided information on the nature and objectives, together with other information on the foundations whose executives were members. The latest in this series includes a short history of its origination, growth, and development.[20]

The European Foundation Centre (EFC) is another continent-spanning organization located in Europe. The seeds for the emergence of the EFC are to be found in the founding and activities of the earlier European Cultural Foundation (ECF).[21] Established by Denis de Rougement in Geneva, Switzerland, in 1954, the ECF was created to promote European cooperation in a wide variety of fields. The foundation moved its headquarters to Amsterdam, Netherlands, in 1960, where it launched the organization of a host of meetings in various European countries on a wide variety of topics. By the 1970s, under the leadership of Raymond Georis, it had also established a network of associated institutes and centers active in sixteen European countries. One of these institutes, the European Cooperation Fund, was set up in 1977 with offices located at 51 Rue de la Concorde, Brussels, Belgium. Against this background seven European foundations,[22] including the European Cultural Foundation, met at the fund's offices in 1989 and organized the European Foundation Centre. Since its origination the offices of the EFC have continued to be located at the 51 Rue de le Concorde address in Brussels, Belgium. Its present director, John Richardson, has served in an official capacity in other national and international organizations, including treasurer of the World Alliance for Citizen Participation (CIVICUS). As now constituted:

The European Foundation Centre (EFC) was set up to promote and underpin the work of foundations and corporate funders active in and with Europe. . . . [T]he EFC today has a membership of over 160 independent funders and serves a further 7,000 organisations linked through networking centers in thirty-five countries worldwide.[23]

INTERPHIL, an acronym for the International Standing Conference on Philanthropy, was organized in 1969 in Geneva, Switzerland, by four Genevans and five executives from the Giovanni Agnelli Foundation, Charities Aid Foundation, Fondation Europeene de la Culture, Stifterverband fur die Deutsche Wissenschaft, and Fomento de Entidades Beneficas. Headquarters was located in Geneva until a move was made to England in 1972. INTERPHIL remained there until 1994, when it moved back to Geneva, where it has since remained. During the period 1975 to 1986 the then head of the Charities Aid Foundation, Dick Livingston Booth, also served as chairman of INTERPHIL. The move to England was due, in part, to Booth's interest in having both organizations located in England.

Several statements outline INTERPHIL's purpose and makeup:

"INTERPHIL" is a combination of the two words "international" and "philanthropy" and is a synthesis of all that these words imply. It is established to promote the principles and the practices of philanthropy and is a voluntary, nongovernmental, nonprofit association working for the good of the community.[24]

INTERPHIL promotes the development of civil society, and specifically the idea and practice of modern philanthropy, i.e., private giving for community purposes. It thus complements the actions of other international bodies which focus on voluntary work. Its concern extends to NGOs, foundations and charities, fund-raising, corporate giving, legislation, fiscal policy, information exchange, capacity building, institutional development, advocacy and international cooperation. It has individual as well as corporate members.[25]

INTERPHIL's governance consists of a General Assembly of all members where policy is determined and carried out by a board of directors consisting of a few elected directors and the usual officials. There are two advisory bodies: Council of Governors and International Advisory Council. Since its inception the major activity of INTERPHIL has been the convening of some twenty-five conferences worldwide on a variety of philanthropic topics. Examples include International Philanthropy, Strasbourg,

France, 1977; Voluntary Sector in Eastern Europe, Budapest, Hungary, 1989; and Philanthropy and Business, Tallinn, Estonia, 1996. In addition to the views expressed and the discussions taking place at such conferences, a number of awards and prizes are made there. Complementing such activities has been the issuance of sporadic publications such as *Philanthropy International*. INTERPHIL has, over the years, also acted in a consultative capacity to various international bodies such as the United Nations and the Council of Europe.

By the 1990s, however, a growing skepticism concerning IN-TERPHIL's past role and future function had developed. The following excerpt from a 1990 article reflects this view:

Interphil's critics, including several financial supporters and long-time members, say the organization has lacked the compelling vision and strong direction needed to propel it to the philanthropic front lines. They wonder whether an organization that has struggled for years in relative obscurity and with scarce resources can emerge as a leader to help channel the energies now driving private voluntary efforts in Eastern Europe, the Soviet Union, Latin America, and elsewhere.

Since its founding two decades ago, Interphil has operated on a shoestring budget and has been heavily dependent on volunteers. Its annual budget is still less than $60,000, and it employs only a small part-time staff at its secretariat in Yalding, England.

Interphil's mission—to promote the principles and practices of philanthropy worldwide—is a lofty one, but its more down to earth achievements have reflected its scant resources. The organization, which has several hundred individual and institutional members representing more than 50 countries, has sponsored several major international conferences on philanthropy, most recently in New York City last October. It has also convened smaller regional or specialty meetings on various topics, such as a gathering in Budapest last summer to discuss philanthropy in Eastern Europe.[26]

At the same time, however, optimistic views as to the future were expressed:

Prodded both by world events and by potential supporters, Interphil's leaders have drafted a long-range strategic plan that calls for substantial increases in its staff and budget, a more aggressive drive for new members, and greater support from the philanthropic community.

"Interphil has been plagued over the years with incredible problems, but has really turned the corner," says Donald S. Rickerd, chairman of its board of directors and president of the Max Bell Foundation in Toronto. "It now has a golden opportunity to make a major step forward to strengthen its staffing and to improve its fund raising. We have very good prospects in both those regards."[27]

Despite such views, a group of European and U.S. foundation leaders, particularly William S. White, president of the Charles Stewart Mott Foundation, at various meetings, particularly one in Budapest in 1988, saw the need for a new organization of worldwide scope. By 1993 a group of philanthropic leaders, coalescing around Independent Sector in Washington, D.C., took the lead in establishing in that year a new entity, the World Alliance for Citizen Participation (CIVICUS), at a meeting in Barcelona, Spain.

Since these events, a newly restructured board of directors for INTERPHIL has been installed, a series of reforms has been undertaken, including the move of its headquarters from England back to Geneva, and INTERPHIL has continued its activities. Too, it has gone on record expressing a willingness to cooperate with all of its sister organizations, specifically including CIVICUS.

NEAR EAST AFRICA

In Turkey a Third Sector Foundation of Turkey has been organized, but the only, now outdated, directory of Turkish foundations was published in 1978 by an individual foundation.[28] Israel does not have a national foundation center, but the Van Leer Jerusalem Institute has recently published a work that, in addition to papers on international philanthropy, describes foundation operations in Israel.[29] South Africa has recently established a Southern Africa Grantmakers Association, and New York's Institute of International Education published three works in the 1990s of a directory and explanatory nature concerning the identity and activities of foundations active in South Africa.[30]

ASIA PACIFIC

Earlier directories of Australian foundations were published by an Australian educational research council.[31] The latest (1996) directory, however, was published by the Australian Association of Philanthropy predecessor to present-day Philanthropy Australia, with offices located in Melbourne, Australia. New Zealand has a foundation center, Philanthropy New Zealand, with offices located in Wellington, New Zealand, and it has compiled directories on computer disks. A 1978 foundation directory of New Zealand was published by a New Zealand educational research council, and another was published in 1987 in association with an individual foundation.[32]

In 1987 a Centre for the Advancement of Philanthropy was set up in New Delhi, India, by a group of Indian industrialists. The center's establishment was aided and facilitated by the interest and support of the Ford Foundation. In 1985 the foundation sponsored a two-day meeting to explore ways of encouraging more corporate giving for philanthropic purposes in India. Also, at the time of its founding the foundation made a $75,000 support grant to the center. The center's activities have included advocating the cause of philanthropy to the Indian government, to public bodies, and to the media. The center has published a newsletter and sponsored a number of international conferences in furthering these objectives. In 1991, for example, in association with the U.S. Council on Foundations, the center sponsored such a conference, which was reported in detail in its newsletter.[33]

The Philippines has a League of Corporate Foundations and an Asia-Pacific Philanthropy Consortium, both with offices located in Manila. A now outdated *Philippine Directory of Foundations* was published there by a separate foundation in 1974.[34]

With its stupendous economic revival and growth after World War II, Japan's industrialists and corporations in the period from the 1970s to the 1990s set up an increasing number of foundations. A national association and two national centers were established during that period to serve Japanese foundation interests: Japan Association of Charitable Corporations, Japan Foundation Center, and Japan Center for International Exchange.

The Japan Association of Charitable Corporations was founded in 1972 to offer consultative services and other forms of aid to its members, consisting of foundations and other voluntary groups. By the 1980s there were about 1,200 members, growing in the 1990s to some 1,500 members. The association made the first survey of Japanese foundations, and the results were published in Japanese in 1982. The book, which included a Part II directory of fifty major Japanese foundations, occasioned so much interest at home and abroad that a translated English version was made and published in 1983.[35]

The Toyota Foundation took the lead among other Japanese foundations and corporations in the establishment in 1985 of the Foundation Library Center of Japan, now Japan Foundation Center. It thereupon assumed responsibility for the amassing of data and publication of subsequent directories and other material on Japanese foundations. In 1988, 1995, and 1998 it published directories, and in 1995 it also published one dealing with grants and grant making. All of these publications were in Japanese.[36] In 1994 and 1996 two other directories in English were published under center auspices.[37]

The Japan Center for International Exchange was founded in 1975. With offices in Tokyo headed by its president, Tadashi Yamamoto, and one in New York under executive director Peter Kamura, the Center was set up to facilitate communication between the United States and Japan. In line with its purpose the center has developed an extensive exchange program between the nationals of both countries, particularly political leaders, and has acted as the convener and secretariat for a number of regional and international meetings. For example, in 1993 the center undertook a survey covering fifteen countries in the Asia Pacific area. The results of the survey were circulated to participants in it and formed the basis for a follow-up symposium by them held in Osaka, Japan, in 1994. The survey and proceedings of the symposium in turn formed the basis for the previously referred-to publication *Survey Report. Research Institutions, NGOs, and Philanthropy in Asia Pacific.* This very informative and wide-ranging *Report*, brought out under the supervision of President

Yamamoto, is the latest in this gentleman's longtime scholarly efforts in the philanthropic field. He was praised, for example, by President Masabe Watanabe of the Japan Association in his Preface to the association's 1983 publication of *Philanthropy in Japan '83*: "We would like to express our sincere appreciation to Mr. Tadashi Yamamoto, representative of Japan Center for International Exchange, Director, for his valuable cooperation in supervising and promotion of this book."

THE AMERICAS

Canada has seen the continuous establishment of foundations from 1918 onward since the establishment in that year of the Massey Foundation, Canada's oldest foundation. Although not nearly as sizable in number, size of assets, and grants as neighboring U.S. counterparts, Canadian foundations have played and are playing a significant role in Canadian philanthropy. Detailed information about them and their programs and activities even as late as the 1970s, however, was hard to come by. A book published in 1975 complained:

> If corporations are taciturn about their donation activities, Canadian foundations are downright clandestine. . . . [M]ost retain an attitude of privacy about their affairs that borders on arrogant concealment. Money held in public trust is viewed as a private resource—"It's our money, not theirs." Canadian foundations are generally inaccessible to the public, their purposes obscure, their decision-making process mysterious, and their boards and staff distant and uncommunicative. They have become symbols of secret wealth.[38]

The voicing of such sentiments led to the successful movement, dovetailing with similar views expressed by some of the larger Canadian foundations, for the establishment of the Canadian Centre for Philanthropy in 1980. Under the initial executive directorship of Allan Arlett, the centre began and has maintained close contact with the U.S Foundation Center and the Council on Foundations. As a partial result of such contact, early praiseworthy efforts of the Canadian Centre included the compilation and publication in financial and other journals of facts and figures about Canadian foundations.[39] Another was the publication of editions of a Canadian directory of foundations, including the latest, twelfth, 1996–1997 edition.[40]

In addition to the directories, the centre publishes an array of pamphlets and books of interest to Canadian foundations and to other charitable and nonprofit organizations and recently designed a code of ethics for Canadian charities. This code was in part an attempt to fend off the possibility of increased governmental regulation proposed in a preliminary report by a Committee of Canada's Voluntary Sector Roundtable.[41] It appears that much of the demand for such regulation was brought on by major charity scandals in the United States in the past decade. President Patrick Johnston was named president and CEO of the center in 1995, and today he and officials of the center are in the forefront in the ongoing debate to try to work out a consensual policy as to government oversight and regulation of foundations and other charities. It is interesting to note, in view of U.S. experience, that much of the debate centers on the creation of a governmental body such as England's Charity Commission or the creation of a private organization to take on such responsibilities similar to those (i.e., responsibilities) advocated by the U.S. Filer Commission.[42]

Manuel Arango led in the founding of the Mexican Center on Philanthropy (CEMEFI) in 1988. From its inception the center established and has maintained close ties with its U.S. counterparts. In 1992, for example, it signed a joint declaration with the U.S. Council of Foundations . In the words of President James A. Joseph of the council, this declaration was aimed at improving "the legal and social atmosphere for private giving and foundation creation" in the United States and Mexico. He added that it "represents a private sector attempt to further the initiatives begun by our governments to bring our economies and societies closer together."[43] Also, in 1993 the Mexican Center pledged $200,000 for the support of CIVICUS when the latter was founded. In 1990 the center published the first edition of the *Directory of Philanthropic Institutions*, which lists some 600 Mexican philanthropic institutions operating with offices in Mexico and a further 300 foreign ones operating there. This directory was followed in 1995 with an updated second edition in the same format as the first.[44]

In Central and Latin America foundation study and attendant directories were largely unexplored and undocumented until the 1968 publication of *Philanthropic Foundations in Latin America*.[45] Beginning in 1974, a number of directories were published in and on individual Latin American countries, together with one on Latin American and one on Central American countries in general.[46] Although considerable sentiment has been expressed in the past for the creation of a center to compile information leading to an up-to-date foundation directory dealing with all of the Central and Latin American countries, it has yet to come to fruition.

An account of the panoply of U.S. foundations, associations, and centers located in the United States and more or less involved in international affairs has been related, particularly in Chapters 4 and 7. There remain to be discussed in more detail two organizations and one assemblage, international in scope, originating and headquartered or centering in the United States: World Alliance for Citizen Participation (CIVICUS), International Society for Third-Sector Research (ISTR), and International Meeting of Associations Serving Grantmakers (IMAG).[47]

As described earlier, the genesis for the World Alliance for Citizen Participation (CIVICUS) was in large part due to the expressed need among philanthropic leaders for the establishment of a new international organization. A number of such leaders were officially linked to, or associated with, Independent Sector (IS). Significantly, Brian O'Connell, then president of IS, announced in 1991 that:

representatives of voluntary organizations worldwide would meet next month to discuss the creation of an international coalition of non-governmental groups and foundations. The exploratory effort, supported by ten U.S. grantmakers, was prompted by a growing thirst for information about, and contacts within, American philanthropy.[48]

By 1993 representatives of a cadre of donors and charities from nineteen countries had begun the organization of a group expected to adopt the name World Alliance for Citizen Participation (CIVICUS). Financial support for it in the amount of over $2.5 million had been pledged by a number of U.S. and foreign foundations and related organizations. Following the selection of an initial board of trustees, the board held its organizational meeting in Barcelona, Spain, in May 1993, where an initial agenda for its operations was agreed on. One of the first items on that agenda was the drafting of plans for its first World Assembly on Citizen Participation, to be held in Mexico City, Mexico, in January 1995. With attendance of more than 350 persons from fifty-five countries, the emphasis in speeches and discussion at this first assembly was placed upon the hope that CIVICUS would be the catalyst for the forming of activist civic organizations in regions that had long discouraged such forms of popular expression. By the time of the meeting, too, Miklos Marschall, former deputy mayor of Budapest, had been appointed the first executive director of CIVICUS.[49]

Six years after its beginnings CIVICUS had compiled an impressive record: a growing number of publications, including its newsletter, *CIVICUS World*; expanding membership that by 1998 totaled over 400 members in eighty countries; and the convening of a second World Assembly in 1997 in Budapest, Hungary.[50] As to the future, in addition to the efforts outlined in its initial mission statement, a priority has been placed upon the development of strong and effective regional groups within the CIVICUS framework. Also, emphasis has been placed upon continuous building up of its worldwide membership base. To that end, a detailed plan has been adopted[51] that it is believed, will form a major part of the program and discussion at the third World Assembly scheduled for Manila, Philippines, in 1999. In the meantime, Miklos Marschall is returning to his Budapest home after seeing CIVICUS through its fledgling period. He has been succeeded by Kumi Naido of the Republic of South Africa as secretary-general of the organization.

Reflecting the relative lack of academic and scholarly concern with the role of NGOs and the voluntary sector internationally, it is understandable why the International Society for Third Sector

Research (ISTR) was also established only recently. Founded originally in 1992 in Indianapolis, Indiana, with the unwieldy title International Research Society for Voluntary Associations, Nonprofit Organizations and Philanthropy, its name was changed to the simpler International Society for Third Sector Research (ISTR) within a short time after its establishment. The society was governed by an interim board of directors composed of eleven members, only two of whom were from the United States, until the holding of an inaugural conference in Pecs, Hungary, in the summer of 1994. At that meeting the organization was officially chartered, and a permanent board of directors was elected. A mission statement was adopted that ISTR would provide a forum and promote research and teaching for those involved in the study of philanthropy, particularly at the international level.

Although a significant number of its members had always been located outside the United States, ISTR headquarters office, under the direction of executive secretary Margery B. Daniels, was opened at Johns Hopkins University, Baltimore, in 1993. By 1994 a quarterly learned journal, *Voluntas,* had been founded and began publication with editorial offices located at the London School of Economics in England, together with a newsletter, *Inside ISTR.* Following its initial conference, successive biennial conferences have followed: Mexico City, Mexico (1996) and the latest in Geneva, Switzerland (1998). Accompanying this ongoing activity was a growth in membership, which now stands at about 550.

As its title suggests, the International Meeting of Associations Serving Grantmakers (IMAG) was just that—a meeting held in Oaxaca, Mexico, in February 1998. Funded by thirteen foundations from around the globe, the meeting seems to have been the first international meeting convened for the exclusive purpose of helping associations and centers committed to helping foundations and other grant makers. An examination of the agenda for the meeting shows that it provided a unique opportunity for the "old-timers" to help "newcomers" among the some eighty representatives of associations and centers from twenty-six countries gathered there. Also, it enabled the former to see their work from the different perspective provided by the latter. Although still in an embryonic stage, IMAG may well be the potential wave of the future for both the associations and centers and the foundations active in, or embarking upon, the international scene.

Commentary

The fact that people have devoted accumulated wealth for charitable and socially useful purposes in all places and in all ages has been noted in the early pages of this study. The reason basically appears to stem from these people's ethical and religious beliefs, particularly those connected with views on life and death, from which grew a moral urge to share such wealth in order to help others. Varying rudimentary organizational forms of foundations emerged in earlier times and different places to implement such beliefs and views. In England, beginning in the 1600s, this moral urge to help others was accompanied by the gradual development of a legal system that has continued to foster and favor such organizational means for giving. This favorable English attitude carried over into its colonies, while in the case of French and other European colonies influenced by the Napoleonic/French legal tradition the establishment and operation of foundations were inhibited. In the case of the United States, the philanthropic impulse with its ethical and religious base and the not-to-be-overlooked impetus to memorialization, in conjunction with the influence of the facilitating legal structure developed in England, seem to be the major reasons for the emergence in the late nineteenth and early twentieth centuries of that unique institution, the U.S. foundation. Since that time, particularly in the past fifty years, there has been a vast increase in disposable wealth acquired by many Americans, which, when tied to the philanthropic impulse, has seen a stupendous growth and expansion of foundations in the United States. During this period the increase in wealth in this country has been geographically widespread, occurring in all sections of the country and resulting in considerable growth in the number and assets of foundations in areas where they had not previously existed in significant numbers.

Such expansion and growth of foundations were not arrived at without opposition. In the first few decades of the twentieth century the concentration of the economy into powerful units and the tremendous wealth for that time acquired by industrialists such as Rockefeller and Carnegie occasioned clamorous opposition from liberals when they created and began operating foundations. Conversely, the perceived communist/socialist menace of the 1950s, which in large part sparked the creation of the Cox and Reece Committees, was brought on by conservatives. Congressman Patman's long-running investigation of the 1960s and early 1970s had a mixture of liberal/conservative thinking in its formation and operation and was populist in its underpinnings. Although the results of such investigations figured largely in the later passage of various regulatory measures affecting foundations, a generally favorable U.S. fiscal, tax, and regulatory climate for foundations has prevailed and is undoubtedly a significant factor in their continuing growth and expansion. Furthermore, there have been no more major governmental investigations or studies of foundations such as those of the 1950s, 1960s, and 1970s. Since those decades most of the public and the vast majority of our elected representatives from either the Right or the Left of the political/economic spectrum have not appeared any longer to be afraid of alleged foundation menaces to the United States. The period was, of course, by and large a very prosperous one in the country, and toward its close the eventual worldwide collapse of communism appeared to end any threat to the capitalistic free enterprise system of the United States. The emergence of new and powerful economic combines in the United States and the acquisition of vast new wealth by the likes of

Messrs. Annenberg, Buffet, Gates, Packard, Soros, Templeton, Turner, and Walton and the foundations they have projected or have created and are operating have been accepted with little or no outcry from the Left or the Right.

Less obvious are several other factors inhibiting seriously crippling criticism of foundations and conversely stimulating their growth and expansion. Changing public perception admits of the possibility that there are limits in the ability of government to solve many societal problems. A host of politicoeconomic liberals as well as conservatives increasingly have embraced the view that nongovernmental organizations, including foundations and to a somewhat lesser extent smaller units of government offer better hope for solution of many current problems rather than perceived overreliance on the national government. Closely tied in with these factors appears to be the conscious emulation of the traditional foundation structure by institutions setting up their own foundations. The notable expansion in this type demonstrates that they have appropriated and applied quite effectively the characteristics of the genuine foundation. For example, institutionally related foundations on college and university campuses, particularly among state supported ones, have provided these institutions with venture capital not as entangled with the bureaucratic restrictions with which many are encumbered. Another example is seen in the federal government itself. Our National Science Foundation can engage and has engaged in many undertakings that older government departments with cabinet status were loath to venture into. Even in the case of the entry of governmentally related foundations into the controversial areas of the arts and humanities, while criticism has caused restrictions to be placed on them, they have survived.

In addition to the developments previously touched on, a major and what appears to be an overlooked reason for foundation growth and expansion in the United States since the 1950s lies in our foundations' responses to the internal and external criticism of their structure and operation extending back to the 1950s and in some cases earlier. In the last fifty years most of the principals connected with our larger and most significant foundations and many in the smaller ones have not only questioned and criticized many aspects of their own structure and operation but welcomed and even encouraged criticism and arguments for changes in and of foundations from external sources. The primarily foundation-funded Peterson and Filer studies of the late 1960s and 1970s of philanthropy and foundations are examples par excellence of this approach. The outcome has been that foundations have embraced many of these ideas and views and made changes accordingly.

Visible results are strikingly clear in foundation response in two areas: (1) the need for much more information and publicity about foundations and their operations and (2) the need to diversify the personnel associated with the operation of foundations. Albeit hesitatingly and haltingly, foundation officials provided much of the funding needed to set up organizations that undertook the amassing of data and research materials dealing with foundations and then encouraged scholars to enter the field of philanthropic and foundation study. Such efforts have resulted in a significant proliferation of publications about foundations in the past fifty years. Nevertheless, bearing in mind the earlier paucity of information available to the public and in view of the constant growth, expansion, and increasing scope of foundation activities over recent decades, foundation scholars see a real need for the augmentation of research on, and information and publications dealing with, them into the future.

A similar revolution took place in the population makeup of foundation personnel, much of it due to a conscious effort on the part of many foundation officials to diversify the gender, ethnic, and geographical makeup of their trustees and staff. Such changes, of course, were spurred on at a time when movements for similar change were producing upheavals in our society at large, the gender and ethnic Civil Rights movements being obvious examples.

Turning to U.S. government supervision or oversight of foundations, one starts with the fact that until the 1970s such supervision can only be characterized as neglect. Legislation requiring foundations to file annual returns and placing a few restrictions on the economic side of their activities was passed in the 1940s and 1950s only as incidentals to tax legislation. Enforcement was placed without much consideration of alternatives in the hands of a then-inattentive Internal Revenue Service. The Tax Reform Act of 1969, which made major changes in this situation, inevitably raised serious concern among our philanthropic leaders as to the future functional status of foundations in the United States. Their deliberations resulted in a movement to create a regulatory or advisory body modeled on that of the British Charity Commission. There was an important reservation on the part of most such advocates, however: such a commission would be a *private* one, albeit with a public character. Also, although a strident minority called for the elimination of the IRS as the supervisory body for foundations, such advocates counseled leaving the existing supervisory role of the IRS intact. On all counts the movement for a new supervisory or advisory body has gotten nowhere. It can be argued that foundations can't eat their cake and have it, too; that is, they can't have a private advisory commission paid for out of public funds. Those with such a point of view can point to the setting up and dissolution of such a private commission in 1977 at the beginning of the administration of President Jimmy Carter.

At the present time some political leaders and figures are calling for the outright scrapping or serious revision of the current income tax codes. The possible passage of such legislation brings into question the supervisory role of the IRS vis-à-vis foundations. One notes that the Canadian government and the voluntary sector there are presently engaged in serious debate about the proper supervisory body for foundations in that country. Perhaps the time has now arrived for a similar effort in the United States to reach a consensus as to what our governmental supervisory/oversight structure of foundations should be.

The final development, probably the most salient and far-reaching consequence to be commented on, is the international activities of U.S. foundations. In addition to other motives, an outstanding and differentiating motive for the early activities abroad of some major foundations seems to stem from the fact that their founders and their founders' businesses were engaged in extensive commercial dealings of one kind or another abroad: Rockefeller in oil; Carnegie in steel; Eastman in photography; and so on. Much of the giving of such foundations in the period before World War II centered on the ameliorative physical aspects, for example, more and better food production and medical care for populations there. Following World War II our dramatically stepped up involvement worldwide and across the board with all peoples and nations, the desire to prevent further cataclysmic wars, and thereby a resultant perceived need to vastly increase our pool of persons knowledgeable of other countries and regions of the world occasioned continuous growth in international activities by U.S. foundations. These reasons also accounted for the continuing support at home for "foreign area studies" and similar programs.

Such significant interest and growth in international activities of U.S. foundations have very recently led to their support for the establishment and operation of foreign foundation centers and associations, together with international organizations linking them. A most recent example of such sponsorship was the February 1998 ad hoc International Meeting of Associations Serving Grantmakers (IMAG). The attendance of many individuals from around the globe and the scope of the meeting, however, augur that IMAG may blossom into a permanent International Association Serving Grantmakers (IASG). The explanation for this proliferation of support for such organizations appears to be the belief of many associated with our major foundations that replication of our philanthropic/foundation structure abroad will provide one of the best hopes, if not the best hope, for the fostering there of the network of organizations ultimately needed for the establishment abroad of what George Soros calls the "Open Society."

Perhaps no better description can be found of the new interconnectedness of the world's nations and peoples in all aspects brought on by the technological revolution, which foundations and other bodies operating on the international scene must face, than that offered by President Susan V. Berresford of the Ford Foundation. She encompasses the vast changes in the term "globalization" and devotes most of her message in the 1997 Foundation Annual Report to the impact of this globalization and the Ford Foundation's response to it:

Globalization describes the rapid and accelerating worldwide movement of technology, goods, capital, people, and ideas. The term reflects a more comprehensive level of interaction than has occurred in the past, suggesting something different from the word "international." . . .
The impact of globalization is evident in the increasing worldwide support for concepts like human rights and in what one writer has called "global democracy fever." We also see it in the speedy transmission of popular culture—music, art, and cuisine, for example—from one part of the world to another. And it is clear in the trillions of dollars in financial transactions that banks now process electronically each day as money moves around the world.[1]

Notes

INTRODUCTION

1. For example, a 1970s study, *Foundations, Private Giving and Public Policy: Report and Recommendations of the Commission on Foundations and Private Philanthropy.* University of Chicago Press, Chicago, 1970, pp. 3–4, questioned, "was there an agreed upon definition of a foundation?" and replied, "There was not." In delving for needed facts on foundations, it complained: "Information gaps of every kind abounded."

2. See John Simon Guggenheim Memorial Foundation, *Reports of the President and Treasurer.* New York, 1989–1996. See, particularly, *Report of the President,* 1996, pp. 19–20.

3. See pamphlet bibliographies, Russell Sage Foundation, New York, 1915, 1920, 1922, 1924, and 1926; *American Foundations for Social Welfare.* Russell Sage Foundation, New York, 1930, 1938; Shelby M. Harrison and F. Emerson Andrews, *American Foundations for Social Welfare.* Russell Sage Foundation, New York, 1946; *American Foundations and Their Fields.* Twentieth Century Fund, New York, 1931, 1932, and 1935; *American Foundations and Their Fields*, vol. 4. Raymond Rich Associates, New York, 1939 and vol. 5, 1942; Wilmer Shields Rich and Neva R. Deardorff (eds.), *American Foundations and Their Fields,* vol. 6. Raymond Rich Associates, New York, 1948; Wilmer Shields Rich, "Foundations and Community Trusts," *Social Work Year Book.* New York, 1954, pp. 233–241; Wilmer Shields Rich, *American Foundations and Their Fields.* American Foundations Information Service, New York, 7th ed., 1955; H. V. Hodson (ed.), *The International Foundation Directory.* Europa, London, Editions 1–8, 1974, 1979, 1983, 1986, 1991, 1994, 1996,

1998; Harold M. Keele and Joseph C. Kiger (eds.), *Foundations*. Greenwood Press, Westport, Connecticut, 1984; and Kiger, Joseph C. (ed.), *International Encyclopedia of Foundations*. Greenwood Press, Westport, Connecticut, 1990.

4. For a detailed discussion of the foregoing and related topics, see Joseph C. Kiger, *Operating Principles of the Larger Foundations*. Russell Sage Foundation, New York, 1954.

CHAPTER 1

1. See William E. H. Lecky, *History of European Morals*, vol. II, chap. 4. George Braziller, New York, 1955. See also James A. Joseph, *The Charitable Impulse. Wealth and Social Conscience in Communities and Cultures Outside the United States*. Foundation Center, New York, 1989 and Robert H. Bremner, *Giving: Charity and Philanthropy in History*. Transaction Publishers, New Brunswick, New Jersey, 1994.

2. *The Li Ki*. A Collection of Treatises on the Rules of Propriety or Ceremonial Usages. Trans. James Legge, in *The Sacred Books of the East*, F. Max Muller (ed.), vol. 27. Clarendon Press, Oxford, England, 1885, pp. 243–244.

3. Ernest V. Hollis, "Evolution of the Philanthropic Foundation," *Educational Record* 20, (October, 1939), p. 575.

4. Ibid., p. 576.

5. James H. Breasted, *Ancient Records of Egypt*. University of Chicago Press, Chicago, 1927, vol. 1, pp. 151–152.

6. F. Emerson Andrews, *Philanthropic Giving*. Russell Sage Foundation, New York, 1950, p. 33.

7. Jacob R. Marcus, *The Jew in the Medieval World*. Sinai Press, Cincinnati, 1938, pp. 364–365.

8. Ernest V. Hollis, "Evolution of the Philanthropic Foundation," *Educational Record* 20 (October 1939), p. 578.

9. Andrews, p. 34.

10. Hollis, p. 579.

11. William Langland, *The Vision of Piers the Plowman*, trans. into modern English W. W. Skeats. Chatto and Windus, London, 1931, p. 114.

12. Danby Pickering, The *Statutes at Large* from the Thirty-ninth of Q. Elizabeth to the Twelfth of K. Charles II, inclusive. Printed at Cambridge University, 1763, vol. 7, p. 43.

13. Wilbur K. Jordan, *Philanthropy in England, 1480–1660: A Study of the Changing Pattern of English Social Aspirations*. Russell Sage Foundation, New York, 1959, p. 153.

14. See David Owen, *English Philanthropy, 1660–1960*. Belknap Press of the Harvard University Press, Cambridge, 1964. It should be noted that Jordan and Owen volumes cited and this work are primarily

concerned with England, Wales, and, to a degree, Northern Ireland. Lack of large accumulations of surplus wealth and differences in governmental/legal structures precludes Scotland.

15. For discussion of this divergence, see M. Michel Pomey, "Fondations," *Encyclopedia Universalis*, vol. 7, 1971, pp. 134–138. See also Klaus Neuhoff and Uwe Pavel (eds.), *Trusts and Foundations in Europe, A Comparative Survey*. Bedford Square Press, England, 1971. Pomey, who also wrote the article on France in the Neuhoff-Pavel work, states therein: "Traditionally, foundations in France have always been regarded with a certain amount of suspicion by the Government. . . . The result is that the charitable or philanthropic sector [i.e., including the foundations] has never really developed very much," p. 191.

16. For a brief history of the foundation, see Joseph C. Kiger (ed.), "International Foundation for the Survival and Development of Humanity," in *International Encyclopedia of Foundations*. Greenwood Press, New York, 1990, pp. 237–238.

17. See Kevin F. F. Quigley, *For Democracy's Sake: Foundations and Democracy Assistance in Central Europe*. Woodrow Wilson Center Press, Washington, D.C., 1997; Daniel Siegel and Jenny Yancey, *The Rebirth of Civil Society. The Development of the Nonprofit Sector in East Central Europe and the Role of Western Assistance*. Rockefeller Brothers Fund, New York, 1992.

18. For a recent article dealing with this question, see Masha Gessen, "The Rebirth of Russian Charity," *The American Benefactor* 1, no. 1 (Spring 1997), pp. 123–126.

19. For a brief general account of their history and character, see F. Emerson Andrews, "On the Nature of the *vaqf*," *Foundation News* 5 (September 1964), pp. 6–7. See also, Yediyildiz Bahaeddin, *Institution du Vaqf au XVIIIe siècle en Turquie: Etude socio-historique*. Société d'Histoire Turque, Ankara, Turkey, 1985.

20. See Minoru Tanaka and Takako Amemiya, *Philanthropy in Japan '83*. Japan Association of Charitable Organizations, Tokyo, 1983. This volume in English contains a brief history of philanthropic and foundation development in Japan and a Part II Directory of fifty foundations, members of the Japan Association, with a considerable size of endowments.

21. Tadashi Yamamoto, "Japan's Philanthropic Development in the Asia Pacific Context," in *Survey Reports. Research Institutions, NGOs, and Philanthropy in Asia Pacific*. Japan Center for International Exchange, Tokyo, 1994, p. 2.

22. Rebecca M. Davis, "Toyota Foundation," in Kiger, *International Encyclopedia of Foundations*, p. 158. For a 1991 book examining the major legal and functional framework of Japanese foundations, particularly the corporate relationship and aspect, see Nancy R. London,

Japanese Corporate Philanthropy. Oxford University Press, New York, 1991.

23. "An Integrative Report," in *Survey Reports*, p. 4.

24. Ibid., p. 21.

CHAPTER 2

1. For example, the classic 1947 case of New York University's purchase and operation of a spaghetti company as a nonprofit organization resulted in an investigation by the Ways and Means Committee of the U.S. House of Representatives. As a result, Congress' Revenue Act of 1950 regulated mixtures of philanthropy, including foundations and business, and prohibited self-dealing between the two.

2. *Industrial Relations*. Final Report and Testimony Submitted to Congress by the Commission on Industrial Relations, U.S. Senate, 64th Congress, 1st Session, Senate Document 415. Government Printing Office, Washington, D.C., 1916, testimony of John Haynes Holmes, vol. 8, pp. 7916–7933.

3. Ibid.; see testimony of Samuel Gompers, pp. 7638–7657.

4. Joseph C. Kiger, *Operating Principles of the Larger Foundations*. Russell Sage Foundation, New York, 1954, p. 91.

5. Helen Hill Miller, "Investigating the Foundations," *The Reporter* 9, no. 9 (November 24, 1953), pp. 37–40.

6. U.S. House of Representatives, 82d Congress, 2d Session, *Final Report of the Select Committee to Investigate Foundations and Other Organizations*. House Report No. 2514. Government Printing Office, Washington, D.C., 1953.

7. See, for example, U.S. House, 82d Congress, 2d Session, *Hearings before the Select Committee to Investigate Tax-Exempt Foundations and Comparable Organizations*. Government Printing Office, Washington, D.C., 1953. Statement of Russell C. Leffingwell, p. 380, and Donald Young, p. 390.

8. *Final Report of the Select Committee to Investigate Foundations and Other Organizations*, p. 11.

9. B. Carroll Reece, *Congressional Record*, vol. 99, no. 141 (July 27, 1953), p. 10188.

10. Ibid., p. 10190.

11. "Another Stupid Inquiry," *New York Times*, July 5, 1954, p. 10.

12. 83d Congress, 2d Session, House Report No. 2681, *Report of the Special Committee to Investigate Tax-Exempt Foundations and Comparable Organizations*. Government Printing Office, Washington, D.C., 1954, p. 226. The following note printed on the foregoing page refers to this addendum: "Mr. Goodwin's added remarks were not received in time to be included in this printing of the report, but it will be included when

the report is reprinted." An unpublished copy of this addendum is on deposit at the Foundation Center, New York City.

13. Wright Patman, *Congressional Record* 107, no. 73 (May 2, 1961), p. 6560.

14. U.S. House of Representatives, Select Committee on Small Business, 87th through 91st Congress, *Chairman's Reports. Tax Exempt Foundations and Charitable Trusts: Their Impact on Our Economy.* Government Printing Office, Washington, D.C., 1962 through 1969, Installments 1 through 7.

15. U.S. House of Representatives, Committee on Banking and Currency, Subcommittee on Domestic Finance, 92nd Congress, 2d Session, *Staff Report. Tax-Exempt Foundations and Charitable Trusts: Their Impact on Our Economy.* Government Printing Office, Washington, D.C., 1972, Installment 8.

16. U.S. House of Representatives, Select Committee on Small Business, 88th Congress, 2d Session, *Hearings before Subcommittee No. 1 Foundations.* Government Printing Office, Washington, D.C., 1964.

17. U.S. House of Representatives, Select Committee on Small Business, 90th Congress, 2d Session, *Hearings before Subcommittee No. 1 Foundations.* Government Printing Office, Washington, D.C., 1967.

18. U.S. Department of the Treasury, *Treasury Department Report on Private Foundations.* Government Printing Office, Washington, D.C., 1965.

19. Ibid., p. 10.

20. Alan Pifer, "Foundations at the Service of the Public," *Annual Report for 1968.* Carnegie Corporation of New York, New York, 1968, pp. 8–9.

21. U.S. House of Representatives, Committee on Ways and Means, 91st Congress, 1st Session, *Hearings. Tax Reform.* Government Printing Office, Washington, D.C., 1969, Parts 1 and 2.

22. U.S. Senate, Committee on Finance, 91st Congress, 1st Session, *Hearings. Tax Reform Act of 1969.* Government Printing Office, Washington, D.C., 1969.

23. *Foundations, Private Giving and Public Policy: Report and Recommendations of the Commission on Foundations and Public Policy.* University of Chicago Press, Chicago, 1970. See also, *A Summary of Findings and Recommendations.* University of Chicago Press, Chicago, 1970.

24. U.S. Department of the Treasury, *Giving in America: Report of the Commission on Private Philanthropy and Public Needs.* Government Printing Office, Washington, D.C., 1977.

25. U.S. Department of the Treasury, *Research Papers Sponsored by the Commission on Private Philanthropy and Public Needs*, vols. 1–5. Government Printing Office, Washington, D.C., 1977.

26. Ibid., vol. 1, part 1, the Donee Group Report and Recommendations, pp. 49–85.

CHAPTER 3

1. Amos G. Warner, *American Charities. A Study in Philanthropy and Economics*. Thomas Y. Crowell, New York, 1894, p. 325.

2. See particularly, Andrew Carnegie, *The Gospel of Wealth and Other Timely Essays*. Century and Co., New York, 1900.

3. Frederick P. Keppel, *The Foundation: Its Place in American Life*. Macmillan, New York, 1930, p. 108.

4. For example, see U.S. House, 82d Congress, 2d Session, *Hearings before the Select Committee to Investigate Tax-Exempt Foundations and Comparable Organizations*. Government Printing Office, Washington, D.C., 1953, statement of Alfred P. Sloan, Jr., pp. 453–475.

5. U.S. House, 82d Congress, 2d Session, House Report No. 2514, *Final Report of the Select Committee to Investigate Foundations and Other Organizations*. Government Printing Office, Washington, D.C., 1953, p. 3.

6. The Foundation Center also publishes an annual *Foundation Directory Part 2*. This volume includes foundations with assets from $1 million to less than $2 million or making annual grants from $50,000 to less than $200,000. The two directories together now provide information on more than 16,000 of the largest active grant-making foundations in the United States. In addition, see Loren Renz, Steven Lawrence, and John Kendzior, *Foundation Giving: Yearbook of Facts and Figures on Private, Corporate and Community Foundations,* 9th ed. Foundation Center, New York, 1999, which since 1990, presents and interprets facts and figures on foundations.

7. Two recent books dealing with the pros and cons of such thinking are: John M. Hood, *The Heroic Enterprise: Business and the Common Good*. Free Press, New York, 1996 and Jerome L. Himmelstein, *Looking Good and Doing Good: Corporate Philanthropy and Corporate Power*. Indiana University Press, Bloomington, 1997.

8. See C. Howard Hopkins, *History of the Y.M.C.A. in North America*. Association Press, New York, 1951.

9. F. Emerson Andrews, *Corporation Giving*. Russell Sage Foundation, New York, 1952, p. 28. This same volume contains a short chapter dealing with the organization and operation of company foundations at that time.

For earlier works dealing, in part, with this type of foundation see Beardsley Ruml and Theodore Geiger, *The Five Percent*. National Planning Association, Washington, D.C., 1951; Beardsley Ruml and Theodore Geiger (eds.), *The Manual of Corporate Giving*. National Planning Association, Washington, D.C., 1952. For a later work see James F. Harris and Anne Klepper, *Corporate Philanthropic Public Service Activities.* The Conference Board, New York, 1976.

10. Jane Anne Morris, "Let's Ban Corporate Giving," *The Chronicle of Philanthropy* (November, 28, 1996), pp. 36–37.

11. Stan L. Friedman,"Charity, Know Thy Corporate Sponsor—and Thyself," *The Chronicle of Philanthropy* (October 30, 1997), p. 70. In the same vein see an earlier article, Lindley H. Clark Jr., "The Business of Business Isn't Charity," *Wall Street Journal* 199, no. 22, February 2, 1982, p. 31.

12. Jennifer Moore and Grant Williams, "Corporate Giving, the Buffet Way," *The Chronicle of Philanthropy* (November 13, 1997), pp. 1, 14–16.

13. *The Chronicle of Philanthropy* (January, 15, 1998), pp. 16–17. A recent article—Amy E. Barrett and Regan Good, "America's 25 Most Generous Companies," *The American Benefactor* 2 (Summer 1998), pp. 30–45—touched on this aspect of corporation giving.

14. "Private Profit, Public Gain. Corporate Philanthropy in America," supplement to *The Atlantic Monthly* (September, 1990), p. 4.

15. Houston Industries Incorporated, *HI Quarterly,* 2d quarter report (1997), p. 2.

16. Lucent Technologies, *Annual Report* (1997), p. 64.

17. For a brief history of the Cleveland Foundation and information about Goff, see William Rudman, "The Cleveland Foundation,"in Harold M. Keele and Joseph C. Kiger (eds.), *Foundations.* Greenwood Press, Westport, Connecticut, 1984, pp. 79–83.

18. For this and other information on the early community foundations, see Frank D. Loomis, *Community Trusts of America 1914–1950.* National Committee on Foundations and Trusts for Community Welfare, Chicago, 1951. See also F. Emerson Andrews, *Philanthropic Foundations.* Russell Sage Foundation, New York, 1956, pp. 32–33.

19. Monica Langley,"You Don't Have to Be a Rockefeller to Set Up Your Own Foundation. Investors Pour $1.5 Billion into Fidelity's Gift Fund: What Will the IRS Do? Tax Breaks to Study Lobsters," *Wall Street Journal* (February 12, 1998), p. 8. For an earlier article dealing with the same issue, see Stephen G. Greene, "Financial Titans' Move into Charity," *The Chronicle of Philanthropy* (November 28, 1996), pp. 1, 26–27, 30.

20. See Jennifer Moore, "Officials of Funds That Invite Donor's Advice Brace for Federal Scrutiny," *The Chronicle of Philanthropy* (January 28, 1999), p. 11.

21. See Wilmer Shields Rich and Neva R. Deardorff, *American Foundations and Their Fields*, vol. 6, Raymond Rich Associates, New York, 1948, p. 13. See also pp. 12–14, 182–241.

22. See *Foundation Directory*, 1st ed. (1960), pp. xxiv–xxv; 4th ed. (1971), pp. xiv, 532; 6th ed. (1997), pp. x–xi.

23. For the relationship of foundations and labor unions, see Richard Magat, "Will Foundations Join the Unions," *The Chronicle of Philanthropy* (January 11, 1994), pp. 39–40; Richard Magat, *Unlikely Companions: Organized Labor and Philanthropic Foundations*. Institution for Social and Policy Studies, New Haven, Connecticut, 1997; Richard Magat, *Unlikely Partners. Philanthropic Foundations and the Labor Movement*. Cornell University Press, Ithaca, New York, 1998; and his Letter to the Editor, "Charities Shouldn't Treat Unions as if They Were Lepers," *The Chronicle of Philanthropy* (August 13, 1998), pp. 42–43.

24. Thomas J. Billitteri, "Putting Faith in a Trust Company, Presbyterian Fund Raising Charity Creates For-Profit Subsidiary to Manage Assets and Perform a Range of Financial Services," *The Chronicle of Philanthropy* (January 15, 1998), p. 29.

25. Ibid., p. 31. For additional information, see Douglas Brackenridge, *The Presbyterian Church (U.S.A.) Foundation: A Bicentennial History*. Geneva Press, Louisville, 1999.

26. For a recent work describing the rationale and legal intricacies of such conversions with case studies of nine hospitals and Blue Cross and Blue Shield Plans included, see Judith E. Bell, Harry M. Snyder, and Christine C. Tien, *The Public Interest in Conversions of Nonprofit Health Charities*. Consumers Union and Milbank Memorial Fund, New York, 1998. See also *Grantmakers in Health: Findings from the 1998 Survey of Foundations Created by Health Care Conversions*. Grantmakers in Health, Washington, D.C., 1999.

27. Joseph F. Phelan (ed.), *College and University Foundations: Serving America's Public Higher Education*. Association of Governing Boards of Universities and Colleges, Washington, D.C., 1997, p. 33.

28. For a brief history of the founding, growth, and activities of the University of Mississippi Foundation see its *Annual Report, 1995–1996*.

29. See, for example, Thomas C. Meredith, "The Foundation as an Institutional Resource: A President's View," in Phelan, pp. 219–228.

30. Ransdell, Gary A., "The Foundation's Behavior as a Cornerstone of Trust," in Phelan, pp. 193–200.

31. Full title, Vannevar Bush, *Science: The Endless Frontier. A Report to the President on a Program for Postwar Scientific Research*. Government Printing Office, Washington, D.C., 1945. This report has been published in other editions since this initial one.

32. For the founding and early history of the Foundation see, J. Merton England, *A Patron for Pure Science. The National Science Foundation's Formative Years, 1945–1957*. National Science Foundation, Washington, D.C., 1982. See also, Elbridge Sibley, *Social Science Research Council: The First Fifty Years*. Social Science Research Council, New York, 1974

and "Social Science Research Council," in Joseph C. Kiger (ed.), *Research Institutions and Learned Societies*. Greenwood Press, Westport, Connecticut, 1982.

33. *Report of the Commission on the Humanities*. American Council of Learned Societies, Council of Graduate Schools in the United States, United Chapters of Phi Beta Kappa, New York, 1964.

34. Ibid., p. 8.

35. This law was subsequently upheld by an 8-to-1 decision of the U.S. Supreme Court in its 1997–1998 term. See, Jennifer Moore, "Supreme Court Upholds 'Decency' Standard for Arts Grants; Other End-of-Term Rulings," *The Chronicle of Philanthropy* (July 16, 1998), p. 51.

36. Elizabeth T. Boris, "Creation and Growth: A Survey of Private Foundations," in Teresa Odendahl (ed.), *America's Wealthy and the Future of Foundations*. The Foundation Center, New York, 1987, p. 92.

CHAPTER 4

1. For a recent report on this technology development and usage see "Grantmakers Technology Report," Council on Foundations, Washington, D.C., 1998.

2. By the 1950s the terms "philanthropist" and "philanthropoid" were in common usage in foundation circles. The former was used to designate those who amassed the money and set up foundations, while the latter was for those who were employed to administer foundations and dispense their funds. For an earlier use of "philanthropoid" see, Frederick P. Keppel, *The Foundation: Its Place in American Life*. Macmillan, New York, 1930, p. 58.

3. See Final Report and Testimony Submitted to Congress by the Commission on Industrial Relations. U.S. Senate, 64th Congress, 1st Session. Senate Document 415, *Industrial Relations*. Government Printing Office, Washington, D.C., 1916, testimony of William H. Allen, vol. 9, pp. 8327–8342; Morris Hillquit, vol. 9, pp. 8262–8286; John Haynes Holmes, vol. 8, pp. 7916–7933; George W. Kirchwey, vol. 9, pp. 8215–8229; John R. Lawson, vol. 8, pp. 8003–8013, vol. 9, pp. 8017–8040; and Amos Pinchot, vol. 9, pp. 8041–8052.

4. Ibid., testimony of Andrew Carnegie, vol. 9, pp. 8286–8297; Charles W. Eliot, vol. 8, pp. 7964–7986; Jerome D. Greene, vol. 9, pp. 8137–8183; George W. Perkins, vol. 8, pp. 7598–7626; John D. Rockefeller, Jr., vol. 8, pp. 7763–7895; John D. Rockefeller, Sr., vol. 9, pp. 8297–8304.

5. Ibid., testimony of George W. Perkins, vol. 8, p. 7599.

6. Ibid., testimony of John D, Rockefeller, Sr., vol. 9, p. 8298.

7. Keppel, pp. 56–57.

8. Eduard C. Lindeman, *Wealth and Culture: A Study of One Hundred Foundations and Community Trusts and Their Operations during the Decade 1921–1930*. Harcourt, Brace, New York, 1936, p. 51.

9. For an analysis of the state situation at that time, see Eleanor K. Taylor, *Public Accountability of Foundations and Charitable Trusts*. Russell Sage Foundation, New York, 1953, particularly pp. 23–76.

10. An exception was a rare, 1909 booklet accessed and filed under an appellation different from philanthropic foundations or foundations, which was an attack on the Carnegie Foundation for the Advancement of Teaching and the General Education Board: Warren A. Candler, *Dangerous Donations and Degrading Doles, or a Vast Scheme for Capturing and Controlling the Colleges and Universities of the Country*. Privately Printed, Atlanta, 1909.

11. *Report of the Committee on the Law and Practice Relating to Charitable Trusts*, Cmd.8710. Her Majesty's Stationery Office, London, England, 1952, hereafter referred to as the Nathan Report for the chairman of the committee, Lord Nathan.

12. F. Emerson Andrews, *Philanthropic Foundations*. Russell Sage Foundation, New York, 1956, Foreword, p. 3.

13. *Report of the Princeton Conference on the History of Philanthropy in the United States*. Russell Sage Foundation, New York, 1956.

14. For citations to these earlier publications, see Introduction (note 3, herein).

15. For an account of the center's establishment and its operations to the 1970s by its first chief executive officer, see F. Emerson Andrews, *Foundation Watcher*. Franklin and Marshall College, Lancaster, Pennsylvania, 1973, particularly pp. 173–260.

16. For a detailed discussion of the role of RAGs, see Lauren Cook, "Something for Everyone," *Foundation News and Commentary* (January/February, 1995), pp. 16–17.

17. See, Stephen G. Greene, "Grants Seek to Encourage Growth in Organized Philanthropy," *The Chronicle of Philanthropy* (January 28, 1999), p. 10.

18. See, for example, Arnaud C. Marts, *Philanthropy's Role in Civilization: Its Contribution to Human Freedom*. Harper and Brothers, New York, 1953; John Price Jones, *The American Giver: A Review of American Generosity*. Inter-River Press, New York, 1954; John J. Schwartz, *Modern American Philanthropy: A Personal Account*. John Wiley and Sons, New York, 1994.

19. Internet, Independent Sector, "About IS," p. 2, viewed March 10, 1998.

20. Internet, Independent Sector, "Home Page," p. 1, viewed March 10, 1998.

21. Internet, Independent Sector, "Organizational Plan 1996–2000," p.1, viewed March 10, 1998.

22. For a brief history of the founding of the institute and its leaders and activities until 1982, see Sidney Hyman,"Aspen Institute for Humanistic Studies," in Joseph C. Kiger (ed.), *Research Institutions and Learned Societies.* Greenwood Press, Westport, Connecticut, 1982, pp. 137–142.

23. Internet, Aspen Institute, Nonprofit Sector Research Fund, "Home Page," p. 1, viewed March 10, 1998.

24. Internet, National Committee for Responsive Philanthropy, "NCRP Homepage," viewed March 12, 1998.

25. Internet, Capital Research Center, "Our Mission," p. 1, viewed March 10, 1998.

26. See, for example, Martin Olasky, *Philanthropically Correct: The Story of the Council on Foundations*. Capital Research Center, Washingotn, D.C., 1953.

27. For a special issue providing details on the program and articles on the study of philanthropy in the undergraduate college and university curriculum, see Association of American Colleges, *Liberal Education* 74, no. 4 (September/October 1988).

28. This publication is a prime source for the history and operation of the center. For example, a brief account of the establishment and first fifteen years of service of the center can be found in the Fall 1990 issue, p. 8.

29. Susan Gray, "Harvard Will Use $10-Million Gift for New Center for Non-Profit Study," *Chronicle of Philanthropy* (May 1, 1997), p. 10.

30. For a recent article dealing with the emergence of ARNOVA together with that of other organizations interested in the study of philanthropy, including foundations, see Stanley N. Katz, "Where Did the Serious Study of Philanthropy Come from, Anyway?" *Nonprofit and Voluntary Sector Quarterly* 28, no. 1 (March 1999), pp. 74–82.

31. For a historiographical review that includes the major publications on U.S. independent foundations up until 1988 see, Joseph C. Kiger, *Historiographic Review of Foundation Literature, Motivations and Perceptions*. Foundation Center, New York, 1987. Generally excluded from the *Review* are works dealing with community or company foundations, and no note is taken of articles. The Biliography herein also excludes articles and generally includes major publications dealing with private foundations.

For a 1987 bibliography on American philanthropy that treats articles as well as books and that includes a section on foundations, see Daphne Niobe Layton, *Philanthropy and Voluntarism: An Annotated Bibliography*. The Foundation Center, New York, 1987.

For a current bibliographic resource, with over 16,000 citations, with some 3,000 entries for searches on "foundations," see the Foundation Center's Web site—Literature of the Nonprofit Sector Online.

32. Ellen Condliffe Lagemann, *The Politics of Knowledge: The Carnegie Corporation, Philanthropy, and Public Policy.* Wesleyan University Press, Middletown, Connecticut, 1989, pp. 323–324.

33. Nicholas Lemann, "Citizen 501 (c) (3). An Increasingly Powerful Agent in American Life Is Also One of the Least Noticed," *Atlantic Monthly* (February 1997), pp. 18, 20.

34. Stephen G. Greene, "New Survey Says Most Americans Endorse Foundations but Know Little About Them," *The Chronicle of Philanthropy* (December 17, 1998), p. 37.

CHAPTER 5

1. For discussion of the legal status and the role and function of trustees in the operation of foundations and nonprofit and voluntary organizations, see Donald R. Young, *Trusteeship and the Management of Foundations.* Russell Sage Foundation, New York, 1969; John W. Nason, *Trustees and the Future of Foundations.* Council on Foundations. New York, 1977; Brian O'Connell, *The Board Member's Book. Making a Difference in Voluntary Organizations.* Foundation Center, New York, 1985; John Carver, *Boards That Make a Difference and Board Leadership.* Jossey-Bass, San Francisco, 1990; and Peter F. Drucker, *Managing the Non-profit Organization: Practices and Principles.* HarperCollins, New York, 1990.

2. For brief histories of them and their metamorphoses, see Joseph F. Wall, "Carnegie Endowment for International Peace," pp. 172–176; Franklin H. Portugal, "Carnegie Institution of Washington," pp. 176–179; Patricia Piety, "Charles F. Kettering Foundation," pp. 184–188 in Joseph C. Kiger (ed.), *Research Institutions and Learned Societies.* Greenwood Press, Westport, Connecticut, 1982.

3. For a 1997 survey report and comparison of staffing patterns at differing foundations, see Loren Renz, Crystal Mandler, and Rikard Treiber, *Foundation Giving, Yearbook of Facts and Figures on Private, Corporate, and Community Foundations,* 8th ed. Foundation Center, New York, 1998, pp. 18, 21, 44, 51, 58.

4. Leonard P. Ayres, *Seven Great Foundations.* Russell Sage Foundation, New York, 1911, pp. 18–19, 50, 77–78.

5. Frederick P. Keppel, *The Foundation: Its Place in American Life.* Macmillan, New York, 1930, pp. 61–74.

6. Eduard C. Lindeman, *Wealth and Culture. A Study of One Hundred Foundations and Community Trusts and Their Operations during the Decade 1921–1930.* Harcourt, Brace, New York, 1936, p. 33.

7. Ibid., pp. 45–46. Harold C. Coffman, *American Foundations; A Study of Their Role in the Child Welfare Movement*. Association Press, New York, 1936 (drew essentially the same conclusions as the Lindeman work).

8. Lindeman, p. 44.

9. *Final Report of the Select Committee to Investigate Foundations and Other Organizations,* p. 10.

10. Ibid., p. 11.

11. Ibid.

12. *Report of the Special Committee to Investigate Tax-Exempt Foundations and Comparable Organizations*, particularly, pp. 22–60.

13. Ibid., p. 38.

14. F. Emerson, Andrews, *Philanthropic Foundations*. Russell Sage Foundation, New York, 1956, p. 76.

15. Ibid., pp. 67–68.

16. Ibid., p. 133.

17. *Treasury Department Report on Private Foundations*, pp. 9–10.

18. U.S. House of Representatives, 89th Congress, 1st Session, Vol. 1 and 2, Committee Print. *Written Statements by Interested Individuals and Organizations on Treasury Department Report on Private Foundations; Issued on February 2, 1965, Submitted to Committee on Ways and Means.* Government Printing Office, Washington, D.C., 1965.

19. *Report of the Commission on the Humanities,* p. 8.

20. Ben Whitaker, *The Philanthropoids. Foundations and Society.* William Morrow, New York, 1974, pp. 88–89.

21. Ibid., pp. 92–93.

22. *Foundations, Private Giving, and Public Policy: A Summary of Findings and Recommendations.* University of Chicago Press, Chicago, 1970, pp. 89–90.

23. Ibid., p. 138.

24. Ibid., pp. 137–139.

25. "The Donee Group Report and Recommendations," vol. I, Part I, p. 65, *Research Papers. Sponsored by the Commission on Private Philanthropy and Public Needs.*

26. Ibid., p. 66.

27. U.S. Department of the Treasury, *Giving in America: Report of the Commission on Private Philanthropy and Public Needs.* Government Printing Office, Washington, D.C., 1977, p. 171. For a commission article expounding this position in more detail see Lawrence M. Stone, "The Charitable Foundation: Its Governance," *Research Papers* 3, pp. 1723–1737.

28. *Giving in America: Report of the Commission on Private Philanthropy and Public Needs,* pp. 170–171.

29. Stephen G. Greene, "Women Gain on Foundation Staffs but Not on Boards," *The Chronicle of Philanthropy* (September 4, 1990), p. 25.

30. Althea K. Nagai, Robert Lerner, and Stanley Rothman, *Giving for Social Change: Foundations, Public Policy, and the American Political Agenda.* Praeger, Westport, Connecticut, 1994, p. 52.

31. "Foundation Management and Governance," *The Chronicle of Philanthropy* (May 1, 1997), p. 33.

32. *The 1997 Grantmakers Salary Report.* Council on Foundations, Washington, D.C., 1997.

33. *Report of the Study for the Ford Foundation on Policy and Program.* Ford Foundation, Detroit, November, 1949, pp. 132–133.

CHAPTER 6

1. A history of English philanthropy, including the origination and supervision of foundations from 1480 to 1960, is to be found in Wilbur K. Jordan, *Philanthropy in England, 1480–1660: A Study of the Changing Patterns of English Social Aspirations.* Russell Sage Foundation, New York, 1959 and David Owens, *English Philanthropy 1660–1960.* Belknap Press of Harvard University Press, Cambridge, 1964. These cited volumes and Chapter 1 of the present study are primarily concerned with England, Wales, and, to a degree, Northern Ireland. Lack of large accumulations of surplus wealth and differences in governmental/legal structures preclude Scotland.

2. *Report of the Committee on the Law and Practice Relating to Charitable Trusts,* Cmd. 8710. Her Majesty's Stationery Office, London, England, 1952, p. 31.

3. Ibid., p. 98.

4. Lord Beveridge, *Voluntary Action.* Macmillan, New York, 1948.

5. *Report of the Committee on the Law and Practice Relating to Charitable Trusts,* p. 1.

6. For example, the number of commissioners was increased to five.

7. See John Murawski and Grant Williams, "Turning to Charities for Taxes," *The Chronicle of Philanthropy* (May 18, 1995), pp. 1, 34–37.

8. Corporation Excise Tax of 1909, ch. 6, #38, 36 Stat. 113.

9. Marion R. Fremont-Smith, *Foundations and Government.* Russell Sage Foundation, New York, 1965, p. 65. This volume, pp. 64–70, 161–162, contains a succinct description of the formation of federal tax law in the regulation of charitable organizations.

10. *Statement of the Rockefeller Foundation and the General Education Board before the Special Committee to Investigate Tax Exempt Foundations. House of Representatives—83rd Congress.* Rockefeller Foundation, New York, 1954, p. 9.

11. Irving Warner, "If They Drop the Tax Deduction, I Won't Mourn," *The Chronicle of Philanthropy* (January 28, 1992), pp. 35–36.

12. Gilbert M. Gaul and Neill A. Borowski, *Free Ride: The Tax-Exempt Economy*. Andrews and McMeel, Kansas City, Missouri, 1993.

13. See Chapter 2 for an account of the origination and conduct of these congressional investigations.

14. Fremont-Smith, pp. 436–437. For an earlier work on the same topic, see Eleanor K. Taylor, *Public Accountability of Foundations and Charitable Trusts*. Russell Sage Foundation, New York, 1953.

15. David Ginsburg, Lee R. Marks, and Roland P. Wertheim, "Federal Oversight of Private Philanthropy," *Research Papers Sponsored by the Commission on Private Philanthropy and Public Needs,* vol. 5, Regulation, p. 2575.

16. *Foundations, Private Giving, and Public Policy: A Summary of Findings and Recommendations.* University of Chicago Press, Chicago, 1970, p. xii.

17. Ibid., pp. 2–3.

18. Ibid., pp. xvii–xviii.

19. *Foundations, Private Giving, and Public Policy: A Summary of Findings and Recommendations.* University of Chicago Press, Chicago, 1970, p. 7.

20. Two reports emanating from such conferences were George Nebolsine, *Fiscal Aspects of Foundations and Charitable Donations in European Countries*. European Cultural Foundation, Amsterdam, Netherlands, 1963; *Foundations and Government. Report of an International Conference of Charitable Foundations and Similar Institutions.* Ditchley Foundation, Endstone, Oxford, England, 1966.

21. John J. Corson and Harry V. Hodson (eds.), *Philanthropy in the 70's: An Anglo-American Discussion.* Council on Foundations, New York, 1973, p. 14.

22. Ibid., p. 12.

23. Ibid., p. 50.

24. Ibid., p. 51.

25. Thomas J. Billiterri, and Vince Stehle, "Brilliant Deduction," *The Chronicle of Philanthropy* (August 13, 1998), pp. 24–27.

26. U.S. Department of the Treasury. *Giving in America: Report of the Commission on Private Philanthropy and Public Needs.* Government Printing Office, Washington, D.C., 1977, pp. 190–191.

27. Ibid., p. 167.

28. Ibid., p. 214.

29. Ibid., pp. 214–216. The same charges were leveled against the IRS in the 1990s. See Elizabeth Macdonald, "The Kennedys and the IRS," *Wall Street Journal,* January 28, 1997, p. A16. Such charges have been consistently denied by IRS officials. See, for example, Jon Craig and

Grant Williams, "IRS Fights Charges of Political Bias," *The Chronicle of Philanthropy* (March 6, 1997), p. 53.

30. Ibid., pp. 215–216.

31. *Research Papers Sponsored by the Commission on Private Philanthropy and Public Needs,* vol. I, Part I, The Donee Group Report and Recommendations, pp. 76–79.

32. U.S. Department of the Treasury, *Giving in America*, p. 135.

33. Urban C. Lehner, "Treasury Stuns New Philanthropy Panel with Word That It Doesn't Have a Future," *Wall Street Journal* (April 11, 1977), p. A8.

34. See Joel L. Fleishman, "To Merit and Preserve the Public's Trust in Not-for-Profit Organizations: The Urgent Need for Regulatory Reform," in Charles T. Clotfelter and Thomas Ehrlich (eds.), *The Future of Philanthropy in a Changing America*. Indiana University Press, Bloomington, 1998.

35. Stephen G. Greene and Grant Williams, "IRS Rules Campaign Funds May Go to Foundations," *The Chronicle of Philanthropy* (September 6, 1994), p. 47.

36. Grant Moore, "New Rules for Charity Disclosure," *The Chronicle of Philanthropy* (October, 16, 1997), pp. 37–41; and "IRS Is Urged to Make Some Revisions in Plan to Enforce Disclosure Law" (February 12, 1998), pp. 41–42.

37. See Grant Williams, "Stopping Excessive Benefits," *The Chronicle of Philanthropy* (August 13, 1998), pp. 29–33. This article includes pertinent excerpts from the proposed IRS regulations.This same issue of the *Chronicle* contains another article calling for more stringent regulations than the ones proposed by the IRS. See Pablo Eisenberg, "The IRS Must Slam the Door on High Salaries," pp. 43–44. See also, Grant Williams, "Intermediate Opinions, Charities Give Preliminary Thumbs-Up to Proposed IRS Regulations on Financial Abuses, but Wait for Further Clarification," *The Chronicle of Philanthropy* (January 28, 1999), pp. 23–25.

38. "IRS Plan to Reorganize Could Aid Charity Regulators," *The Chronicle of Philanthropy* (February 12, 1998), p. 47.

39. "Return of the Future. Disclosure Law and Internet Access Spur New Focus on Charity Tax Forms," *The Chronicle of Philanthropy* (December 17, 1998), pp. 1, 31–33.

40. These differences are summarized by Barbara Shenfield, "A Summary of the Debates" under the heading Influencing Public and Political Opinion, in Corson and Hodson, pp. 8–11.

41. For a general discussion of that role, see Joseph C. Kiger, *Operating Principles of the Larger Foundations*. Russell Sage Foundation, New York, 1954, pp. 45–66. For two recent works on that role see Mary Anna Culleton Colwell, *Private Foundations and Public Policy: The Political*

Role of Philanthropy. Garland Pub., New York, 1993 and Judith Sealander, *Private Wealth and Public Life: Foundation Philanthropy and the Reshaping of American Social Policy from the Progressive Era to the New Deal.* Johns Hopkins University Press, Baltimore, 1997.

42. See, for a recent example, Debra E. Blum, Stephen G. Greene, and Grant Williams, "IRS Reverses Position, Recognizes Kemp Group," *The Chronicle of Philanthropy* (January 15, 1998), p. 47.

43. U.S. House, *Hearings before the Special Committee to Investigate Tax-Exempt Foundations and Comparable Organizations,* Part I, 83d Congress, 2d Session, Government Printing Office, Washington, D.C., 1954. See particularly the testimony of Norman A. Sugarman, assistant commissioner of the Internal Revenue Service, pp. 418–463.

44. U.S. Department of the Treasury, *Giving in America,* pp. 181–182.

45. See U.S. House of Representatives, 81st Congress, 2d Session, House Report 3138, *General Interim Report of the Select Committee on Lobbying Activities.* Government Printing Office, Washington, D.C., 1950, pp. 1–67. See also, U.S. House of Representatives, 81st Congress, 2d Session, House Report 3239, *A Report of the Select Committee on Lobbying Activities.* Government Printing Office, Washington, D.C., 1950, Part I, pp. 1–58 and Part 2, Minority Views, pp. 1–11.

46. See *General Interim Report,* pp. 14–15.

47. See Althea K. Nagai, Robert Lerner, and Stanley Rothman, *Giving for Social Change: Foundations, Public Policy, and the American Political Agenda.* Praeger, Westport, Connecticut, 1994, p. 156.

48. See Joseph C. Kiger (ed.), "American Enterprise Institute for Public Policy Research," *Research Institutions and Learned Societies,* Greenwood Press, Westport, Connecticut, 1982, pp. 56–59. See also James Allen Smith, *The Idea Brokers. Think Tanks and the Rise of the New Policy Elite.* Free Press, New York, 1991, pp. 176–180.

49. *General Interim Report,* p. 61.

50. Ibid., p. 66. There were in this document other references and observations expounding these same points of view. See, for example, pp. 15, 30, 46.

51. U.S. House, *A Report of the Select Committee on Lobbying Activities,* Part 2, p. 11.

52. *Congressional Quarterly Almanac,* 104th Congress, 2d Session, vol. LII, p. , D-26, 1996.

53. Steven Rathgeb Smith, and Michael Lipsky, *Nonprofits for Hire: The Welfare State in the Age of Contracting.* Harvard University Press, Cambridge, 1993. See also Bob Smucker, *The Nonprofit Lobbying Guide,* 2d ed. Independent Sector, Washington, D.C., 1999.

54. Throughout the 1990s *The Chronicle of Philanthropy* was filled with numerous articles on the issue. Articles on the issue also appeared

at that time in such publications as *Forbes, Foundations News and Commentary,* and the *Wall Street Journal.*

55. J. J. Pickle, "Make Charities Earn Their Tax Exemption," *The Chronicle of Philanthropy* (September 19, 1996), p. 57.

56. William Montague, "New Curbs Sought on Political Activity by Non-Profit Groups," *The Chronicle of Philanthropy* (April 23, 1990), p. 25. See, also pp. 22–23, 26.

57. For an article urging such action, see Leslie Lenkowsky, "Congress: Revise Rules on Advocacy by Charities," *The Chronicle of Philanthropy* (February 25, 1999), pp. 49–50.

58. *Impact of Tax Restructuring on Tax-Exempt Organizations.* Council on Foundations and Independent Sector, Washington, D.C., April, 28, 1997.

59. *Helping Canadians Help Canadians: Improving Governance and Accountability in the Voluntary Sector.* Panel on Accountability and Governance in the Voluntary Sector, May, 1998, Ottawa, Ontario, Canada, particularly, Chapter 8, "A New Voluntary Sector Agency," pp. 40–44.

60. *Building on Strength: Improving Governance and Accountability in Canada's Voluntary Sector. Final Report.* Panel on Accountability and Governance in the Voluntary Sector, Ottawa, Ontario, Canada, 1999.

61. Ibid., p. 58.

62. Stephen G. Greene, "Canadian Charities Urged to Adopt Codes of Conduct," *The Chronicle of Philanthropy* (February 25, 1999), p. 43.

CHAPTER 7

1. The term "international activities," herein covers foundation expenditures made abroad or in the United States having an international content or context, that is, those aiding foreign governments, students, research, conferences, publications, libraries, and so on.

2. See Franklin Parker, *George Peabody: A Biography.* Vanderbilt University Press, Nashville, Tennessee, 1971, pp. 124–135.

3. Eduard C. Lindeman, *Wealth and Culture.* Harcourt, Brace and Co., New York, pp. 122–123; Shelby M. Harrison and F. Emerson Andrews, *American Foundations for Social Welfare.* Russell Sage Foundation, New York, 1946, p. 79; Wilmer Shields Rich, *American Foundations and Their Fields*, 7th ed. American Foundation Information Service, New York, 1955, p. xxxvi.

4. For more extensive discussion of foreign activities by foundations based on the *Questionnaire,* see Joseph C. Kiger, *Operating Principles of the Larger Foundations.* Russell Sage Foundation, New York, 1954, pp. 70–74.

5. Amy P. Longsworth, "Rockefeller Brothers Fund," in Harold M. Keele and Joseph C. Kiger (eds.), *Foundations*. Greenwood Press, Westport, Connecticut, 1984, p. 363.

6. *Foundations, Private Giving, and Public Policy: A Summary of Findings and Recommendations*. University of Chicago Press, Chicago, 1970, pp. 81–82.

7. Henry Romney, "The Rockefeller Foundation," in Keele and Kiger, *Foundations*, p. 371.

8. *Report of the Study for the Ford Foundation on Policy and Program*, p. 25.

9. Joseph C. Kiger, "Foundations and International Affairs," *Foundation News* 6, no. 4 (July 1965), p. 67.

10. Oona Sullivan, "The Ford Foundation," in Keele and Kiger, p. 129.

11. David A. Hamburg, "A Perspective on Carnegie Corporation's Program, 1983–1997," Carnegie Corporation of New York, *Annual Report,* 1996, p. 16.

12. Ibid., p. 19.

13. "International Foundation for the Survival and Development of Humanity," Joseph C. Kiger (ed.), *International Encyclopedia of Foundations*. Greenwood Press, Westport, Connecticut, 1993, p. xii, 237–238.

14. For much additional information for foundation giving for these purposes in 1988, see *Search for Security*. ACCESS, Washington, D.C., 1989.

15. Marina Dundjerski, "A Boom Year: Ford's Giving to Rise 18%," *The Chronicle of Philanthropy* (May 1, 1997), pp. 1, 12–13. See also, "President's Message," *1997 Annual Report,* Ford Foundation, 1997.

16. For this and other information resulting from the study, see Loren Renz, Josefina Samson-Atienza, Trinh C. Tran, and Rikard R. Treiber, *International Grantmaking: A Report on U.S. Foundation Trends*. Foundation Center, New York, 1997. See also Loren Renz, "International Grant Making by U.S. Foundations: Issues and Directions in the 1990s," *Nonprofit and Voluntary Sector Quarterly,* 27, no. 4 (December 1998), pp. 507–521.

17. For an autobiographical and aptly titled book telling about his life, philosophy, and the establishment and conduct of the foundations he created, see George Soros, *Underwriting Democracy*. Free Press, New York, 1991.

18. Kevin F. F. Quigley, *For Democracy's Sake: Foundations and Democracy Assistance in Central Europe*. Woodrow Wilson Center Press, Washington, D.C., 1997, pp. 100–101. This book also provides an excellent bibliography listing the more important recent books and articles dealing with assistance programs in Central and also Eastern Europe, particularly the role played there by U.S. and other foundations.

For an earlier briefer, but somewhat broader, account of aid for the region, see Daniel Siegel and Jenny Yancey, *The Rebirth of Civil Society: The Development of the Nonprofit Sector in East Central Europe and the Role of Western Assistance.* Rockefeller Brothers Fund, New York, 1992.

19. For a more detailed account on the 1998 giving of the foundation see Stephen G. Greene, "Ted Turner Maps Out His Sphere of Influence," *The Chronicle of Philanthropy* (June 4, 1998), pp. 9–10, 12.

20. Alex Kucxynski, "The Very Rich Pay to Learn How to Give Money Away," *New York Times* (May 3, 1998), pp. 1–48.

21. For a thorough discussion of the pros and cons of this aspect of foundation operations, see Ben Whitaker, *The Philanthropoids: Foundations and Society.* William Morrow, New York, 1974, pp. 144–166.

22. Quoted in Merle Curti, *American Philanthropy Abroad: A History.* Rutgers University Press, New Brunswick, New Jersey, 1963, p. 335.

23. Henry T. Heald, "The Painstaking Ascent," *Ford Foundation Annual Report,* Ford Foundation, New York, 1963, pp. 2–3.

24. U.S. House, *Final Report, Select Committee to Investigate Foundations and Other Organizations,* p. 12.

25. *Foundations, Private Giving, and Public Policy,* p. 69.

26. For the worldwide growth and importance of these nonprofit organizations, see Lester Salamon, "The Rise of the Nonprofit Sector," *Foreign Affairs,* 73, no. 4 (July/August, 1994), p. 114.

CHAPTER 8

1. "Charities Aid Foundation (CAF)," in Joseph C. Kiger (ed.), *International Encyclopedia of Foundations.* Greenwood Press, Westport, Connecticut, 1990, p. 248.

2. *The Chronicle of Philanthropy* (September 18, 1997), p. 13, and (October 16, 1997), p. 13.

3. Leonie Baldwin, comp., *The Irish Funding Handbook,* 3d ed. Directory of Social Change, London, 1994.

4. Klaus Neuhoff, "Donors' Association for the Promotion of Sciences and Humanities in Germany," in Kiger, *International Encyclopedia of Foundations,* p. 92.

5. Ibid., p. 93.

6. Klaus Neuhoff and Uwe Pavel (eds.), *Trusts and Foundations in Europe, a Comparative Survey, 1971* and *Bericht Stifterverband fur die Deutsche Wissenschaft.* Die Gemeinschaftsaktion der Wirtschaft, Essen, Germany, 1992.

In addition to the Stifterverband directory, three more comprehensive directories of German foundations, all in German, emanated from other sources: Ute Berkel, Klaus Neuhoff, Ambros Schindler, and Erich Steinsdorfer, *Stiftungshandbuch.* Foundation Handbook, 3d ed. Nomos Verlagsgesellschaft, Baden-Baden, West Germany, 1989; *Maecenata Stiftungsfuhrer: 1111 Forderstiftungen*. Maecenata Management GmbH, Munich, Germany, 1994; and *Verzeichnis der Deutschen Stiftungen*. Verlag Hoppenstedt GmbH, Darmstadt, Germany, 1994.

7. *The Week in Germany*, "Foundations Urge Tax Changes" (May 29, 1998), p. 6.

8. See "Foundation of France," in Kiger, *International Encyclopedia of Foundations*, pp. 82–83.

9. See *Foundations*. Ministre de l'Interieiur, Journal Officiel de la Republique Française, Paris, France, 1971 and 1980.

10. For a report on this conference see George Nebolsine, *Fiscal Aspects of Foundations and of Charitable Donations in European Countries*. European Cultural Foundation, Amsterdam, Netherlands, 1963.

11. See Michel Didisheim, "King Baudouin Foundation," in Kiger, *International Encyclopedia of Foundations*, pp. 17–20.

12. Franco Agnelli (ed.), *Guide to European Foundations*. Giovanni Agnelli Foundation, Milan, Italy, 1973 (English edition available through Columbia University Press) and Franco Agnelli (ed.), *Le Fondazioni Italine. Con un saggio sulle fondazioni private nell ' ordiname giurdico di Dante Cosi*. Milan, Italy, 1973.

See also, Davide Gucci, *Le fundazione: perche crearle e comme gestirle*. Edizioni FAG s.r.l., Assago, Italy, 1995.

13. *Directorio de las Fundaciones Españolas*. Madrid, Spain, Centro de Fundaciones, 1986 and 1994.

14. See *Memoria de gestion 1998* (Annual Report), Confederacion Española de Fundaciones, Madrid, Spain, 1998.

15. See *Guia das fundaçoes Portugesas* (Portuguese Foundations Guide), 2d ed. Fundacao Oriente, Lisbon, Portugal, 1993.

16. See *Saatiohakemisto* (Finnish Foundations). Finnish Cultural Foundation, Helsinki, Finland, 1977.

17. See Peter Balazs (ed.), *Alapitvanyi Adattar* (Hungarian Foundation Directory), published in Hungarian with English translation side-by-side. Hungarian Foundation Centre, Budapest, Hungary, 1992 and Peter Balazs, *Alapitvanyi Adatta* (Hungarian Foundation Directory), vol. 3. Hungarian Foundation Centre, Budapest, Hungary, 1994.

18. The European foundations represented included four from Germany: Fritz Thyssen Stiftung, Max Planck Institut fur Europaeische Rechtsgeschichte, Stiftung Volkwagenwerk, and Alfried Krupp von Bohlen und Halbach Stiftung. The six others were the Leverhulme Trust and Nuffield Foundation from Great Britain, the Fondazione Giovanni Agnelli and Fondazione Adriano Olivetti from Italy, the Fundaçao Caloueste Gulbenkian from Portugal, and the Bernard van Leer Foundation from the Netherlands.

19. These members were Gotthard Gambke, Volkswagen Stiftung, Germany; Ubaldo Scassellati, Fondazione Giovanni Agnello, Italy; Willem H. Welling, Bernard van Leer Foundation, Netherlands; and Peter O. Williams, Wellcome Trust, Great Britain.

20. See Frank Niepoth, "A Bird's Eye View of the Club," *Foundation Profiles,* 6th ed. The Hague Club, The Hague, Netherlands, 1995, pp. 7–19.

21. Jill Adler, "European Cultural Foundation," in Kiger, *International Encyclopedia of Foundations*, pp. 178–181.

22. The seven European foundations' founding members of EFC were Charities Aid Foundation (United Kingdom), European Cultural Foundation (Netherlands), Fondation de France (France), Fundaçao Oriente (Portugal), Juliana Weizijn Fonds (Netherlands), King Baudoin Foundation (France), and Stifterverband fur die Deutsche Wissenschaft (Germany).

23. Pamphlet *Members, Associates, Networks, 1997*. European Foundation Centre, Brussels, Belgium, 1997.

24. *Philanthropy International.* INTERPHIL, Geneva, Switzerland, April 1994, p. 8.

25. "What Is INTERPHIL?" INTERPHIL, Geneva, Switzerland, October 1994, p. 1.

26. Stephen G. Greene, " 'Interphil' Group Eyed as Potential Leader of World Philanthropy," *The Chronicle of Philanthropy* (January 8, 1990), p. 5.

27. Ibid., p. 5.

28. See Engin Ural, *Foundations in Turkey*. Development Foundation of Turkey, Ankara, Turkey, 1978.

29. See Dorothy Harman (ed.), *Modes of Foundation Operations in Israel*. Van Leer Jerusalem Institute, Jerusalem, Israel, 1997.

30. See Ann McKinstry Micou, *South African Trusts / Foundations*. 1991; *The Donor Community in South Africa: A Directory*. 1993; and *The U.S. Independent Sector as It Relates to South African Initiatives: A Directory*. 1993. Each of these works was published by the Institute of International Education, New York.

31. See E. K. Hart, *Directory of Philanthropic Trusts in Australia*. 1974; *Philanthropic Trusts in Australia,* 3d ed. 1981; and *Philanthropic Trusts in Australia*. 5th ed. 1987. Each of these works was published by the Australian Council for Educational Research, Hawthorn, Victoria, Australia.

32. See *A Directory of Philanthropic Trusts in New Zealand*, 2d ed. New Zealand Council for Educational Research, Wellington, New Zealand, 1978 and 3d ed. in association with J. R. McKenzie Trust Board, Wellington, New Zealand, 1987.

33. "International Conference on Corporate Philanthropy," *Philanthropy. Newsletter of the Centre for the Advancement of Philanthropy*. Centre for the Advancement of Philanthropy, New Delhi, India (March, 1991), pp. 1–4.

34. Narzalina Z. Lim, *Philippine Directory of Foundations*. SCC Development and Research Foundation, Manila, Philippines, 1974.

35. Minoru Tanaka and Takako Amemiya, *Philanthropy in Japan '83*. Japan Association of Charitable Corporations, Tokyo, 1983.

36. *Directory of Grant-Making Foundations: Guide to Private Grant Sources*. Foundation Library Center of Japan, Tokyo, 1988, 1995, 1998. *Directory of Grant-Making Foundations: Summary of Current Grant Awards*. Foundation Library Center of Japan, Tokyo, 1995.

37. Katherine E. Jankowski (ed.), Foundation Library Center of Japan, *Inside Japanese Support: Descriptive Profiles and Other Information on Japanese Corporate Giving and Foundation Giving Programs*, 3d ed. Taft Group, Detroit,, 1994 and *Directory of Grant-Making Foundations in Japan 1996*. Japan Foundation Center, Tokyo, 1996.

38. Samuel A. Martin, *An Essential Grace: Funding Canada's Health Care, Education, Welfare, Religion, and Culture*. McClelland and Stewart, Toronto, Canada, 1985, p. 260. See also Samuel A. Martin, *Financing Humanistic Service*. McClelland and Stewart, Ltd., Toronto, Canada, 1975, particularly pp. 104–119.

39. See, for example, Allan Arlett and Ingrid van Rotterdam, "The Power of Giving, What's What in Canada's World of Foundations," *The Financial Post*, March 9, 1987, p. 13.

40. Rose van Rotterdam (ed.), *Canadian Directory to Foundations and Grants: 1996/97*, 12th ed. Canadian Centre for Philanthropy, Toronto, Canada, 1996.

41. *Helping Canadians Help Canadians:Improving Governanace and Accountability in the Voluntary Sector*, Panel on Accountability and Governance in the Voluntary Sector, Ottawa, Ontario, Canada, 1998.

42. Stephen G. Greene, "A Crossroads for Canadian Charities. As Demand for Service Rises So Does Debate on Regulations, Ethics," *The Chronicle of Philanthropy* (August 27, 1998), pp. 1, 29–31.

43. "U.S., Mexican Foundations Sign Accord to Spur Giving," *The Chronicle of Philanthropy* (November 17, 1992), p. 14.

44. *Directory of Philanthropic Institutions*, 1st ed. Mexican Center on Philanthropic Institutions, Mexico City, Mexico, 1990 and *Directory of Philanthropic Institutions 1995/1996*, 2d ed. Mexican Center on Philanthropy, Mexico City, Mexico, 1995.

45. Ann Stromberg (ed.), *Philanthropic Foundations in Latin America*. Russell Sage Foundation, New York, 1968.

46. *Fundaciones Privadas de Venezuela*. Eugenio Mendoza Foundation, Caracas, Venezuela, 1973; Antonieta M. de Lopez and Luisa E. M.

de Pulido (eds.), *Latin American Foundations*. Eugenio Mendoza Foundation, Caracas, Venezuela, 1974; *National Directory of Private Philanthropic Institutions and Social Development*. Accion en Colombia, Bogotá, Colombia, 1974; *Argentine Directory of Foundations* (in Spanish). Jose Maria Aragon Foundation, Buenos Aires, Argentina, 1980; *Guia de Fundaciones y Organismos Afines de Centroamerica*. Fundacion Arias para la Paz el Progreso Humano, San José, Costa Rica, 1992.

47. A World Congress on Philanthropy, designed to be a triannual forum for philanthropy worldwide, held meetings in Toronto, Canada, in 1988 and in 1991 in Miami, Florida. Since then no further meetings by the congress have been held, and it appears to be defunct.

48. Kristin A. Goss, "Charities See Collaboration on Social Problems as Essential—but Full of Pitfalls," *The Chronicle of Philanthropy* (October 22, 1991), p. 12.

49. For a detailed report of the meeting, see Stephen G. Greene, "Promoting Participation by Citizens Worldwide," *The Chronicle of Philanthropy* (January 26, 1995), pp. 6–8. For a presentation at the time of Marschall's views and hopes for CIVICUS together with a biographical sketch of him, see Louis L. Knowles, "A Conversation with Miklos Marschall," *Foundation News & Commentary* (January/February, 1995), pp. 13–15.

50. For a report on the assembly, see Stephen G. Greene, "Civic Virtue vs. 'McWorld,'" *The Chronicle of Philanthropy* (October 16, 1997), pp. 15–17.

51. "Strategic Plan 1998–2000," CIVICUS World Alliance for Citizen Participation, Washington, D.C., 1998, pp. 1–19.

COMMENTARY

1. Susan V. Berresford, "Responding to Globalization," *Ford Foundation Annual Report*, Ford Foundation, New York, 1997, p. 1.

Bibliography

Alchon, Guy, *The Invisible Hand of Planning: Capitalism, Social Science and the State in the 1920's*. Princeton University Press, Princeton, New Jersey, 1985.

Andrews, F. Emerson, *Foundation Watcher.* Franklin and Marshall College, Lancaster, Pennsylvania, 1973.

Andrews, F. Emerson, *Philanthropic Foundations.* Russell Sage Foundation, New York, 1956.

Andrews, F. Emerson, *Philanthropic Giving.* Russell Sage Foundation, New York, 1950.

Appreciations of Frederick Paul Keppel. Columbia University Press, New York, 1951.

Arnett, Jan Corey, Robert Matthews, and Barbara H. Kehrer, *Evaluation for Foundations: Concepts, Cases, Guidelines, and Resources.* Jossey-Bass, San Francisco, 1993.

Arnove, Robert F. (ed.), *Philanthropy and Cultural Imperialism: The Foundations at Home and Abroad.* G. K. Hall, Boston, 1980.

Ayres, Leonard P., *Seven Great Foundations.* Russell Sage Foundation, New York, 1911.

Bahaeddin, Yediyildiz, *Institution du Vaqf au XVIIIe siécle en Turquie: Etude socio-historique.* Société d'Histoire Turque, Ankara, Turkey, 1985.

Barnard, Harry, *Independent Man: The Life of Senator James Couzens.* Charles Scribner's Sons, New York, 1958.

Barzun, Jacques, *The House of Intellect.* Harper and Bros., New York, 1959.

Baxter, Christie I., *Program-Related Investments: A Technical Manual for Foundations.* John Wiley and Sons, New York, 1997.

Becker, Stephen, *Marshall Field III.* Simon and Schuster, New York, 1964.

Bellant, Russ, *The Coors Connection: How Coors Family Philanthropy Undermines Democratic Pluralism.* 2d ed. South End Press, Boston, 1991.

Berle, Adolf A., *Leaning against the Dawn: An Appreciation of the Twentieth Century Fund and Its Fifty Years of Adventure in Seeking to Influence American Development toward a More Effectively Just Civilization, 1919–1960.* Twentieth Century Fund, New York, 1985.

Berliner, Howard A., *A System of Scientific Medicine: Philanthropic Foundations in the Flexner Era.* Tavistock, Pub., New York, 1985.

Berman, Edward H., *The Influence of the Carnegie, Ford, and Rockefeller Foundations on American Foreign Policy: The Ideology of Philanthropy.* State University of New York Press, Albany, 1983.

Bremner, Robert H., *American Philanthropy.* University of Chicago Press, Chicago, 1960.

Bremner, Robert H., *Giving: Charity and Philanthropy in History.* Transaction, New Brunswick, New Jersey, 1994.

Brown, E. Richard, *Rockefeller Medicine Men: Medicine and Capitalism in America.* University of California Press, Berkeley, 1979.

Building on Strength. Improving Governance and Accountability in Canada's Voluntary Sector. Final Report. Panel on Accountability and Governance in the Voluntary Sector, Ottawa, Ontario, Canada, 1999.

Bullock, Mary Brown, *An American Transplant: The Rockefeller Foundation and Peking Union Medical College.* University of California Press, Berkeley, 1980.

Cameron, Frank, *Cottrell: Samaritan of Science.* Doubleday, New York, 1952.

Candler, Warren A., *Dangerous Donations and Degrading Doles or a Vast Scheme for Capturing and Controlling the Colleges and Universities of the Country.* Privately printed, Atlanta, Georgia, 1909.

Carnegie, Andrew, *Autobiography of Andrew Carnegie.* Houghton, Mifflin, Boston, 1920.

Carnegie, Andrew, *The Gospel of Wealth and Other Timely Essays.* Century, New York, 1900.

Carver, John, *Boards That Make a Difference and Board Leadership.* Jossey-Bass, San Francisco, 1990.

Castle, Alfred L., *A Century of Philanthropy. A History of the Samuel N. and Mary Castle Foundation.* Hawaiian Historical Society, Honolulu, 1992.

Cieply, Michael A., *The Hearsts: Family and Empire.* Simon and Schuster, New York, 1981.

Clotfelter, Charles T., and Thomas Ehrlich (eds.), *The Future of Philanthropy in a Changing America.* Indiana University Press, Bloomington, 1998.

Cluff, Leighton E., *Helping Shape the Nation's Health Care System: A Report on the Robert Wood Johnson's Program Activities, 1972–1989.* Robert Wood Johnson Foundation, Princeton, New Jersey, 1989.

Collier, Peter, and David Horowitz, *The Rockefellers: An American Dynasty.* New American Library, Bergenfield, New Jersey, 1977.

Colwell, Mary Anna Culleton, *Private Foundations and Public Policy: The Political Role of Philanthropy.* Garland, New York, 1993.

Coon, Horace, *Money to Burn: What the Great American Philanthropic Foundations Do with Their Money.* Longmans, Green, and Co., New York, 1938.

Corson, John J., and Harry V. Hodson (eds.), *Philanthropy in the 70's: An Anglo-American Discussion.* Council on Foundations, New York, 1973.

Cueto, Marcos (ed.), *Missionaries of Science: The Rockefeller Foundation and Latin America.* Indiana University Press, Bloomington, 1994.

Cuninggim, Merrimon, *Private Money and Public Service: The Role of Foundations in American Society.* McGraw-Hill, Inc., New York, 1972.

Curry, J. L. M., *A Brief Sketch of George Peabody and a History of the Peabody Fund through Thirty Years.* John Wilson, Cambridge, Massachusetts, 1989.

Curti, Merle, *Philanthropy Abroad: A History.* Rutgers University Press, New Brunswick, New Jersey, 1963.

Curti, Merle, and Roderick Nash, *Philanthropy in the Shaping of American Higher Education.* Rutgers University Press, New Brunswick, New Jersey, 1965.

Drucker, Peter F., *Managing the Non-Profit Organization: Practices and Principles.* HarperCollins, New York, 1990.

Durden, Robert F., *The Dukes of Durham, 1865–1920.* Duke University Press, Durham, North Carolina, 1975.

Edie, John A., *Foundations and Lobbying: Safe Ways to Affect Public Policy. A Complete Guide for Private and Community Foundations.* Council on Foundations, Washington, D.C., 1991.

Embree, Edwin R., and Julia Waxman, *Investment in People: The Story of the Julius Rosenwald Fund.* Harper and Bros., New York, 1949.

Ettling, John, *The Germ of Laziness: Rockefeller Philanthropy and Public Health in the New South.* Harvard University Press, Cambridge, 1981.

Ferguson, Mary E., *China Medical Board and Peking Union Medical College: A Chronicle of a Fruitful Collaboration.* China Medical Board of New York, New York, 1970.

The First Twenty-Five Years: The Story of a Foundation. W. K. Kellogg Foundation, Battle Creek, Michigan, 1956.

Flexner, Abraham, *Abraham Flexner: An Autobiography*. Simon and Schuster, New York, 1960.

Flexner, Abraham, *Henry S. Pritchett. A Biography*. Columbia University Press, New York, 1943.

Flexner, Abraham, with Esther S. Bailey, *Funds and Foundations: Their Policies, Past and Present*. Harper and Bros., New York, 1952.

Fosdick, Raymond B., *Chronicle of a Generation: An Autobiography*. Harper and Bros., New York, 1958.

Fosdick, Raymond B., *John D. Rockefeller, Jr., a Portrait*. Harper and Bros., New York, 1956.

Fosdick, Raymond B., *The Story of the Rockefeller Foundation*. Harper and Bros., New York, 1952.

Fosdick, Raymond B., with Henry F. Pringle and Katherine Douglas Pringle, *The Story of the General Education Board*. Harper and Row, New York, 1962.

The Foundation Directory. Editions 1 through 21. Foundation Center, New York, 1960–1999. 21st ed., 1999.

Foundations and Government. Ditchley Paper No. 9. Ditchley Foundation, Endstone, Oxford, England, 1966.

Foundations, Private Giving, and Public Policy: Report and Recommendations of the [Peterson] *Commission on Foundations and Private Philanthropy*. University of Chicago Press, Chicago, 1970.

Freeman, David F., *The Handbook on Private Foundations*. Council on Foundations, Washington, D.C., 1981.

Fremont-Smith, Marion R., *Foundations and Government: State and Federal Law and Supervision*. Russell Sage Foundation, New York, 1965.

Freund, Gerald, *Narcissism and Philanthropy: Ideas and Talent Denied*. Viking, New York, 1996.

Gates, Frederick T., *Chapters in My Life*. Free Press, New York, 1977.

Gaul, Gilbert M., and Neill A. Borowski, *Free Ride: The Tax-Exempt Economy*. Andrews and McMeel, Kansas City, Missouri, 1993.

Geiger, Roger L., *To Advance Knowledge: The Growth of American Research Universities, 1900–1940*. Oxford University Press, New York, 1986.

Glenn, John M., Lillian Brandt, and F. Emerson Andrews, *Russell Sage Foundation, 1907–1946*. Russell Sage Foundation, New York, 1947. 2 vols.

Goulden, Joseph C., *The Money Givers*. Random House, New York, 1971.

Gray, George W., *Education on an International Scale: A History of the International Education Board, 1923–1938*. Harcourt, Brace and Co., New York, 1941.

Gurda, John, *The Bradley Legacy: Lynde and Harry Bradley, Their Company, and Their Foundation.* Lynde and Harry Bradley Foundation, Milwaukee, Wisconsin, 1992.

Guzzardi, Walter, Jr., *The Henry Luce Foundation: A History, 1936–1986.* University of North Carolina Press, Chapel Hill, 1988.

Haislip, Bryan, *A History of the Z. Smith Reynolds Foundation.* John F. Blair, Winston-Salem, North Carolina, 1967.

Harr, John Ensor, and Peter J. Johnson, *The Rockefeller Conscience: An American Family in Public and in Private.* Charles Scribner's Sons, New York, 1991.

Harrison, Shelby M., and F. Emerson Andrews, *American Foundations for Social Welfare.* Russell Sage Foundation, New York, 1946.

Harvey, A. McGehee and Susan L. Abrams, *"For the Welfare of Mankind" The Commonwealth Fund and American Medicine.* Johns Hopkins University Press, Baltimore, 1986.

Heimann, Fritz R. (ed.), *The Future of Foundations.* Prentice-Hall, Englewood Cliffs, New Jersey, 1973.

Helping Canadians Help Canadians: Improving Governance and Accountability in the Voluntary Sector. Panel on Accountability and Governance in the Voluntary Sector. Ottawa, Ontario, Canada, 1998.

Hendrick, Burton J., *The Life of Andrew Carnegie.* Doubleday, Doran, Garden City, New York, 1931.

Hersch, Burton, *The Mellon Family: A Fortune in History.* William Morrow, New York, 1978.

Hewlett, Richard Greening, *Jessie Ball du Pont.* University Press of Florida, Gainesville, 1992.

Hobhouse, Arthur, *The Dead Hand: Addresses on the Subject of Endowments and Settlements of Property.* Chatto and Windus, London, 1880.

Hodson, H. V. (ed.), *The International Foundation Directory.* Europa, London, Editions 1–8, 1974, 1979, 1983, 1986, 1991, 1994, 1996, and 1998.

Hollis, Ernest V., *Philanthropic Foundations and Higher Education.* Columbia University Press, New York, 1938.

Hopkins, Bruce R., and Jody Blazek, *Private Foundations: Tax Law and Compliance.* John Wiley and Sons, New York, 1997.

Hutchins, Robert M., *Freedom, Education and the Fund: Essays and Addresses, 1946–1956.* Meridian Books, New York, 1956.

Jarchow, Merrill E., *Amherst H. Wilder and His Enduring Legacy to Saint Paul.* North Central, St. Paul, Minnesota, 1981.

Jenkins, Edward C., *Philanthropy in America. An Introduction to the Practice and Prospects of Organizations Supported by Gifts and Endowments 1924–1948.* Association Press, New York, 1950.

Jonas, Gerald, *The Circuit Riders: Rockefeller Money and the Rise of Modern Science.* W. W. Norton, New York, 1989.

Jones, John Price, *The American Giver: A Review of American Generosity*. Inter-River Press, New York, 1954.

Jordan, Wilbur K., *Philanthropy in England, 1480–1660: A Study of the Changing Patterns of English Aspirations*. Russell Sage Foundation, New York, 1959.

Joselit, Jenna Weissman, *Aspiring Women: A History of the Jewish Foundation for Education of Women*. Jewish Foundation for Education of Women, New York, 1996.

Keele, Harold M., and Joseph C. Kiger (eds.), *Foundations*. Greenwood Press, Westport, Connecticut, 1984.

Kelly, Frank K., *Court of Reason: Robert Hutchins and the Fund for the Republic*. Free Press, New York, 1981.

Keppel, Frederick P., *The Foundation: Its Place in American Life*. Macmillan, New York, 1930.

Kiger, Joseph C., *Historiographic Review of Foundation Literature: Motivations and Perceptions*. Foundation Center, New York, 1987.

Kiger, Joseph C., *Operating Principles of the Larger Foundations*. Russell Sage Foundation, New York, 1954.

Kiger, Joseph C. (ed.), *International Encyclopedia of Foundations*. Greenwood Press, Westport, Connecticut, 1990.

Kiger, Joseph C. (ed.), *International Encyclopedia of Learned Societies and Academies*. Greenwood Press, Westport, Connecticut, 1993.

Kiger, Joseph C. (ed.), *Research Institutions and Learned Societies*. Greenwood Press, Westport, Connecticut, 1982.

Kilman, Ed, and Theon Wright, *Hugh Roy Cullen: A Story of American Opportunity*. Prentice-Hall, New York, 1954.

Kincaid, Cliff, and William T. Poole (eds.), *The Playboy Foundation: A Mirror of the Culture?* Capital Research Center, Washington, D.C., 1992.

Kiser, Clyde V., *The Milbank Memorial Fund: Its Leaders and Its Work, 1905–1974*. Milbank Memorial Fund, New York, 1974.

Kohler, Robert E., *Partners in Science: Foundations and Natural Scientists, 1900–1945*. University of Chicago Press, Chicago, 1991.

Koskoff, David E., *The Mellons: The Chronicle of America's Richest Family*. Crowell, New York, 1978.

Lagemann, Ellen Condliffe, *The Politics of Knowledge: The Carnegie Corporation, Philanthropy, and Public Policy*. Wesleyan University Press, Middletown, Connecticut, 1989.

Lagemann, Ellen Condliffe, *Private Power for the Public Good. A History of the Carnegie Foundation for the Advancement of Teaching*. Wesleyan University Press, Middletown, Connecticut, 1983.

Lagemann, Ellen Condliffe (ed.), *Philanthropy and Education*. Teachers College Press, Columbia University, New York, 1992.

Lankford, John, *Congress and the Foundations in the Twentieth Century.* Wisconsin State University, River Falls, 1964.

Laski, Harold J., *The Dangers of Obedience and Other Essays.* Harper and Bros., New York, 1930.

Layton, Daphne Niobe, *Philanthropy and Voluntarism: An Annotated Bibliography.* Foundation Center, New York, 1987.

Lenzner, Robert, *The Great Getty: The Lives and Loves of J. Paul Getty-Richest Man in the World.* Crown, New York, 1985.

Lindeman, Eduard C., *Wealth and Culture: A Study of One Hundred Foundations and Community Trusts and Their Operations during the Decade 1921–1930.* Harcourt, Brace and Co., New York, 1936.

Lomask, Milton, *Seed Money: The Guggenheim Story.* Farrar, Straus and Co., New York, 1964.

Lord, Mary E., and Bruce Seymour II (eds.), *Foundations in International Affairs: Search for Security.* ACCESS-D.C., Washington, D.C., 1996.

Ludmerer, Kenneth M., *Learning to Heal: The Development of American Medical Education.* Basic Books, New York, 1985.

Macdonald, Dwight, *The Ford Foundation: The Men and the Millions.* Reynal, New York, 1956.

Madison, James H., *Eli Lilly: A Life, 1885–1977.* Indiana Historical Society, Indianapolis, 1989.

Magat, Richard, *Unlikely Companions: Organized Labor and Philanthropic Foundations.* Institution for Social and Policy Studies, New Haven, Connecticut, 1997.

Magat, Richard, *Unlikely Partners: Philanthropic Foundations and the Labor Movement.* Cornell University Press, Ithaca, New York, 1998.

Marts, Arnaud C., *Philanthropy's Role in Civilization: Its Contribution to Human Freedom.* Harper and Bros., New York, 1953.

McGuire, William, *Bollingen: An Adventure in Collecting the Past.* Princeton University Press, Princeton, New Jersey, 1982.

McIlnay, Dennis P., *Foundations and Higher Education: Dollars, Donors, and Scholars.* George Kurian Books, New York, 1991.

McIlnay, Dennis P., *How Foundations Work: What Grantseekers Need to Know About the Many Faces of Foundations.* Jossey-Bass, San Francisco, 1998.

Miller, Howard S., *Dollars for Research: Science and Its Patrons in Nineteenth-Century America.* University of Washington Press, Seattle, 1970.

Miller, Russell, *The House of Getty.* Henry Holt, New York, 1985.

Nagai, Althea K., Robert Lerner, and Stanley Rothman, *Giving for Social Change: Foundations, Public Policy, and the American Political Agenda.* Praeger, Westport, Connecticut, 1994.

Nason, John W., *Foundation Trusteeship: Service in the Public Interest.* Foundation Center, New York, 1989.

Nason, John W., *Trustees and the Future of Foundations.* Council on Foundations, New York, 1977.

Nelson, Ralph L., *The Investment Policies of Foundations.* Russell Sage Foundation, New York, 1967.

Nevins, Allan, *John D. Rockefeller: The Heroic Age of American Enterprise.* Charles Scribner's Sons, New York, 1940, 2 vols.

Nevins, Allan, *Study in Power: John D. Rockefeller, Industrialist and Philanthropist.* Charles Scribner's Sons, New York, 1953, 2 vols.

Nevins, Allan, with the collaboration of Frank Ernest Hill, *Ford.* Scribner, New York, 1954–1963, 3 vols.

Nielsen, Waldemar A., *The Big Foundations.* Columbia University Press, New York, 1972.

Nielsen, Waldemar A., *The Golden Donors: A New Anatomy of the Great Foundations.* Truman Talley Books, E. P. Dutton, New York, 1985.

Nielsen, Waldemar A., *Inside American Philanthropy: The Dramas of Donorship.* University of Oklahoma Press, Norman, 1996.

O'Connell, Brian, *The Board Member's Book. Making a Difference in Voluntary Organizations.* Foundation Center, New York, 1985.

Odendahl, Teresa (ed.), *America's Wealthy and the Future of Foundations.* The Foundation Center, New York, 1987.

Olasky, Martin, *Philanthropically Correct: The Story of the Council on Foundations.* Capital Research Center, Washington, D.C., 1953.

Owen, David, *English Philanthropy, 1660–1960.* Belknap Press of Harvard University Press, Cambridge, 1964.

Parker, Franklin, *George Peabody: A Biography.* Vanderbilt University Press, Nashville, Tennessee, 1971.

Phelan, Dale, *Samuel Fels of Philadelphia.* Drake Press, Philadelphia, 1969.

Pifer, Alan, *Philanthropy in an Age of Transition: The Essays of Alan Pifer.* Foundation Center, New York, 1984.

Poweell, Horace B., *The Original Has This Signature—W. K. Kellogg.* Prentice-Hall, Englewood Cliffs, New Jersey, 1956.

Quigley, Kevin F. F., *For Democracy's Sake: Foundations and Democracy Assistance in Central Europe.* Woodrow Wilson Center Press, Washington, D.C., 1997.

Reeves, Thomas C., *Freedom and the Foundation: The Fund for the Republic in the Era of McCarthyism.* Alfred A. Knopf, New York, 1969.

Reeves, Thomas C. (ed.), *Foundations under Fire.* Cornell University Press, Ithaca, New York, 1970.

Renz, Loren, Josefina Samson-Atienza, Trinh C. Tran, and Rikard R. Treiber, *International Grantmaking: A Report on U.S. Foundation Trends.* Foundation Center, New York, 1997.

Renz, Loren, Steven Lawrence, and John Kendzior, *Foundation Giving: Yearbook of Facts and Figures on Private, Corporate and Community Foundations,* Editions 1 through 9. Foundation Center, New York, 1990–1999. 9th ed., 1999.

Report of the Committee on the Law and Practice Relating to Charitable Trusts, Cmd. 8710. Her Majesty's Stationery Office, London, England, 1952.

Report of the Princeton Conference on the History of Philanthropy in the United States. Russell Sage Foundation, New York, 1956.

Richards, William C., and William J. Norton., *Biography of a Foundation. The Story of the Children's Fund of Michigan, 1929–1954.* Detroit, 1957.

Rockefeller, John D., *Random Reminiscences of Men and Events.* Doubleday, Doran, Garden City, New York, 1937.

Salamon, Lester A., and Kenneth P. Voytek, *Managing Foundation Assets: An Analysis of Foundation Investment and Payout Procedures and Performance.* Foundation Center, New York, 1989.

Sarnoff, Paul, *Russell Sage the Money King.* I. Oblensky, New York, 1965.

Savage, Howard J., *Fruit of an Impulse: Forty-Five Years of the Carnegie Foundation, 1905–1950.* Harcourt, Brace and Co., New York, 1953.

Schwartz, John J., *Modern American Philanthropy: A Personal Account.* John Wiley and Sons, New York, 1994.

Sealander, Judith, *Private Wealth and Public Life: Foundation Philanthropy and the Reshaping of American Social Policy from the Progressive Era to the New Deal.* Johns Hopkins University Press, Baltimore, 1997.

Siegel, Daniel, and Jenny Yancey, *The Rebirth of Civil Society: The Development of the Nonprofit Sector in East Central Europe and the Role of Western Assistance.* Rockefeller Brothers Fund, New York, 1992.

Sloan, Alfred P., Jr., *Adventures of a White Collar Man.* Books for Libraries Press, Freeport, New York, 1940.

Smith, Dean, *The Flinn Legacy: The Story of Arizona's Flinn Foundation.* Flinn Foundation, Phoenix, Arizona, 1996.

Smith, James Allen, *The Idea Brokers: Think Tanks and the Rise of the New Policy Elite.* Free Press, New York, 1991.

Smith, Steven Rathgeb, and Michael Lipsky, *Nonprofits for Hire: The Welfare State in the Age of Contracting.* Harvard University Press, Cambridge, 1993.

Smucker, Bob, *The Nonprofit Lobbying Guide.* 2d ed. Independent Sector, Washington, D.C., 1999.

Soros, George, *Underwriting Democracy.* Free Press, New York, 1991.

Spencer, Rae MacCollum, *The Gift of Imaginative Leadership: Harry Galpin Stoddard, Affectionately called "Mr. Worcester" 1873–1969.* Privately printed, Worcester, Massachusetts, 1972.

Stanfield, John H., *Philanthropy and Jim Crow in American Social Science.* Greenwood Press, Westport, Connecticut, 1985.

The Stern Fund: The Story of a Progressive Family Foundation. Institute for Media Analysis, New York, 1992.

Stone, Deanne, *Hands-On Grantmaking: The Story of the Boone Foundation.* Council on Foundations, Washington, D.C., 1998.

Struckhoff, Eugene C., *The Handbook for Community Foundations: Their Formation, Development, and Operation.* Council on Foundations, New York, 1977.

Taylor, Eleanor K., *Public Accountability of Foundations and Charitable Trusts.* Russell Sage Foundation, New York, 1953.

Tobias, Andrew, *Fire and Ice: The Story of Charles Revson.* William Morrow, New York, 1976.

Tobin, Gary A., Amy L. Sales, and Diane K. Tobin, *Jewish Family Foundations Study.* Maurice and Marilyn Cohen Center for Modern Jewish Studies. Waltham, Massachusetts, 1996.

U.S. Congress, *Congressional Record: Containing the Proceedings and Debates.* Government Printing Office, Washington, D.C., 1874– .

U.S. Congress, House of Representatives. Committee on Banking and Currency. Subcommittee on Domestic Finance. *Staff Report. Tax-Exempt Foundations and Charitable Trusts: Their Impact on Our Economy.* 92d Congress, 2d Session. Government Printing Office, Washington, D.C., 1972. Installment 8.

U.S. Congress, House of Representatives. Committee on Ways and Means. *Hearings. Tax Reform.* 91st Congress, 1st Session. Government Printing Office, Washington, D.C., 1969, Parts I and II.

U.S. Congress, House of Representatives. Select (Buchanan) Committee on Lobbying Activities. *General Interim Report.* 81st Congress, 2d Session. House Report No. 3138. Government Printing Office, Washington, D.C., 1950.

U.S. Congress, House of Representatives. Select (Buchanan) Committee on Lobbying Activities. *Report.* 81st Congress, 2d Session. House Report No. 3239. Government Printing Office, Washington, D.C., 1950, Part I, and Part II, Minority Views.

U.S. Congress, House of Representatives. Select (Cox) Committee to Investigate Foundations and Other Organizations. *Final Report.* 82d Congress, 2d Session. House Report No. 2514. Government Printing Office, Washington, D.C., 1953.

U.S. Congress, House of Representatives. Select (Cox) Committee to Investigate Tax-Exempt Foundations and Comparable Organizations. *Hearings.* 82d Congress, 2d Session. Government Printing Office, Washington, D.C., 1953.

U.S. Congress, House of Representatives. Select (Patman) Committeee on Small Business. *Chairman's Reports. Tax-Exempt Foundations and Charitable Trusts: Their Impact on Our Economy.* 87th through 91st Congress. Government Printing Office, Washington, D.C., 1962 through 1969. Installments 1 through 7.

U.S. Congress, House of Representatives. Select (Patman) Committee on Small Business. *Hearings before Subcommittee No. 1 Foundations.* 88th Congress, 2d Session. Government Printing Office, Washington, D.C., 1964.

U.S. Congress, House of Representatives. Select (Patman) Committee on Small Business. *Hearings before Subcommittee No. 1 Foundations.* 90th Congress, 2d Session. Government Printing Office, Washington, D.C., 1967.

U.S. Congress, House of Representatives. Special (Reece) Committee to Investigate Tax-Exempt Foundations and Comparable Organizations. *Hearings.* 83d Congress, 2d Session. Government Printing Office, Washington, D.C., 1954, Parts I and II.

U.S. Congress, House of Representatives. Special (Reece) Committee to Investigate Tax-Exempt Foundations and Comparable Organizations. *Report.* 83d Congress, 2d Session. House Report No. 2681. Government Printing Office, Washington, D.C., 1954.

U.S. Congress, Senate. (Walsh) Commission on Industrial Relations. *Final Report and Testimony.* 64th Congress, 1st Session. Senate Document No. 415. Government Printing Office, Washington, D.C., 1916. 11 vols.

U.S. Congress, Senate. Committee on Finance. *Hearings. Tax Reform Act of 1969.* 91st Congress, 1st Session. Government Printing Office, Washington, D.C., 1969.

U.S. Department of the Treasury. *Treasury Department Report on Private Foundations.* Government Printing Office,Washington, D.C., 1965.

U.S. Department of the Treasury. *Giving in America: Report of the* [Filer] *Commission on Private Philanthropy and Public Needs.* Government Printing Office, Washington, D.C., 1977.

U.S. Department of the Treasury. *Research Papers. Sponsored by the* [Filer] *Commission on Private Philanthropy and Public Needs.* Government Printing Office, Washington, D.C., 1977, 5 vols.

Wall, Bennett H., and George S. Gibb, *Teagle of Jersey Standard.* Tulane University, New Orleans, 1974.

Wall, Joseph Frazier, *Andrew Carnegie.* Oxford University Press, New York, 1970.

Warner, Amos G., *American Charities. A Study in Philanthropy and Economics.* Thomas Y. Crowell, New York, 1894.

Weaver, Warren S., *U.S. Philanthropic Foundations: Their History, Structure, Management, and Record.* Harper and Row, New York, 1967.

Wheeler, Sessions A., *Gentleman in the Outdoors: A Portrait of Max C. Fleischmann.* University of Nevada Press, Reno, 1985.

Whitaker, Ben, *The Foundations: An Anatomy of Philanthropic Societies.* Pelican Books, New York, 1979.

Whitaker, Ben. *The Philanthropoids: Foundations and Society.* William Morrow, New York, 1974.

Wilson, Emily Herring, *For the People of North Carolina: The Z. Smith Reynolds Foundation at Half-Century, 1936–1986.* University of North Carolina Press, Chapel Hill, 1988.

Wooster, James W., *Edward Stephen Harkness, 1874–1940.* Commonwealth Fund, New York, 1949.

Wooster, Martin Morse, *The Great Philanthropists and the Problem of Donor Intent.* Capital Research Center, Washington, D.C., 1994.

Wormser, René A., *Foundations: Their Power and Influence.* Devon-Adair, New York, 1958.

Young, Clarence H., and William A Quinn, *Foundation for Living: The Story of Charles Stewart Mott and Flint.* McGraw-Hill, Inc., New York, 1963.

Young, Donald R., and Wilbert Moore, *Trusteeship and the Management of Foundations.* Russell Sage Foundation, New York, 1969.

Zurcher, Arnold, *The Management of American Foundations: Administration, Policies, and Social Role.* New York University Press, New York, 1972.

Zurcher, Arnold J., and Jane Dustan, *The Foundation Administrator: A Study of Those Who Manage America's Foundations.* Russell Sage Foundation, New York, 1972.

Index

About the Author

JOSEPH C. KIGER is Professor of History Emeritus and Director of the Program on Foundations and Comparable Organizations at the University of Mississippi. He is the author or coauthor of several works, including *Foundations* (Greenwood, 1984), *Historiographic Review of Foundation Literature* (1993), and *International Encyclopedia of Foundations* (Greenwood, 1993).

ISBN 0-313-31223-0

90000>

EAN

9 780313 312236

HARDCOVER BAR CODE